C000135911

797,885 Books

are available to read at

www.ForgottenBooks.com

Forgotten Books' App
Available for mobile, tablet & eReader

ISBN 978-1-330-12498-7
PIBN 10031919

This book is a reproduction of an important historical work. Forgotten Books uses
state-of-the-art technology to digitally reconstruct the work, preserving the original format
whilst repairing imperfections present in the aged copy. In rare cases, an imperfection in
the original, such as a blemish or missing page, may be replicated in our edition. We do,
however, repair the vast majority of imperfections successfully; any imperfections that
remain are intentionally left to preserve the state of such historical works.

Forgotten Books is a registered trademark of FB &c Ltd.
Copyright © 2017 FB &c Ltd.
FB &c Ltd, Dalton House, 60 Windsor Avenue, London, SW19 2RR.
Company number 08720141. Registered in England and Wales.

For support please visit www.forgottenbooks.com

1 MONTH OF
FREE
READING

at

www.ForgottenBooks.com

By purchasing this book you are eligible for one month membership to ForgottenBooks.com, giving you unlimited access to our entire collection of over 700,000 titles via our web site and mobile apps.

To claim your free month visit:

www.forgottenbooks.com/free31919

* Offer is valid for 45 days from date of purchase. Terms and conditions apply.

English
Français
Deutsche
Italiano
Español
Português

www.forgottenbooks.com

Mythology Photography **Fiction**
Fishing Christianity **Art** Cooking
Essays Buddhism Freemasonry
Medicine **Biology** Music **Ancient
Egypt** Evolution Carpentry Physics
Dance Geology **Mathematics** Fitness
Shakespeare **Folklore** Yoga Marketing
Confidence Immortality Biographies
Poetry **Psychology** Witchcraft
Electronics Chemistry History **Law**
Accounting **Philosophy** Anthropology
Alchemy Drama Quantum Mechanics
Atheism Sexual Health **Ancient History
Entrepreneurship** Languages Sport
Paleontology Needlework Islam
Metaphysics Investment Archaeology
Parenting Statistics Criminology
Motivational

THE SIX-HOUR DAY
& OTHER INDUS-
TRIAL QUESTIONS

BY

LORD LEVERHULME

WITH AN INTRODUCTION BY

VISCOUNT HALDANE OF CLOAN

EDITED BY

STANLEY UNWIN

NEW YORK
HENRY HOLT AND COMPANY
1919

MOUNT PLEASANT BRANCH

HD8390
.L4
1919

TRANSFER
D. C. PUBLIC LIBRARY
SEPT. 10, 1940

(All rights reserved)

366008

DISTRICT OF COLUMBIA PROPERTY

EDITOR'S FOREWORD

WHEN Lord Leverhulme gave me permission to reprint in book form a collection of his Addresses, I had no conception of the mass of material from which I should be called upon to make a selection. The wide range of the subjects and the diversity of the audiences are alike remarkable. Whether he is addressing a learned society, a meeting of business men, a boys' or girls' school, a men's brotherhood, or a gathering of his own employees, his gifts of lucid exposition, concrete and often homely illustration and apt anecdote never fail him. One thing he has never learnt—how to be dull. It was, indeed, surprising to find that one so immersed in business and occupied with enterprises in all parts of the world had found time for so much activity of this character. But the explanation was simple ; Lord Leverhulme prescribes a Six hour Day, but he manages to work sixteen.

In the following selection I have confined myself largely to addresses dealing with Industrial questions, and in particular to those which treat of the two subjects which lie nearest to his heart and upon which he has had most to say—Co-partnership and the Six-hour Day. But space has been found under the heading " Education and Business " for some characteristic speeches of a lighter order.

For the most part no changes have been made in the original text, but to avoid undue repetition, references to the

Six-hour Day and Co-partnership have been, omitted from addresses concerned principally with other subjects.

The two opening essays on the " Six-hour Day " have been specially written for the volume and embody Lord Leverhulme's considered views on this all-important subject. They demonstrate that in the opinion of one of the most enlightened capitalists and foremost business administrators in this country a Six-hour Day is no mere chimera but a practical and necessary step in the Reconstruction after the War. If this volume serves to focus attention upon this one attainable ideal, its most important purpose will have been achieved.

                                        STANLEY UNWIN.

CONTENTS

CONTENTS

INTRODUCTION

By VISCOUNT HALDANE

TRUTH does not stand still. What is enough for one generation may prove inadequate when that generation has done its work and a new one has arrived. He would be bold who ventured to say that any plan for settling the relations between labour and capital could be reckoned on to prove sufficient in times ahead, merely because it would improve the state of things to-day.

None the less it is an event of importance when a captain of industry on a colossal scale has planned out a means towards the end of making things work in his own time, and has so far put Co-Partnership into successful operation. The pages of this book set forth not only the broad conclusions to which Lord Leverhulme has come about reform in the relations of capital to labour in great productive undertakings, but the book describes the fashion in which he has actually sought to apply these conclusions in his own very large works. It is this feature in the exposition that gives it much more than an academic importance. There will doubtless be many questions raised, and many who will assert that the point which he has reached falls short by much of the end of a journey the whole of which they wish to accomplish. But it cannot but be to the good to have before us the record which the book contains of a great attempt at progress. Lord Leverhulme's endeavour has been to interest labour in the results which modern direction of labour and of the capital employed is accomplishing. His principle is progressive profit-sharing on the part of labour. He describes the system under which the worker is given a share in profits without being subjected to the temptations and uncertainties of the common type of shareholder. He says frankly that his motive has been no merely sentimental one, but the desire to do what is at once best for his business and at the same time beneficial and just to those employed in it.

It is plain that the conception which underlies Lord Leverhulme's conclusions about productive undertakings is very different from that put forward more than half a century ago by Karl Marx. The socialists of those days taught that labour was the real source of wealth, and that the competition for employment brought about by increase of population enabled the monopolist who chanced to own capital to dictate rates of wages tending towards the minimum that would avert bare starvation. For them the obvious and only remedy was the abolition of private ownership of capital, including land. But the advent on a large scale of the modern banking system, and particularly of the joint-stock company, has to some extent changed the premises of the syllogism. Capital is now no monopoly. It is a widely diffused commodity which can be hired in the open market at a moderate interest by any one who can command public confidence. The particular form of capital which is called land is not in reality in a different position. We are rapidly tending to the general opinion that it must not be withheld where it is required, and that all the owner is entitled to is its market value. Capital, including land, is therefore to-day becoming an instrument of which he who can really wield it can get the use freely. It does not create wealth. That is created by the unlocking of the potential energy stored up in the world beneath, around, and above us, and by the conversion of this potential into kinetic energy in its appropriate form. Coal, for instance, enables men to produce heat and steam, and the energy of steam is turned into electricity. But labour is for this purpose only an instrument, no more adequate by itself to the task than is capital. What impels both is participation in thought-out and complete operation, and what is the fountain and origin of the activities of both is mind. The initiation and direction cannot be given either by the mere capitalist or the mere labourer. As progress takes place, as increase of output becomes more and more essential, as competition sets in, only to be met by fresh invention, it becomes plain that no industry can stand still. If it is to succeed it must be constantly adapted, and to this end not only mind but trained mind, and the increasing command of scientific knowledge and invention, are essential. The director who has genius will accordingly always possess something of the power of a monopolist.

Now, how is this new form of peril to be met ? To begin with, it cannot be wholly met. Nature will always produce men and women of quite unequal capacity for direction, and a few with talent for it which will give them colossal advantages in the competition for the foremost place. In the second place, I do not think that we need worry ourselves over the fact that we cannot prevent nature from denying us equality in this particular form of talent. As civilization progresses, if the minimum standards are raised as regards the home and the means of living, if knowledge is more widely diffused and higher ideals prevail, inequality in wealth will count for less than it does to-day. What are called " values " will change ; I mean those ends which people judge as conclusively best in themselves, and to be chosen without question.

Men and women, relieved from the grinding pressure of poverty, and having enough to live on, may well prefer, as the main thing that counts in life, to know more rather than to have more wealth. The possessions of the millionaire may, in days to come, count for less to the average man than under existing conditions. And here comes in the real point of Lord Leverhulme's ideal of a six-hour day. The labour of such a day must be concentrated if it is to bring a sufficiency in wages. But if it does bring such a sufficiency it leaves leisure for the things of the soul.

One of the nascent ideas which are taking root in this country, an idea which is being fostered in particular by the Workers' Educational Association, is adult education. We have forgotten too often that a man's mind can be developed in a high degree comparatively late in life. Under sufficient stimulus of ideas he can acquire a freedom of spirit which is just as important to him as his bodily liberty. For freedom is the essential characteristic of mind at its best, the freedom which enables it to detach itself and to choose freely; to be the spectator of time and of eternity, and to abstract, if need be, from its own pain and even from its own death. We want to produce in this country a generation of an outlook large enough to see things steadily and to see them whole. If the doctrine which underlies Lord Leverhulme's conclusions is right, the production of such a generation is of high importance for industry itself as well as for spiritual ends. Now the six-hour day is a means to the attainment of this object.

But the conception of direction as the source of wealth has another application. Probably it is best that in the supreme command of every great industrial undertaking there should be a single great intelligence. Unity of conception and of execution is not, in its highest form, easy to produce cooperatively. We have seen something of this truth in connection with the armies in this war. But just as even in an army devolution can be carried very far and with great advantage, if the level of general intelligence is high enough, so it is in industry. The object ought always to be to get the operations that are merely mechanical performed by machines in relief of men, and to entrust to the men in charge of them the duty of arriving at a result by their own intelligence and initiative rather than by mere rule of thumb. So only are initiative and invention to be stimulated. So only is labour to be relieved of the monotony which always comes in when the mind is not called on to play any real part.

In other words, the object should surely be to make the workman in the future more of a director of instruments than a labourer, and to unite hand and brain as of necessity implying each other. Monotony will at least be diminished when men feel that they have always to be thinking when they act, and that the occupation of the workman depends on knowledge and skill, and belongs to what is truly a profession. It will require education and training to bring this about, but, if it can be done, even partially, it will give more freedom of the spirit and it will give something more besides. It will afford an opening for exceptional talent, and for its development to the man who possesses it. For the factory and the mine will tend to become places where there is a gradation of direction, dependent on capacity for directing. It will be open to every man to rise, and it will be in the interest of the organization as a whole that he should have the chance of rising, and of so bringing to bear his own special gift To this end not only do Lord Leverhulme's six-hour day but his profit-sharing arrangement also seem to lend means. And in the nation as a whole the tendency will be to substitute for the existing aristocracy of wealth a new aristocracy, an élite of talent, the members of which will always be changing, and which will be open to the humblest if only he renders himself capable of entering it.

Such a reorganization of industry and of society can only come gradually. But the gradual process of its evolution may produce results more rapidly than people are apt to think. It is not only the new earnestness of spirit about education and the things of the soul that promises much. It is the new and impressive demand to bring production up to the level of the scientific standards which are now being reached. As Lord Leverhulme says, our waste of energy by not developing electrical processes and machinery is a hindrance. We seem, however, to be in sight of great reforms in this connection which may enormously diminish the waste of coal and water-power which has obtained hitherto. With a copious and well-distributed national system of distribution of electrical current from great central generating stations, instead of its inadequate and costly supply from the multitude of little generators which are strewed about the country to-day, a vast improvement becomes conceivable. If this were done, much reduction in standing charges would be possible, together with greatly increased production and much improved wages. The energy furnished could be employed mainly in the day for giving power, and at night largely for giving light. But it would at least be easier to provide for the continuous operation in different forms of a uniform electrical current which would make practicable the provision required for the introduction of a succession of short shifts for those employed in production.

In these matters, which are of such tremendous importance for the future of our nation, the Government and the great captains of industry, such as Lord Leverhulme, must play their part. Much thought and much guarding against inertness and the selfishness of the individual are required. But, after all, what is most important is a high level of intelligence and interest in our people. And it will not be enough to confine this intelligence and this interest to things that are only material, however important. Further ideals are required—ideals of knowledge, ideals of beauty, and ideals of conduct. The whole man must be kept in view throughout. The spiritual leaders, in Churches and in Parliament and elsewhere, must co-operate. For it is not by bread alone that man can live.

But the soul cannot be saved unless the body is attended to, and it is because I think that the result of Lord Leverhulme's striving will be, if he succeeds, to better the condition of both soul and body that I have ventured by his desire to write these introductory lines in his book, and especially to that part of it which considers the six-hour day.

THE SIX-HOUR DAY

2

INTRODUCTORY. THE INDUSTRIAL SITUATION

WHEN this world-war is over we shall be confronted with problems which, whilst in no way new, will be presented in new and acute forms. How shall we, as an empire, emerge from this ordeal? Are we to continue a progressive democracy or sink into the slough of Socialism and Anarchy? The decision will rest not with the Socialists or Anarchists; not with politicians or Governments, but with the business men and working men of the Empire. Hitherto on both sides there has been a disastrous exhibition of short-sightedness and of greed, or lack of knowledge of those economic laws on which all solid well-being must and can only rest. Every increase in wages and shortening of hours has been resisted by business men as a raid on their ability to meet competition and make reasonable profits. And every attempt by business men to increase output and reduce costs has been met by the workers with sullen indifference or the active opposition of " ca' canny " methods.

Now we shall, after the war, ·be entering upon the most fateful and critical stage of our Empire's career. This war has thrown all previous rules and practices into the melting-pot. How will the Empire emerge? Are we to attempt after the war to restore old decayed, wrong, and ruinous practices, or is there to be a radical recasting of all our business and labour methods? It has been truly said that " to govern and in turn to be governed is the only form of true liberty." In a true democracy and in this sense there is no governing class and no class that is governed: all classes govern, and all classes in turn serve alike and together. All classes serve one master—the only master whose service all liberty-loving citizens can be proud to serve—and that is their country's welfare.

Amidst all this confusion and clash of arms, this return to conditions of savage barbarism, our great encouragement and confidence are that the British Empire stands solid and united to face her foes, and loyal to our King as Sovereign of the British race at home and in our Colonies as never before in her history. Some timid people, suffering from an attack of cold feet, nervously ask, " What about Labour ? " The answer we can fin{ , most clearly written in our history is, " Trust Labour wl oleheartedly and wisely, and all will be well." A good and wise lover of the cause of Labour can never be a bad or undesirable citizen of the British Empire. And it will be our own fault if, by distrust and suspicions, we make him so. Let us never forget that the British spirit responds best when trusted, and can only become stupid, morose, and bad when distrusted and viewed with suspicion. This nation as a whole has never yet really trusted Labour. We have always borne a mental attitude of suspicion and distrust towards Labour. Well, this attitude won't help us, and is doomed to most serious failure and may bring possible disaster to the Empire. We have, with unbounded success, trusted our Colonies and other sections of the community that make up the British Empire, and, when we have done so, all has been well. We have even trusted the Boers in South Africa, who were so recently at war against us ; and now who amongst us dare to-day to come forward and say that our trust has not been amply and fully repaid by the loyalty and devotion to the British Empire of our South African brothers, Boer or Briton ? Distrust and suspicion can only breed distrust and suspicion, whilst confidence and trust inspire confidence and trust. The sympathy of every right-thinking man or woman is with those who toil ; with those who produce the necessities and comforts of life ; with those who bear the burden and heat of the day in whatever position they may be working : employer-capitalists or employee-workers.

Our national future stability has its sure foundation in the fact that both employer-capitalist and employee-worker are each becoming more and more intelligent every year that passes. The day is fast coming when both will be intelligent enough to recognize that their interests are identical and that the prosperity of either depends on the prosperity of both.

Life is not merely a respite between the sentence of death which is passed on all life at birth and the execution of that sentence. Every healthy human being seeks for happiness, and has to find happiness in supplying the wants of the body with food, clothing, and shelter. And equally happiness can only be found in feeding mind and soul with ideals of beauty, art, and learning. Happiness of the lasting, permanent type, without after shadows of regrets or ghosts of repentances, is the only good, and everything that tends to produce such happiness in men and women is good, and to do whatever produces this state and condition is to achieve the highest possible gain for the Empire and the whole of mankind.

Our industries progress, science progresses, but we have little or no corresponding progress in conditions of comfort of the workers. The employee-worker lags behind in that culture, education, social and economic well-being which he ought to enjoy under modern conditions of civilization. Our manufacturing towns are squalid and overcrowded, with ugly dwellings, without gardens. They are unlovely congestions, without beauty or possibility of refinement, and the great bulk of the workers remain at a relatively low state of betterment. The individual Home is the solid rock and basis of every strong, intelligent race. The more homes there are and the better these homes are, the more stable and strong the nation becomes. Men and women who get up to go to work before daylight and return from that work after dark, cannot find life worth living. They are simply working to earn enough one day to prepare themselves to go to work again the next day. Their whole life is one grey, dull, monotonous grind, and soon their lives become of no more value to themselves or the nation than that of mere machines.

Every year the workers become more intelligent and more acute reasoners. Think of the intelligence required in the workers to produce a modern locomotive or a greyhound of the Atlantic, or to work and operate the same, and to make and operate all the thousands of different types of machines now producing and working for the good of man. And each succeeding year demands still higher intelligence to produce still higher, better, and more complex mechanical utilities.

The requirements of our ancestors were few, but as civilization advances, not only do the wants of the body for variety in food, raiment, and shelter increase, but as the mind and soul expand, the intellectual horizon widens and the higher plane of living demands more and more leisure to feed its hunger for better conditions of life.

In the dark ages that are past, man believed in the supernatural as the direction in which he should search to satisfy his super-wants. To meet disease and death, primitive man believed in charms, magics, fetishes, and incantations. In chemistry he sought for the transmutation of base metals into gold, and his idea of mechanics was a search for perpetual motion ; and as to Governments, he relied on the Divine Right of Kings and Infallibility of Popes.

Are we not equally ignorant and equally doomed to disappointment if to-day the employer-capitalist relies on the magic of the " perpetual motion " fetish of long hours of toil, with low wages for employee-workers ; and are we not also doomed to disappointment if to-day the employee-workers rely on the " Philosopher's Stone " of " ca' canny " and the " transmutation " of restriction of output into the " Elixir of Life " ?

The struggle of science and right thinking against ignorance and prejudice during the dark ages was long and bitter, but to-day no chemist is seeking for the " Elixir of Life " or trying to discover the " Philosopher's Stone." And equally our present-day ignorance of those economic laws that govern costs of production will disappear, and we shall learn that by development and encouragement of individual effort for increased output in fewer hours with higher wages we can best serve all mankind and best overcome all obstacles to progress, and so, by taking advantage of discoveries of science in invention and industrial development, supply all our wants with less exertion and secure a greater reserve of leisure to satisfy the hunger of mind and soul.

We are all agreed that the industrial situation has become the most pressing after-war problem to be solved, and that the solution will not be easy, not because there is more poverty in the United Kingdom to-day than ever—as a matter of fact there is less poverty than ever before in our history—but because there is a wholesome Labour unrest and national craving for vastly better conditions of life. The poor are not growing poorer, and the workman of to-day is better off than his employer was two centuries ago. But because— and I rejoice that it is so—the workman is each day becoming more ambitious, his mind and soul are expanding at a greater rate than, under existing conditions—even with higher wages —his leisure time permits him to keep pace with. Each year the workman is becoming a better educated man, with better social outlook. Whilst his social outlook is expanding, the workman in the twentieth century finds himself simply a seller of service, and that he has gradually become a cipher in a most complex industrial system, and has his life absorbed and controlled as a mere unit in a great factory or workshop that leaves him no scope for the exercise of the higher intellectual developments of modern life.

Whilst science is making life more livable and lovable by means of rapid transit and greater range of interests and wider scope, the time of the worker is occupied almost entirely in the provision of food, shelter, and clothing, with little or no leisure time remaining, even if he had the means, to provide for a higher level of living. He sees other sections of the community dashing about in motor-cars and generally living what appear to be, in contrast to his own life, lives of leisure and comfort. So long as the workman's life is passed in monotonous toil in factory and workshop from daybreak to sunset, no wages, however high, can make up for this separation from all that is highest and best in life : the workman is not content to be exhausted in the task of providing food, shelter, and clothing for himself, wife, and children, with practically no leisure for other pursuits.

This is perhaps a subconscious state, and is a condition that the workman himself would probably be unable to put into clear language, but that it exists is plainly shown by the so-called " Labour Unrest," and by the readiness with which a section of the Labour Party is prepared, Samson like, to break the pillars and throw down the whole structure of Society, rather than continue under the present conditions of the workman's life (which hateful conditions are far from being merely and solely a question of wages)—he disregards social usages, awards of umpires, his own Trade Union leaders, and the legal rights of Society, and would seek industrial revolution in order to obtain redress from his present industrial position, and often merely imaginary grievances.

All this "Labour Unrest" arises from the fact that his life in factory and workshop has become one dull, monotonous grind, from schoolage to dotage, and this state of mind is as dangerous to the workman himself as it is to the nation —dangerous to himself, because, while he smarts under the oppression of his lot in life, he does not quite know how to obtain that fullness of life and happiness, comfort and well-being, leisure and advancement for which he hungers.

It is a basic law of all healthy, permanent growth that no one part of a whole can increase and develop without all other parts being symmetrically and proportionately increased and developed. This is equally true of Society as a whole or viewed in sections. No section of Society can enjoy improved conditions without all other sections enjoying improved conditions—otherwise there would be lack of symmetry in the whole and danger of the social tree toppling over at the first gale that tested the strength of the hold of its roots on the solid ground. The future security, or the present danger that menaces the industrial world, will be exactly in proportion to the symmetrical growth or lack thereof in all its parts. We can have no so-called leisured class or moneyed class unless all classes can enjoy the opportunity in their lives of leisure and money in symmetrical proportion. Not in equal proportions, because there is no such thing as equality or uniformity in God's scheme of man or of nature. But nature's and man's Creator never planned that one section should be starved whilst another section be overfed without decay and death resulting. Therefore our problem can only be solved by increasing wealth and increasing leisure. Then equal distribution would have no meaning, because the mere fact of equal distribution would increase neither the total wealth nor the total leisure—in fact, equal distribution would decrease both, by withdrawing the stimulus of reward from those possessed of the power to create wealth and leisure, and would encourage the "leaners" and "apathetics" to cease from all efforts and to make no use of opportunity as a means for development in skill and knowledge for production of wealth.

The power to create wealth is not a power against the

public interest and well-being, any more than is bodily health and strength or great intellectual power. A man is not an enemy of the human race because, by exercise of foresight, thrift, and intelligence, he has accumulated great wealth, any more than is the man who, by temperate living and good habits, accumulates a store of good health, and consequently is fitted to live a long life. It would be as logical, as right, and as reasonable for the consumptives, the weak, the feeble, and the diseased to denounce the healthy and strong as it is for those possessing little or no wealth to denounce the rich and wealthy. And it would be just as effective a cure for consumption, weakness, feebleness, and disease to take steps to reduce the healthy and strong to a state of weakness, feebleness, and disease as it would be a cure for poverty to attempt to conscript the riches of the wealthy.

Take, for instance, the crude Henry George theories that to abolish all property in land by confiscating the rents received from land, and the more recent suggestions of others, that to abolish all ownership in capital by confiscating all interest and profits on capital would abolish poverty, and this wealth, when shared in by all equally, would bring about the millennium. These proposals are shown up in all their grotesque absurdity when we examine the figures, for we then find that their product, on pre-war basis, would, if divided equally, be under 11d. per head per day for each man, woman, and child in the United Kingdom. In this calculation we take, of course, no count of salaries or wages, or of foreign investments, but merely of profits, rents, and interest on capital invested in the United Kingdom.

So that equality or uniformity of wealth is clearly no way to abolish poverty

A man is not a criminal merely because he is wealthy nor is a man a criminal merely because he is weak, feeble, or diseased. A man is not judged merely by his state of health or disease, or his state of wealth or poverty, but by his acts and how he lives, be he healthy or diseased, be he wealthy or poor, and he is also rightly judged by how he came by his health or disease and how he came by his wealth or poverty.

Some men acquired their health and strength, their feebleness, ill-health, or disease from their parents ; others gained their strength and health, or acquired their ill-health, feeble-ness, or disease, by their own acts. Equally, some men inherit their wealth or poverty from their parents, whilst others have gained their wealth or become poor by their own acts. A strong, healthy man can use his health and strength not only for his own benefit and happiness, but also for the good and happiness of others, and so become a gain to the whole human race. Equally, a wealthy man can use his wealth and riches not only for his own benefit and happiness, but also for the good and happiness of others, and so become a gain to the whole human race. The well-being and happiness of the whole human race depend not on equality of health or of wealth, but on each man and woman making the best use of their health or wealth, be either or both little or great, for the production of more health and more wealth. It is only so that gradually all can become healthy and all wealthy. Every advantage must be taken of every opportunity for creation of conditions that make it easier for each man and woman—if they so will—to become more and more healthy and strong, more and more wealthy and happy.

The great end and aim of life is happiness. The happy man or woman is the highest product the world can produce, whatever their state of health or wealth, but health and wealth are great removers of limitations. And that is all that either health or wealth can do for any of us—just remove our limitations and give us a wider scope for usefulness to our fellow-men.

We are forced, therefore, to direct our whole energies to the production of more wealth, and in doing so we must concentrate on machine power and not on human energy. This will enable us to increase wages by creating a larger fund out of which to pay Labour—to increase leisure by reducing costs, so that fewer hours of toil are required to produce more goods, better goods, and cheaper goods by an ever-increasing use of machine power, so that the worker becomes, as he was intended to be, a director of machinery and not himself a machine or part of a machine. The man must be master and controller of the machine, and not the machine be master and so swallow up the mind and personality of the man.

We find all over the world, in the semi-civilized countries as well as in the most highly civilized, that wealth is the greatest, wages are the highest, and hours of labour are the shortest where capital invested in machine power is the greatest per head of the people. This outstanding fact has yet to be learned by both employer-capitalist and employee-worker. The employer-capitalist must get rid of his infatuation for the error that low wages and long hours of toil for the employee-worker mean cheaper production and cousequently higher profits. It is only by the extended use of machine power and the prompt adoption of every labour-saving device that cheaper production can be achieved by obtaining a greater volume of products. And it is only by the paying of the highest possible rate of wages to the employee-worker for the fewest possible number of hours that an adequate demand for this increased volume of products can be found. Leisure increases wants, whilst over-fatigue and long hours decrease wants. The British employee-worker will then recognize the fallacy of restriction of output as a means to social betterment for the workers, and will for ever discard this folly.

Mr. Gompers, the American Labour Leader, has told us that the workman in the United States abandoned the fallacy of restriction of output thirty years ago, which was, by a strange coincidence, about the very period the British workman first began to adopt extensively " ca' canny " and restriction of output; and since 1886 there has been a steady rise in the production per head of the workers in the United States, and an equally steady reduction in the production per head of the workers in the United Kingdom, with the result, as shown by the census of production issued recently, that of the seven million workers in Great Britain, four million were engaged in trades yielding a net annual increased value of only £75 to £100 per head over the value of the material used. In most of the principal industries in the United States the output per worker averages from three to five times that amount.

We have to reconsider our methods and change all this. The power and ability to produce by means of machinery is from a hundred to a thousand times greater than the power to produce by hand labour, and demands from the man less fatigue. Notwithstanding the enormous increase in machinery, and simultaneously in complexity and intricacy of parts of machines, the workman always finds himself master of his machine—the machine cannot master the workman. And further, the better our equipment of machinery, the better and more intelligent our workman becomes. This is shown by the fact that, however high the type of machine may be, man can always improve on the same, so that each year the new machine shows improvements on the old machine. The man who can best effect this improvement is the man who works at the machine. He knows the machine he works with as a rider knows his horse. He understands its peculiarities and its weaknesses, and gradually comes to view it almost as a living creature. Then why do we not get more inventions and suggested improvements from the man working the machine? The reason is that suggestions for improvement require thought, and thought requires leisure, and the present industrial system gives no leisure. To provide more leisure, it can be proved that men properly trained to their task and to working together can accomplish from 50 per cent. to 100 per cent. more work than the same number of ill-selected, badly organized men. Similarly the man working with machinery; the trained, skilled, unfatigued worker can produce a larger volume of product than the fatigued workman. The mastery of the machine can only be accomplished by development of high character as well as high skill in the employee-worker. The obtaining of the most from machines requires the highest intelligence along with highest character, and so we tend to get further from the brutes and nearer to the angels. Without machines, man required mere brute force and strength, with relatively little skill and no special high character or moral laws to guide him. The drunken or debauched workman is incapable of running a modern complicated machine in the factory or a modern high-speed locomotive. He is unable to keep up with the strain that machine or locomotive makes upon him, whilst the steady workman of character is complete master of his job and his machine. The whole tendency of modern machinery is to improve the workman whilst increasing his wages and reducing his hours of labour. A handloom weaver might be semi-drunk and take no harm at his work beyond loss of output. A man driving a horse and cart or carriage may be half drunk, and yet his horse will find home in safety whilst the driver nods a drunken half-sleep. But not so the modern workman, with many and delicate intricate looms to watch and keep running, nor the man on the footplate of the express mail-train locomotive. The drunkard would be an impossibility for these modern machines, and would lack that nerve and steadiness of eye and hand essential to their operation.

The modern machine knows nothing of religion or moral laws, yet it is one of the greatest religious and moral teachers the world has produced in modern times. However far and wide we extend mechanical utilities and machine power, we come finally to the necessity of providing intelligent and careful men for their control and running. Machines cannot run alone, and workmen of skill, high character, and moral conduct are essential to successful control. Man remains man and machine remains machine. Therefore we may look to the future with confidence. All the tendencies of the greater use of machinery are in the direction of improving man. Machinery properly used need not degrade man, but is capable of raising him indefinitely.

Equally, modern industrial conditions improve the employer-capitalist. Modern industrial conditions demand and necessitate an employer of not only high ability, but also of high character.

Can employer-capitalists and employee-workers so conduct productive and distributive industries, so work together, so adjust themselves to new ideals, so govern and serve the Empire, so, in brief, review their own private, selfish ideas on the lines of most enlightened self-interest that they may both realize the truth that in best serving the Empire and the public they will best serve themselves? There never was a greater need for employer-capitalist and employee-worker to exercise the wisest and most enlightened self-interest. There never was such an opportunity for the immediate and prompt exercise of a far-sighted, wise, and enlightened policy. Narrow, selfish greed and cunning on either side would bring this Empire and its peoples to ruin and disaster. The future of civilization and of our Empire, and the future of our race, the happiness and prosperity of our children and our children's children, will depend in no small degree on the wisdom of our employer-capitalists and employee-workers, in whose hands now and after the war lie the guidance and control of our policy.

II

THE SIX-HOUR DAY

THERE exists to-day profound and widespread anti-capitalist and anti-Trade Union labour prejudice and distrust. "A plague on both your houses" says the consumer, who feels uneasy and vaguely suspicious that he is not well and truly served by either. And with this widespread unrest there is the most profound ignorance of the very rudiments of the economics of production, of profits, and of wages.

We may search, with painstaking care and attention, through the present-day writings of those who attempt to deal with industrial conditions and wages and hours of work, whether the writers be Socialists or Trades Unionists, but we shall search in vain for any recognition of the fact that the economical cost of production and volume of product are the all-important factors, or any reference to the fact that over 90 per cent., and possibly even over 95 per cent., of the products of labour are consumed by the employee-workers themselves, and not by the employer-capitalists. So that restriction of output, or the "ca' canny" policy, can only, whatever might be the rate of wages, make wages nominal by reducing their exchange value when measured in terms of clothing, food, and shelter.

At this present moment there is in the mind of many writers and speakers the most shallow and dangerously wrong views as to the patriotism, during war-time, of so-called profits of capital and the patriotism of demands for higher wages of labour. It is not easy to get the public or the employee-worker to recognize that it would be the reverse of patriotic —in fact, absolutely ruinous to the national well-being—for the employer-capitalist to forgo profits during war-time. And it is not easy to get the public or the employer-capitalist to see that it would equally be the reverse of patriotic for the employee-worker to waive demands for higher wages during war-time. The economic truth is that unless the employer-capitalist be able to make reasonably higher profits during war-time than during peace-time, and the employee-worker to earn reasonably higher wages during war-time than during peace-time—the profits to enable the employer-capitalist to expand production to the utmost and to meet post-war contractions and losses, and the wages to enable the employee-worker to meet the higher cost of living, and also the increased cost of higher living—it would be impossible to maintain the industries of the country at concert pitch during the war.

In short, reasonable and fair, full profits to the employer-capitalist, and reasonable, generous, and full wages to the employee-worker during war-time are essential to the maintenance of our Empire's stability and to prevent widespread national and business prostration. How to conduct our industries, how to handle capital and labour, how to run what we may call in brief the business of the Empire during the war, is one of the problems of the war, as it will be our problem after the war is over.

Can we bear our post-war loads and carry the Empire after the war with its trade and commerce back into the cahn safety of prosperity? We can only do so provided all classes and both sexes, following the example set us by our King and Queen, continue to make, after the war, the same sacrifices of ease or comfort, and continue to work as hard and with the same spirit of brotherhood as has been displayed by all classes, without exception, during the war. This will be no easy task; but we can and must face it, and, facing it promptly, it will be easier to accomplish than if we hesitate and procrastinate. Sound principles of finance and our national credit will necessitate our not only paying promptly the interest on our War Loans, but also providing for the repayment of the loans with all possible speed.

Our National Debt at the end of the present financial year, 1918–19, we are told by the Chancellor of the Exchequer, will be about eight thousand millions sterling. Our crushing burden of taxation during the current financial year is estimated to yield about nine hundred millions sterling. Hundreds of thousands of the flower of our manhood will have been killed in battle or will have died of war diseases, or have been permanently maimed or crippled. We have a house famine actually with us, and are exerting every nerve and muscle to prevent a food famine and to provide munitions of war ships for commerce, and ships for war, submarines, aircraft and all known weapons of war for the destruction of life and property. Our programme of social reforms and betterment and of extended education is a long and an overdue one.

And first of all we must learn the most serious importance of the avoidance of waste—waste of child life, waste of adult life, waste of energy, waste of time, waste of opportunity, and, greatest waste of all, the appalling waste caused by over-fatigue of the workers, resulting in inefficiency, bad health, lost time, and premature decay and death.

But we have learned much during the last three years on the subject of fatigue, overwork, and excessively long working hours. We have proved conclusively that prolonged hours of toil, with resulting excessive fatigue, produce, after a certain point, actually smaller results in quantity, quality, and value than can be produced in fewer hours when there is an entire absence of overstrain or fatigue. Fortunately, however, this logical effect of over-long hours of continuous work does not apply, except to a very limited extent, to the case of machinery and mechanical utilities. True, even machinery must have times of rest for cleaning, overhauling, repairs, and lubrication; but these stoppages are not serious, and require only slight intervals that are easily arranged for. Therefore, as we shall require an enormously increased output of goods to replenish stocks that have been allowed to run down, both for our home and export trade, and as we have the machinery available, and which hitherto in most industries has been run for only 48 hours per week, a solution of this one of our difficulties can be best and most readily found by working our machinery for more hours and our men and women for fewer hours.

We must have a six-hour working day for men and women, and by means of six-hour shifts for men and women we must work our machinery twelve, eighteen, or twenty-four hours per day.

We have in the United Kingdom the finest type of work-people in the human race—second to none in the whole world,

If we are to make the most of this rare humanity, and have more of the inventions to which I have alluded, there must be some change in our industrial system of hours of working. We must remember the deadening effect of general factory life. From fourteen years of age to seventy years of age is a long life-span, and if you consider the conditions of attending, for eight hours a day, the same automatic machinery and following the same routine, with its continual deadly, monotonous round of toil, those of us whose employment is varied will realize how this bites into the soul of a man or woman and tends to corrode it. There is not that variety which human life thrives on. The horses of the coaches which went out of London along the level Slough and Windsor road were done up and had to be sold long before the horses that went a similar distance through Highgate, where they climbed the hill to the summit and then trotted down into the valleys with collars loose. And so also those who work in factories with unbroken monotony till tired and weary, only preparing by rest and sleep for the beginning of another similar dull day, must inevitably wear out at a premature age and become enfeebled under such conditions.

Of all welfare work in factories, a proper apportionment of the time is the one that will yield the best results, and is the problem most pressing for solution. Let us take as an illustration of our meaning the position with regard to London and overcrowding. We know the slums of London and the overcrowding of London ; but do we realize that the Metropolitan area, with its 7¼ millions of people, covers the extensive area of 450,000 acres of ground. If, therefore, we had planned for building under ideal conditions of some ten houses to the acre over the whole of this Metropolitan area, instead of having, as we have at present, badly packed slum districts in some quarters and so on, and of badly housing only 7¼ millions of people, we could in that area have provided for housing 22½ millions of people, three times the number, with ideal surroundings for comfort and happiness. It is merely a case of bad packing. Now, I believe this is not an unfair parallel for me to take with regard to working hours. We can get into a working day of six hours all the work we are capable of when that work is monotonous—attending machinery and general work in a factory. To get the work

3

condensed into six hours would enable us to produce not only everything that we require, but to produce it without fatigue.

Not only can we produce, when all ranks and all classes of both sexes are workers for six hours each day for six days each week, all the ships, machinery, factories, houses, and goods we require both for home requirements and for exchange for raw materials through our export markets, but the houses can be built in beautiful garden suburbs ; we can provide adequately for education, mental and physical, and military training for national defence. In addition, all being workers, our burden of taxation will—being then wisely laid on the wealth produced—be borne by all without impoverishment or oppression of any. The only wise, sane basis of taxation is to avoid all tariffs on goods except luxuries, and then solely for revenue purposes, and to raise further revenue mainly by graduated income tax and death duties. The only possible way to produce wealth is by the labour of all classes working shoulder to shoulder together in co-partnership during reasonable hours and without individual over-fatigue or overwork. There must be neither idle overfed and underworked men or women nor overworked, underfed men or women. It has been estimated that less than half of our total population are actual producers of wealth, but if we are, as a nation, to make good the wastage of this war and to maintain our position amongst the nations of the world after we have won complete victory and the unconditional surrender of our enemies, then it will require that all able-bodied men and women from schoolage to dotage, of all ranks and stations, shall be workers for six hours each day for six days each week. There will be no place in the whole British Empire for the idle rich or the idle or " ca'-canny " poor. We cannot consent as a nation to there being any loafers, nor can the British Empire, if it is to continue to exist, become a loafer's paradise.

But the adoption simultaneously, in all industries of the United Kingdom, of a six-hour working day is absolutely impossible and impracticable. As with the acorn that produces the British oak, the growth of the six-hour day movement will be slow, but none the less sure. It can only be adopted in such industries as those in which it will, by its application, give lower costs of production by working machinery for longer hours and humanity, in two or more shifts, for fewer hours. The six-hour day, for instance, is not immediately applicable to agriculture, because at present there is little labour-saving machinery used in agriculture. But already steam and petrol tractors for ploughing, cultivation, seed-sowing, harvesting, and haulage are each succeeding year being more and more used, and it is quite evident that the time will come when a six-hour day and two shifts of workmen will be the most profitable and most economical employment for humanity in agriculture.

It is already applicable without loss to all those industries in which the cost of production in overhead charges is equal in amount to the cost of wages. But in most workshops and factories the cost of production in the form of overhead charges is double or more the cost of wages. In all these latter the six-hour day can be applied forthwith with enormous gains in cost of production, provided the supply of raw material and of labour is available and the demand for products exists.

The six-hour day is already a most urgent and much-needed condition of working hours in all industries where women and girls are employed. It must be remembered that a large proportion of women engaged in industries, whether married or single, have, unlike their fathers and brothers, some housework to do as well as their work in industrial employment. And these hours of housework and the resulting fatigue must be remembered when considering their hours of work in the factory, workshop, or office.

In the textile industries and all others where the cost of overhead charges, such as interest on capital, salaries of partners and managers, repairs and renewals, depreciation, rates and taxes (omitting all taxes on income or profits) is about equal to the cost for weekly wages, the change from a 48-hour week to a 72-hour week of two shifts of 36 hours each would affect the cost of production somewhat as follows :

Working a 48-hour week and assuming that the product was 1,000 items per week at a cost of £1,000 per week for overhead charges and of £1,000 per week for wages, the resulting total cost of production per item, exclusive of raw material and such other proportionate costs as would always be in exact relation to volume produced, would be 40s. per item.

If such textile or other factories adopted the six-hour working day system they would work 72 hours per week in two shifts of 36 hours each shift per week, and assuming that no increase of production per hour worked was achieved, which need not necessarily be the case, and that the wages paid for a 36-hour week were the same as for a 48-hour week, which must always necessarily be the case, then the resulting product would be 1,500 items. The cost of production for overhead charges would not be seriously affected, as machinery almost invariably becomes obsolete before it is worn out, and fixed capital in plant, buildings, and machinery would be the same, the cost of overhead charges would again be £1,000, but the cost for wages would now be £2,000, or a total of £3,000 for 1,500 items, or again a cost, exclusive of raw materials, of 40s. per item.

But supposing, as one is justified in doing by past and present experience, that the unfatigued worker could produce as much in six hours as formerly was produced in eight hours—and we will examine into this later on—then the figures as to cost of production would be somewhat the following, and show a great gain in economical production: 2,000 items would then be produced in a 72-hour week of two shifts of 36 hours each shift at a cost of £1,000 for overhead charges and of £2,000 for wages, a total of £3,000, or of 30s. per item, which would be a reduction of 25 per cent. on cost of production compared with cost when working a 48-hour week. This economy might wisely be used, partly in increased payment to the workers by means of a bonus on production in addition to wages, which wages would be the same for 36 hours as formerly for 48 hours, and the balance to the consumer in reduced selling price of the product—so that practically the whole of the benefits of economy of production would go to the workers first directly in shorter hours of labour with higher total earnings as wages and bonus, and afterwards as consumers in lower cost of living.

The employer-capitalist would not need to share in this economy of production, because his share would come to him on his increased production and quicker turnover of capital, with resulting increase in dividend-earning capacity.

It is clear from this rough and ready calculation that in all industries where overhead charges exceed the portion of cost of production paid as wages to the worker, the advantages would be greater in proportion to the ratio of increase in cost of overhead charges. And equally it is clear that where the cost of overhead charges is less than the portion of the cost of production paid as wages, there would be a resulting increase in cost of production in proportion to the ratio that the lesser cost of overhead charges bore to the cost paid as wages, and that a point would be reached at which the immediate adoption of a 72-hour working week in two shifts of 36 hours each would be impossible and impracticable.

And now as to the possibility of the unfatigued worker producing as much in a 36-hour week as in a 48-hour week, let us refer to the experience of our forefathers as recorded in the debates in Parliament during the passing of the Ten Hours and other Bills, and let us remember also that nowadays, with more or less automatic machinery, increased production per hour by the workers can be effected in two ways : firstly, by the unfatigued workers' increased efficiency, and secondly, by the unfatigued and alert workers being able to attend to a greater number of machines.

At this stage some may be asking themselves, Why not work a 96-hour week in two shifts of 48 hours each ? and in answer to this we can apply the experience of Russia cited by Mr. Romaine Callender in a debate in the House of Commons on the Factory Acts Amendment Bill in 1874. He said :—

The hours worked in Russia were of extraordinary duration— one case being cited when, by a double shift of workers, 132 hours were made per week, yet in this case the production per spindle was barely more than that of an English mill working 60 hours.

Mr. Baxter, in an adjourned debate on the same Bill, also referring to the practice in Scotland at that time of working twelve hours, and when the trade was good some fourteen or fifteen hours a day for a part of the week, said :—

Now, I was so convinced that this could not be a good system, that twelve years ago I issued a peremptory order that no man in my employ should under any pretext whatever be permitted

to work in those premises for more than ten hours a day. And
what was the consequence ?   The very first year—and it has
continued ever since—we turned out more bales in the ten hours
than ever we had done in twelve or fifteen hours.

In the same debate Mr. Hermon, who was, I believe, Member
for Preston, stated :—

There was a very strong opposition to the Sixty Hours Bill, but
it might now be safely said that there was no manufacturer who
wished to repeal it.   He entirely disagreed with the Commissioners
when they said that by giving more time in the evening to the
operatives there would be an increase in debauchery.   No such
effect had followed from the Ten Hours Bill, but, on the contrary,
as soon as it passed, the operatives had improved their position
socially, mentally, and educationally, while it had advanced a
most important branch of national industry.

It is well known in the trade that more bad work accumulated
during the last half-hour or hour than during the whole of the
day.   During this time a drowsiness crept over the factory hands,
so that they became themselves like machines, and almost all
the disputes and unpleasantness that occurred during the day
had their source in the present prolonged hours of labour.

Mr. Mundella, speaking towards the end of the debate,
said :—

The Hon. Gentleman (Mr. Fawcett) contended that if the working
hours were reduced 6 per cent. the outcome would be reduced in
the same proportion unless the machinery or its rate of speed were
increased.   That was, however, an argument which was answered
by Mr. Hugh Mason, who, after he had reduced the hours of labour
without adding a single revolution to the speed of his motive power,
declared that he had not turned out a breadth less in the year
after he had made the change as compared with that which
preceded it.

Miss Victorine Jeans, in her Cobden Club Prize Essay
entitled *Factory Act Legislation : Its Industrial and
Commercial Effects, Actual and Prospective,* states :—

If we had to sum up in a single sentence the general effect
of the Factory Acts on the textile manufactures, we should say
that the legislation tended to enforce everywhere the prin-

ciples of the selection of the fittest ; in other words, it helped to bring about the fittest use of capital, of invention, and of human skill and energy, and therefore it did not diminish production or lower wages, neither probably did it lead to a fall in profits nor a permanent loss of foreign trade. . . .

No nation can long maintain a commercial supremacy unless its labouring class is strong and intelligent.

There are those who will assert to-day, as Mr. Webb does, that the English cotton-spinner finds competition keenest, not where the hours of work are longest, as in Russia and India, but where they are shortest, as in Massachusetts. Certain it is that the most perfect machinery, the largest system of production, the lowest amount of waste time, are all features characteristic of those industries and those countries where the shortest working day obtains.

But our greatest encouragement and inspiration come from reading the various speeches of the late Lord Shaftesbury (then Lord Ashley), when speaking in Parliament on the Ten Hours Bill. The Government of the day resisted the evidence he brought forward to show that the hours of labour could be reduced without economic loss. On May 10, 1844, he spoke to the House as follows :—

Here then springs up a curious and important problem for solution by this House—no, not by this House, for they have already resolved it—but for Her Majesty's Government, who deny our conclusions and oppose themselves to the thrice-recorded wishes of the British Empire. Which is the preferable condition for the people—high wages with privation of social and domestic enjoyment, without the means of knowledge or the opportunities of virtue, acquiring wages which they waste through ignorance of household economy, and placed in a state of moral and physical deterioration ; or lower earnings with increased advantages for mental improvement and bodily health—for the understanding and performance of those duties which now they either know not or neglect ; for obtaining the humble but necessary accomplishments of domestic life and cultivating its best affections ? Clouds of witnesses attest these things—clergy, ministers of every persuasion, doctors, master-manufacturers, and operatives have given, and are ready to give again, the most conclusive evidence, but Her Majesty's Ministers refuse to listen, and will neither adopt the remedy we are proposing nor assist us with one of their own.

Speaking sixteen years afterwards as Lord Shaftesbury in the Town Hall, Manchester, on October 6, 1866, he referred to the agitation for the Ten Hours Bill and to the success of the workers in carrying their point, and the effects on the workers themselves as well as on the nation resulting therefrom. He recalled the attitude the workers had taken up during the agitation. They had said :—

"We are standing for the limitation of the hours of labour as our great right, as the charter of our liberties ; give us but that and you will never hear of sedition in Lancashire ; you will never hear of discontent ; you will see that we are among the most loyal of Her Majesty's subjects, and we shall be both able and willing to discharge every duty that can become a citizen. No more (they had said) shall you hear of disturbances in Lancashire if once that right is conceded, if once our just demands are acknowledged."

Speaking of the better times, Lord Shaftesbury continued :—

I cannot but congratulate you from the very bottom of my heart, and I know you will congratulate me that we are met under such favourable auspices. We are collected together. in this room, not to talk of grievances, nor to devise methods for the purpose of removing them—not to talk of what we shall do, nor of what we fear ; but simply and solely to exchange congratulations that we have, by the blessing of God, attained to the present condition of things, and that the whole of this great country is working in perfect harmony, men with masters and masters with men.

There is no sour feeling, no angry heart, no difficulty existing among them.

And how was this achieved ? Recollect this was achieved without violence, without menace, without strikes, without resort to any extraordinary or illicit means.

God's blessing rested upon so peaceful a course ; and when you obtained your triumph, when you gained your end, I tell you I think in no one part of your career, in all the long agitation we had, did you exhibit a more generous spirit, a truer policy, a more thorough development of that which is the greatest blessing man can have—common sense, than the way in which you took your victory, and the way in which you acknowledged your triumph. There was no boasting, there was no pæan, no crowing of cocks, no cry of victory, no desire to exult, and no saying to

the masters : ". We have carried the victory and will make you feel
you are under our feet." On the contrary, you said : " We
have been enemies, but let us now be friends. We have
come now to the grand point ; you may fancy you may lose,
but only give us a fair chance, only meet us with an open heart
and generous treatment, and you will find that when worked out
the issue will be quite as beneficial to yourselves as it is to the
operatives."

You have that statement from the Chairman, who from his
own experience says that the measure has been beneficial alike
to master and man, to employers and employed ; and so it is, and
in all great works of this kind, in which the real rights of mankind
are concerned, in which the physical and moral interests of the
human race are in jeopardy, in all matters of the kind, depend
upon it, the truer economy is justice and humanity, and when you
have achieved the triumph the truer wisdom is to say, " We
forget the past ; we have been enemies, but for God's sake let us
be friends ; we have in time to prepare ourselves for eternity :
let us have no feuds, no differences, but let us join hands and
go forward, and God will bless the issue."

And coming down to modern times, experience still demon-
strates that working shorter hours with lessened fatigue does
not reduce output, but generally, and with very few exceptions,
tends to increase output.

The Report of Dr. Vernon on the Health of Munition
Workers gives facts which will remove any doubt existing
in the mind of any one as to the six-hour working day. In
that Report he states that from experiments spread over
thirteen and a half months upon the output of workers making
fuses, a reduction of working hours was associated with an increase of production, both relative and absolute. Hours of work
were changed first from a twelve-hour day to a ten-hour day,
and Sunday work abolished. A group of women making
aluminium fuse bodies provided the following results : A
twelve-hour nominal day, after deducting lost time, making
eleven hours net, yielded 100 articles, say, per hour, and
100 totals, say, per week. A ten-hour nominal day, after
deducting lost time, making nine hours net, yielded 134
articles per hour and 111 totals per week. A nominal eight and
a half-hour day, after deducting lost time, making a seven
and a half-hour day net, yielded 158 articles per hour and 109
totals per week, thus proving that an eight and a half-hour

working day, or 52-hour week, yielded more in products, both per hour and per week, than a twelve-hour day or 72-hour week, calculated either per hour or per week.

From other reports also that have been issued since the war began on fatigue of munition workers, we find this astonishing fact—that a larger output, not only per hour but per week, has been made when fewer hours have been worked. Recently an employer stated that in the early days of the war the nominal hours in his factory were 53 for the women; and he was staggered to find that the women were losing an average of 14 hours each per week. Fourteen hours a week was the average lost time for each woman, bringing the actual average time worked by each down to 39 hours, and he said: "Oh, this won't do; we will let the women come an hour later in the mornings, and we will let them go an hour earlier in the evenings," making twelve hours a week reduction. So he made the hours 41 a week, and then he found that the lost time averaged one hour per woman per week; therefore, they were making 40 hours instead of 39 as previously. But he found, in addition, that in the 40 hours that they now worked—this was after deducting lost time—he had an increase in the output in the week of 44 per cent.

Government reports repeat over and over again, from definite experiments, that in a reasonable number of hours the human being turns out its maximum output. Fatigue the human being one day, let the man or woman come fatigued to work the following day, and so on, and after two or three days the output goes down, down, down, and is continually falling. Let the human being work no harder each day than the body can accomplish without fatigue, and he or she will come again fresh the next day; and the output will increase and increase. And it has been found that the increased output by working a reasonable number of hours varied, according to the industry, from 50 per cent. to 120 per cent., and the 50 per cent., it will be seen, agrees very nearly with the figures given in the above record. Therefore, it is not difficult to imagine that with two shifts working six hours each shift, the output might go up 33⅓ per cent. per hour, and so give the same output in a 36-hour week as previously in a 48-hour week.

Sir Robert Hadfield, of Sheffield, stated last year (1917), in the course of an interview :—

At our plants we have reduced working hours with that largely beneficial result which seems to be inevitable. It has become clear that this procedure is even better business than it is humanity. Shorter hours make good men better, and bring the medium workman up to something higher than the old-time average. The hostility of the men to various progressive things was as unfailing as, for instance, their opposition to labour-saving machinery. Now they have learned that the better the tools the better the workman, and that the better the workman the better his pay.

The fact that workmen are not themselves machines is not yet appreciated in its full value.

Mr. Cecil Walton, of Glasgow, than whom there is no one who has a wider experience or speaks with greater authority on the subject of hours, fatigue, and output, has stated in an address given in Glasgow as follows :—

There is only one way of reducing hours of a working day, and that is by increased production. Any attempt to shorten the working day without this must end in national failure.

He cites the following amongst many other proofs of the possibility of greatly increasing output and greatly reducing hours :—

A factory producing 15,000 items a week was divided into six units of machinery, each unit producing 2,500 items per week. It was decided during 1917 to transfer some of these units of machinery to another factory in another part of the country, and to do this in one complete unit of machinery at one time, and to introduce a bonus on output arrangement with the operators. After removal of the first unit it was found that the remaining five units still produced 15,000 items a week. The second, third, and fourth unit were similarly removed, leaving only two units of machinery, and these again and alone produced 15,000 items per week.

And again Mr. Walton has stated :—

If we turn to the authorities on the subject and study the figures as given us with regard to output per head of our indus-trial armies, we are staggered to find that Germany and America produce per worker in the twenty-six principal industries something like five times as much as we do. This sounds a terrible indictment, and it is. But if we study the question closer still, we find it is not a disaster we cannot overcome. Their industrial efficiency is below what it ought to be, and although our own industrial efficiency is lower, still we can so improve our efficiency as to bring ourselves easily in advance of either the German or American scale of industrial efficiency.

He then proceeds to refer to the economy and increased efficiency to be achieved by one only of the many changes possible in our industrial operations—that contemplated in the "All Electric" Scheme,[1] by which it is shown that we are at present paying wages to at least one-half our industrial population for producing waste. It is claimed that by the introduction of such a scheme and the transfer of these producers of waste into the ranks of producers of essentials, we can reduce the working hours of all workers by 50 per cent. without reducing wages or increasing costs. So that the 25 per cent. reduction of hours involved in the scheme of a six-hour day can then become universal with increased wages to the workers and reduced selling prices to the consumer. He concludes with the deduction that this is a clean-cut proposition for which the nation should strive, and that he is quite convinced that by intensive production without fatigue in fewer hours we can greatly increase our production.

But whilst under the scheme for a six-hour day the employee-workers would be working only for six hours each day, the machinery would be working for twelve, eighteen, or twenty-four hours each day, with resulting enormous increase in production at reduced cost.

We need not fear too slow an adoption of the principles of economy of production—our fears are of too hasty adoption before supplies of raw materials, supplies of workers required for increased production are available, as well as increased demand sufficient to absorb all increased production.

[1] By the so-called "All Electric" Scheme it is proposed to burn the coal at the pit mouth, thus saving transport on rails to house or factory or locomotive, recovering the by-products for fertilizers, aniline dyes, and coke, and using the gas in internal combustion engines for generation of electricity, to be conveyed by truck, cables, and wires to wherever required.

We are not likely in any case to move as slowly towards adoption as was the movement towards the Ten Hours Bill, which was first proposed in Parliament in 1802, and only finally carried by Lord Ashley through Parliament in 1850.

It would be useless to increase the output of all the factories in the United Kingdom if we had no purchasers who could absorb the increased output. There are two great factors in increasing demand—one is increased wages and the other is reduced cost. Both these increase the purchasing power of the home-market consumer and equip us the better to compete with the foreigner abroad, by enabling us to supply cheaper articles for export, so that, as a commercial proposition, the six-hour day based on increased production would be absolutely sound, and could be depended upon to result in the increased demand for our products essential to its success. It is stated that a Scotchman once wrongly attributed a quotation from Shakespeare to Robert Burns. On being corrected he replied, " Ah, weel, it was guid enough for Rob tae ha'e written it." It is not known who first said that if one makes but a mousetrap better and cheaper than any one else the whole world will soon beat a path to one's door, but these words are good enough to have been said by the wisest business sage the world ever produced, and to date back to the very first dawn of civilized dealings between man and fellow-man.

In addition to the effect of a six-hour working day in giving all that we require in production from our workers, so that we can pay to the workers the same wages for the reduced hours that they receive for the longer hours, it would give us this great additional national advantage : it would enable us the better to solve our after-war problem of employment for the men and women who will then be released from actual war and war supply work.

After the war we shall have a demand, which must be met, for increased supplies of all kinds of products to replenish exhausted stocks both at home and for export markets. This will necessitate, for many years after the war, an increased production, if Great Britain is to retain her home and export trade, amounting to at least 50 per cent. over and above the normal production required in pre-war times. In addition, we shall require to build, it is estimated, at least one million

homes to house the workers under proper reasonable conditions. We shall also require to replenish our mercantile
marine by many millions of tons of new ships.

All these will make a demand upon our labour to such an
extent that it will not be possible immediately to build
additional factories and workshops, or to erect plant and
machinery for the same, in order to provide for the 50 per
cent. increased production demanded. We shall be short of
factories and workshops, but we shall not be short of labour,
for it is estimated that the termination of the war will release
at least 11¼ millions of men and women who are at present
engaged either in active work on the field of battle or in
workshops and factories and transport service necessitated
to supply the army in the field with material and supplies
required for the prosecution of the war.

The raw material we shall require is mainly produced
within the British Empire : therefore, so far as raw materials
are concerned, and so far as labour is concerned, we shall
not be in any serious difficulty, but we shall be in difficulties
with regard to providing the factories and workshops and
machinery required to work up raw materials into the finished
product. We shall have an overwhelming demand for goods :
we shall have the necessary raw material and men and women
required to make the goods, but we shall not have the equipment to manufacture the goods to meet the demand for the
finished product, owing to the lack of workshops, factories,
plant, and machinery.

But even if we could immediately at the close of the war
erect new factories and workshops, we must remember that
it is estimated the cost of building would then be 75 per cent.
more than pre-war rates; and the cost of plant and machinery
would be anything from .100 to 200 per cent. above pre-war
rates. Therefore the erecting of new factories and equipping
with new plant and machinery would seriously handicap our
home manufacturers in their competition with manufacturers
in Neutral and Allied countries, such as Holland and the
United States, in supplying economically the demand in
the Neutral markets of the world, which demand we had
previously very largely ourselves supplied. But by the
adoption of the six-hour working day we could automatically
and immediately increase our production by at least 50

per cent., just as effectively as if we had been able to build 50 per cent. additional factories, workshops, plant, and machinery. And we could do this without making any call on capital or any call on labour for the mere erection of these mechanical utilities.

After the war, therefore, the times will be ripe for the six-hour working day of two shifts. There will be the demand and there will be the labour to meet the demand, and by working double shift we shall have the machinery sufficient to meet all our requirements. The $11\frac{1}{4}$ million men and women released when the war is over cannot be found work on any permanent basis by means of philanthropic effort or subscription lists or good intentions. They can only be provided permanently with employment on sound economic lines of greater economy in production and of a greatly increased demand for products resulting from that economy in production.

The six-hour day would also solve the question of the education of the boy and girl on their first leaving school : it would also solve the question of their physical training ; it would solve the question of military training, so that we could have a trained citizen army ; and it would solve the question of the outlook on life of our workers. Can we fancy anything more sordid than the life of a boy (or girl) who goes into the factory to-day under the stress of modern conditions ? His grandfather probably went to work at eight years of age. The present-day boy goes at fourteen years of age, and from then to seventy years of age (if he survive) he sees nothing but the factory, except for a few holidays, so few that he scarcely knows how to systematize and make the most of them, and his horizon, his whole outlook on life, is so stunted that he cannot live the life he was intended to live. It was never the Creator's intention to send us into this world as so many " hands "—He sent us with imagination, He sent us with the love of the country, He sent us with ideals and outlook, and these are simply stifled under our present industrial system.

How can we wonder at what is called " Labour Unrest " ? If men and women were satisfied to endure quietly such conditions, then we might indeed despair of their future and the future of the British race.

Let us make the most of our English-speaking race, the finest race, in our opinion—of course, we may not be impartial judges as to that—on the face of the globe. Let us face the problem of the boy and girl of fourteen—it is a pressing one. What to do with boys from fourteen to sixteen is a most important problem. We know how, at that age, boys delight in getting into all sorts of scrapes and mischief. The training of boys in Boys' Brigades and the Boy Scout movement, for which we are indebted to General Sir Robert Baden-Powell, has proved a great remedy for that state of affairs. But if we could take the boy and girl at the age of fourteen and give them, say, two hours' schooling in the morning or afternoon, and continue this right on until the age of thirty, what could we not make of them? Evening classes, we know, are a failure. The boy or girl attending these classes after a hard day's work is not in a receptive state of mind for instruction—both mind and body are weary, and therefore the evening classes are not a means to an end—they are a substitute and not a success. Education cannot be completed at fourteen for the very simple reason that the necessary number of hours have not been devoted to it, and the number of subjects have not been covered that ought to be covered. But under the six-hour day scheme these two hours of instruction on alternate mornings and afternoons could be continued from fourteen to eighteen, and from eighteen to twenty-four years of age, during which period the scholars would be receiving instruction of a still higher character, with physical training, and would be learning how to improve in their work. The very fact that during their working hours they are working with their hands would help their brain education, and eventually make them infinitely superior citizens.

These two hours for education and training each day, from fourteen to thirty years of age, must be made absolutely compulsory, must be what we may call " conscripted " for the benefit of the whole nation. From fourteen to eighteen years of age, let it be extended education of what we may call the High School character, together with physical training; from eighteen to twenty four years of age, education of what we may call the Technical and University character, with extended physical training ; from twenty-four to thirty years of age, training for military service, for national service, for the duties of citizenship, preparing for membership of Village and Town Councils, and so on, and general study of all that goes to make for government, of ourselves, for ourselves, by ourselves, which ideal is very often merely a catch phrase. Then each of us after reaching thirty years of age will be a unit in a nation of educated, trained men and women, and within the limits of the law we can be trusted then to make the best use, for whatever appears good to us, of the two hours a day, for we do not think a conscription of time after thirty years of age would serve any useful purpose. The organizing of our time in this way would give us a fully educated nation, a nation capable of assuming responsibility, and with initiative. We should all be the better for it—we should have better bodies and better minds; not even University education could compare with the education which would be obtained under the above conditions simultaneously through hand and eye and brain. The man in the University gets his brain developed, but if he had simultaneously the training of hand which manual industries impose upon those who work in factories, his brain would be better for that discipline and for that training of hand and eye. We should produce under these conditions a population in the United Kingdom more highly trained, more hard-headed, and more practical than ever we can produce with a Public School education followed by that of a University. We believe most thoroughly in the combination of the training of hand and brain and eye simultaneously, and we believe most sincerely that a six-hour working day would solve that modern problem experienced in all our industries of the scarcity of men and women to fill the positions of foremen, managers, and directors. All through our industrial system this scarcity is so great, that unless the nation takes in hand the proper and efficient education of her people, with definite courses of study for definite careers, agriculture will suffer, manufactures will suffer, shipping will suffer, business will suffer, and the progress of the whole Empire will be retarded in competition with other nations.

There is a great desire, and not an unreasonable desire, and certainly a healthy desire, on the part of the workman to take some share in the control of the factory he works in, and it is a desire that should be encouraged; but we

4

cannot take a rank-and-file worker out of the factory to-day and put him on the Board of Directors and expect that he will be able to give valuable help and assistance. He must be trained ; we have all had to be trained. There must be healthy growth and development towards this end, for there can be no sound business without previous training. The desire to have a seat on Boards of Directors and a share in the control of the industries is a healthy sign ; but it would be madness and ruin to the industries of this country if our Boards of Directors were not composed of trained men, and only by better education shall we be able to satisfy that reasonable ambition of the employee-workers.

We should also have, under such a system, a huge trained citizen army, without any of the waste that attaches to the barracks system and ordinary militarism. Let us remember that a standing army is always an incentive to war, whilst equally unpreparedness induces an attack. Into the members of this citizen army would be instilled that love of country and of home that would make them feel that both were worth fighting for, because their conditions of life would be such that they could take pride and pleasure in them.

The girls, too, would be trained in domestic economy and in all that they must know to fit them for their part in life in the highest, fullest, and happiest sense.

Now, human beings who have received all these advantages, at the age of thirty can be trusted to make the best use of their spare time. They will usually have a hobby. The man at thirty will perhaps keep a garden, and he will take a special pride in growing his own vegetables ; and if you consider the millions of cultivators who, if we had some such system, might be raising food-stuffs to-day in this way, what a relief such assistance would prove in the feeding of the people of the British Isles !

We should gain vastly in all directions by the introduction of the six-hour day ; the worker would have opportunities for recreation, for education, and for the achievement of a higher social standing. The term " factory hand "—that most hateful of terms, as if the " hand " possessed no soul, no intellect, and no ambition in life at all—that term would go. The factory employee, no longer a " hand," would go for six hours a day to the factory in the true spirit of service.

He or she would receive for that six hours at least the same pay that he or she now receives for eight hours. Those now receiving one shilling an hour and working eight hours a day would, in future, receive 1s. 4d. per hour and work six hours, and would be able to produce as much in the six hours as is now produced in the eight, while the machinery, running in two six-hour shifts, would produce a vastly increased output.

This is the very rough and crude outline of what we suggest should be done in order to meet industrial conditions after the war. With all modesty and sincerity, the six-hour working day proposal is submitted to careful consideration and vigorous criticism. Out of all this wreckage of war must ultimately come better and more ideal conditions of living for all classes, and under better conditions we can raise from our British stock the finest race the world has hitherto seen, and build up an empire founded on principles of health, happiness, justice, and equal rights for all—an empire that will be the friend of all nations and the enemy of none. Then this war will not have been fought in vain, and fathers, brothers, and sons will not in vain have surrendered their lives ; mothers, wives, and sisters will not in vain have mourned the sacrifice of their dear ones, and Peace, never again to be broken, will smile once more, and kindly Nature will reward our labour with enough and to spare, and with lengthening life, deepening joy, and happiness for all.

III

TOOLS TO THE MEN WHO CAN
USE THEM

HUDDERSFIELD, *January* 19, 1918.

[Addressing a meeting at Huddersfield, Lord Leverhulme expressed the fullest confidence in the leaders of Labour and
the representatives of Labour associations, who, in this crisis
of the nation's history, would help to bring the war to a
successful issue in " a clean peace." He proceeded :].

WE are a democracy, and a democratic country would not
be worthy of its name if it could only think of war and the
winning of wars. We have got to think also of peace, of
what will come to this country when the war is over ; but
surely if we can all trust the cause of Labour and Labour
leaders to-day, we can equally trust Labour and those who
lead Labour to do their duty when the war is over. And I
am convinced we can equally trust the employers and all
sections of the community. There is some sort of nervous
dread about, that when the war is over there will be a cutting
down of wages ; that there will be, as is thought—I do not
agree in it—more workmen than jobs ; and on the other
hand, that there is going to be some attempt to take the tools
from the hands of men that are now using them, and who
are experienced in the use of them, and hand the tools over
to men who are inexperienced in the use of them. I am sure
we would agree that either the cutting down of wages or in
any way the worsening of the present conditions with respect
to earnings would be disastrous to this country ; and it would
be equally disastrous to have our industries taken out of
the hands of those who have conducted them successfully
and handed over to those who are inexperienced because
untrained.

It is a curious fact that this talk of the reorganization of the control of industry should come forward at the time when the great nation, our kindred across the Atlantic, is giving greater consideration to efficiency, and a larger output, and a cheaper cost of production, with higher wages and shorter hours. Now, any mistake on our part in the peaceful lines of commerce when this war is over would be only second as a disaster to a mistake on the field of battle. Either would be irredeemable. If a nation once loses its position in commerce, it requires a matter of centuries to recover it. We have seen commerce in the Mediterranean pass from the Venetians to the Spaniards. Why? Because the Venetians got an idea that they were strong and powerful and could dictate terms to the world. They thought they could make their own rules—selfish rules, entirely for the benefit of the Venetians. The trade passed to Spain, and Spain was in her glory at the time when she began to consider that she had arrived at the point when she could ignore the basis upon which her trade had been built up, and became more narrow and selfish, less considerate of the interests of others. Then the trade passed from Spain to Holland, and Holland, in turn, got to the pinnacle that we enjoy to-day, because although we are only 45 millions of people in this country, we can say with truth that we stand in advance in manufactures, in trade and commerce, of any other nation in the world, whatever its population may be.

Holland, in her turn, lost the trade to England, and we are now at the cross-roads, and have to consider carefully what way we take, or the pre-eminent position of British manufacturers, and the pre-eminent position of the workers, and of interest in them, may pass from our hands to those of other and more alert nations. You remember we are told that above all things we are to desire wisdom. And I do believe myself that what we in Lancashire call " nous," wisdom, is one of those rare faculties which, possessed in full, can take us through life to a realization of our wildest dreams and ambitions. But if we neglect wisdom, and rush to make changes without due consideration—very much like the proverbial bull in the china shop—then we only court wreckage and ruin and disaster.

Now, what are our ambitions? What are the ambitions

of any true democratic people? Surely our ambitions are a
better life for each of us, more equal distribution of wealth,
higher wages in order to attain to a better living, more plentiful supply of all that we require in the way of boots, shoes,
and clothing, better homes—homes with gardens, homes that
are really places in which a soul can live and expand, and
not caves in which we can crouch out of the light. Well,
these things will not drop down from the skies for us. They
are not very much good until we can get them on the earth
on which we live our narrow span of life. There is no other
way. Some people see the curse of Adam in work. I believe
it was the greatest blessing that ever came to us. Of all
people, those without work are the most miserable. That is
no reason why " A " should be worn down and fatigued,
whilst " B ," without much work, apparently gets more than
his fair share of the good things of this world.

There is no logic in that, and I am bound to say I feel it
very intensely that it has to be recorded at the beginning of
the twentieth century that nine-tenths of the wealth of the
United Kingdom—and I believe the same equally applies to
most other countries—should be possessed by less than one-
tenth of the people, and that nine-tenths of the people should
possess only one-tenth of the wealth. That is a system that
cannot be defended for one single moment. But you must
remember this, that through all the centuries we have had
such a system of taxation in this country that the taxes have
not been laid on the backs best able to bear them, but have
been laid on the worker. I remember very well years
ago, when I was a Liberal candidate, pointing out that,
including the rates on the house, and if the man happened
to be a moderate drinker and a moderate smoker, and his
wife enjoyed her cup of tea, and so on, the rates and
taxes collected from the workman were from 4s. to 5s. in the
pound of his income; whilst the contributions of the
wealthy man at that time could not be totalled up to any
more than 1s. in the pound. The income tax at that time
was about 6d. or 8d. in the pound, there was no super-tax,
no graduated death duties, and no excess profits tax.
But now how do we stand? If a man is wealthy, he
has 5s. in the pound to pay in income tax; 3s. 6d. in the
pound super-tax; if he possesses a fortune of a million, it

will have to pay 20 per cent. in death duties. Take the death duties as payable on an insurance basis (that is the easiest way to reckon it), and you will find that it will bring his total taxation to-day (1917–18) up to 12s. 6d. in the pound. We have only had this system a few years; but I venture to say—and this is apart from excess profits tax—that under the present system of taxation it can no longer be said that the wealthy are not bearing their fair share of the burden of the country.

I do not say they are bearing more than they ought to bear; but I feel proud of the fact that the opportunity is now given to each man in the country, whatever his riches may be, whether he is a weekly wage-earner or a wealthy man, to bear his fair share of the burden of the country. The wealthy are bearing it in the form of taxation, and in every other form—by their sons fighting in the trenches, and in all other ways. We never were a more united nation, a more equal nation on the basis of taxation; and we ought to be proud of it. But the echo of the former complaint still reverberates around the land, that the rich are not paying their share. That has ceased to be the fact. And it is not really the fact that land does not pay its fair proportion, that property does not pay its fair share, that the incomes of the wealthy do not pay their fair share. All this we have altered very largely since 1896. The years 1909 and 1910 were the crucial years, when a big advance was made; but the biggest advance of all has been made since the war began. I want us to bear that fact in mind, because, believe me, it has accomplished more to improve the conditions of the people of this country, to raise their spirits, and to give them an outlook on life, than anything in the century preceding it. I am confident and happy to acknowledge that that is so; but our hearts, having begun to show sympathy in one direction, must show it in all. That is the rule of nature. You cannot be warm-hearted and sympathetic in one direction only; you must be in all. You cannot be cold and brutal on one question; you are cold and brutal on all. That is the law of life. We have also seen the Health Insurance Acts, and I had the honour of carrying two bills preceding the Government Acts — the Old Age Pensions Act and the Payment of Members Act—which latter gives the means to

any constituency to select its member without consideration
as to whether he can afford to pay his railway fares
to London and his lodgings when he is in London. Just
think what it has meant to give old age pensions, improved education, medical attendance on school children,
and health insurance. The total expenditure on these—
education, old age pensions, labour bureaux, and health
insurance—is 61 millions a year. That amount is taken out
of the taxes (mainly income tax) and distributed throughout
amongst the workers.

It is thought by some that democracy means absolute
uniformity, and you will notice one of the questions put by
the Prime Minister yesterday, in reply to a questioner, about
the conscription of wealth and the acquisition of wealth,
was not answered by the questioner. The Prime Minister
had asked whether equality of wealth ideal was to apply all
round, whether we were to be bound by the ideal of the skilled
engineer receiving the same wages as the labourer. He was
not answered ; but if equality all round would achieve anything to better the conditions of life, I am sure the skilled
engineer and all of us would agree that a system that made
for the greatest good of the greatest number would be a right
system in a democratic country. But, believe me, human
nature is founded upon very distinct principles. First of
all, we are social. We love to live in communities, in towns.
Very few of us love to live in scattered districts. The men
in the backwoods of Australia are always longing to go to
Sydney, Melbourne, Adelaide, Brisbane, or wherever their
big city may be. But whilst we are social in our habits and
love our fellow-men, we are individualistic in that we love
our own homes. We do not want to have our homes in a
barracks, there to live a barracks life with others. Each one
of us feels that we have an individuality. We are not only
a body, but we have a soul, and our individuality wants room
for expression. I always think the earning power of a man,
whether in the factory or in the office, whether he is or is not
the proprietor of the business, is in proportion to his mental
attributes. As the young tree sends its roots in every direction searching for nourishment and water, so does human
nature send out its roots to feed its soul. If you were to say
that the man in the factory must not do some duty apart

from the workshop, and that the employer must not undertake some task apart from his business, you would cramp
the aspirations and desires of every human being. We have
to attempt to satisfy our souls as well as our bodies by our
effort. Take inspiration for that effort away, and we should
just become automata.

But whilst we recognize these two attributes, there is a
great rule that has been laid down by the greatest Founder
of social institutions the world has ever seen. And He laid
it down two thousand years ago, "Thou shalt love thy neigh-
bour as thyself." If we desire that we would not be crippled
ourselves, then we ought not to cripple our neighbours. We
would like to have room to expand ourselves. So ought
our neighbours, and our neighbours are those we come in
daily contact with in works and in factories We are on a
level as citizens of this country. We are all producers, and
equally consumers, and it is only when we recognize this
that we can consider the idea that there should be some read-
justment of the productive work of the country. There are
those who affirm that industries should be put under Government control. Now, I do not know whether Government
control is going to be called scientific management, whether
it is that this management by a Government would be more
scientific than management by an individual. The only
scientific management that I have any belief in, and under
which as far as I see to-day everything could be successful,
is a knowledge of human nature. You cannot force human
nature. If you set tasks for human nature, as seems to be
the basis of what is called scientific management, it will
surely break down. Human nature can respond enormously
to sympathy, to a kindly touch, to a participation in the
fruits of its industry, to a share of the profits it has helped
to create. The only scientific management there can be, in
my opinion, is that holding between employer and employed,
one to the other, and each for the other; on those lines
only can we have scientific management. Now, is that really
to come about in other ways than we have developed? Supposing we were to take all our industries and hand them over
to the Government. You could no more put in chains and
chain to the business the present proprietor than you could
the present operatives of the machines. Such a thing would

be slavery and unthinkable. Whilst you could take over the machines, the mechanical apparatus, the soul of the owner you could not chain and fasten to the industry. The industry would pass into the hands of men who were not used to the tool, and who had no experience as to how to use it. And remember how narrow the margin is for economical production. Do we ever think for one moment how narrow it is?

Now, I think we were agreed that we want more of all the good things of life if we can only produce them. Ninety per cent. of the consumers of this country are the workmen themselves. I am certain I have not over-stated that. There-fore, under the present system the workman encourages his own production where he lives. I knew a man whose father put him as a draper in his own draper's shop. On the death of the father—the man was then forty—he sold the shop and went to study medicine, took his degree, and served in Edin-burgh as a doctor for the remainder of his life. He is still alive. That man followed not his father, who thought there was nothing finer than the drapery business. If our businesses are going to be nationalized, are we going to be requisitioned to work in our own factory? Are we going to be told that they want so many engineers, so many people in woollen factories, and that they must have them? If that system is going to prevail, in any case, whatever the system may be, it will be a limitation of individual liberty; it will not produce higher wages; it will not produce shorter hours; it will not produce as cheap commodities. Just to refresh our memories! The worker negotiates himself, or through his union, for the highest rate of pay. And the employer knows that the rate is one that he must pay, and produce goods on, either at a profit or at a loss. He knows that if there is a loss, no one will drop a tear over him; he will slide into the Bankruptcy Court, and later on into some forgotten scrap-heap of the world. But when the workman as producer has received his pay, and handed that pay over to his wife, he is now a consumer, and as a consumer, his wife, rightly and properly, and he himself, rightly and properly, must spend that money where he or she can get the best value in quality and price. And, therefore, you have this position—the producer of goods at the risk of the employer, who takes all the risk ; you have the spending of the wages in the cheapest market that the world can provide ; and between these two comes the employer.

Could there be any better system devised by any man placed in a Government office in one of those London hotels, in a department run under a system that they call " minuting," under which a document is sent round, and to which each official adds a little note, and about three months later it comes back, and the whole thing is forgotten ? Under that system, there would be nobody to stand the loss but the consumer. Under that system, if the goods were badly bought, we should still have to pay. And assuming we make this " advance," the outside world would not move at the same speed. If the wages were put up, they would be added to the cost to the consumer, and the consumer would have to bear the cost of those goods, well or badly bought. The success of the business would be no concern of the man in the office : his salary would be assured, and if he was not suitable, his services would be dispensed with, and another man, equally unsuitable, could be put in his place. Then, how deep-rooted in our individual nature is the love of liberty, which gives us the right to expand. If we are chafing at all to-day, it is that we feel we have not sufficient liberty ; that we want more liberty, not less. And any error of wisdom, any lack of " nous " that we might be carried to in a departure of such magnitude, would lead to untold unrest, and our children's children would not call blessings down upon us for it.

The individualistic system is the system we are on to-day. We have the employer, whether he is a limited company or an individual ; he stands between these two great forces— the producer, the wage-earner and consumer—and he has to have a very intense mind to enable him to make a profit between the high rate of wages, ever increasing, the shorter hours, ever reducing, both, I am happy to say, necessary adjuncts to civilization. Between these, and the demand from the consumer for ever better and cheaper goods, he may or may not make a profit. Well, as to the supposed profit, if he does make a profit, I am sure in any case such profit is grossly exaggerated, because our income tax returns do not show (as is known to every one in the business world)

the losses of the unsuccessful. If we had the returns side
by side, as we should have in an ordinary balance-sheet, if
the nation's balance-sheet not only showed the income of
the successful, but the losses of the unsuccessful, you would
be astonished to find that the average earnings of the employers
in this country, over and above the lowest minimum bank
rate of interest on their capital, are so small that you could
not replace them for the same money by salaried men, who
could be depended upon to look so closely after production,
keen buying, and strict economies.

I am convinced of that, and you would find that the profits
of trade and commerce are much less than are imagined.
But suppose that was not the case. Here and there is a man
of extraordinary ability for making money. Generally that
ability comes more from extraordinary ability for avoiding mistakes than from anything else. But there are such men. It is
a faculty that is very rare. I am convinced from my own
observation that there is less than one per 100 people who
would be capable of running a business, however small, and
making a profit in it; that there is less than one in 100,000
who would be capable of running a large business. And you
know the number of men who have made those fortunes
which seem to be so great—the Fords, the Carnegies, the
Rockefellers—they are very few, less than one per hundred
millions out of the 1,200 millions there are in the world. Not
only are they very few, but very largely their fortunes have
been realized through a combination of fortuitous circumstances. Invariably, without a single exception that I know
of, the men who have made these colossal fortunes have
actually made them by special service to the public, and by
producing a cheaper and ever cheaper article. Not one of
them has been able to make money by advancing prices.
The only time that money is made is when, by improved
processes of manufacture, prices can be lowered. You find
that without a single exception. Now, if we change all this,
and we are to have an idea that by putting our industries
on some other footing we should mend matters, I would like
us to consider exactly the basis that we are on before we make
the change. I would like to remind you of this, that we have
not as manufacturers, we have not in my opinion even as
Trade Unions, considered sufficiently the human element in

our industries. The manufacturer has devoted enormous efforts by means of science towards cheaper and ever cheaper production. Why, it is within the lifetime of most of us in this room when electricity was not the useful and beneficial servant of man that electricity is to-day. The power of Niagara ran to waste, and also the power of the Victoria Falls, and the waterways on the Continent and in America. Now, by means of science, we know that that waste power is equivalent to the efforts of millions of human beings, and we have harnessed it and utilized it as our servant.

We have to-day, I believe, in the United Kingdom, by means of steam-power and machinery, the productive capacity of over 1,000 millions of human beings working twenty-four hours a day, and by means of that power we produce, by possibly 14 or 15 millions of human beings, all that could be produced by the thousand million producers without that power. But, as I say, there was in the past a great power running to waste, and some of it is running to waste yet (such as the ocean tides), in spite of us. I venture to say there is not one of us in this room who without fatigue, in terms of thought and organized inspiration and aspiration, is not capable of infinitely more for the common good than we are doing to-day; but we have never been studied; the best has not been brought out of us. We have been made into automata to go to our work at six or seven in the morning and finish at five or six in the evening. And it has become almost a fetish with some of us that the less they can do in that period, not only the easier is it for themselves but the better for their mates, because they will be leaving so much more for their mates. And on the employers' side it has been equally a fetish that the lower the wages paid, the longer the hours worked, the cheaper the product would be. They are both wrong, absolutely wrong. But is it to be wondered at that under this system the idea should have leaped into the minds of some trade unionists as to the restriction of output? I do not know whether you have read recently what has been said by a great Trade Union leader in America. I want you to consider this very carefully, because we are in competition with America. Don't think for a moment that our Allies in the trenches will be our allies in commerce. It is in noble devotion to the cause of democracy that the Americans are throwing themselves into the war. They have no territory in dispute, no object to pursue in European politics. They are doing it from the highest ideals of democracy and to free Europe from the hell of militarism. They are not children who are doing this, and when this war is over, and we come to consider the trade of the world, whatever ideals we have in this country, we shall have to reckon with the ideals the Americans have.

I will read to you what Mr. Gompers, the President of the American Federation of Labour, representing many millions of working men, said in a recent speech : " We are not going to have the trouble here that Britain had through restriction of production." He is speaking for Labour, not for the masters ; but you might think he was speaking for the masters. " There has not been any restriction of output for over thirty years in America. We, in the United States, have followed an entirely different policy." Well, I can say that I have been to America, and found a man in charge of five lathes, automatic machines. I remember asking, when I got back, why a man should not look after five lathes here, and I was told the Union rules were against it. That is a mistake. I do not want you to believe that I think the Unions are not doing good work according to their lights. I have never met a Trade Union official yet who has not impressed me with his sincerity in desiring to do the best for his members ; but it is a mistaken policy, that is all. It is exactly the same as many mistakes on the side of the masters ; but they are both wrong. " We say to the employers "— there is no doubt about letting employers know—" bring in all the improved machinery and new tools you can find. We will help you to improve them still more, and we will get the utmost product out of them ; but what we insist on is the limitation of hours of labour for the individual to eight." This might be my speech if you take the eight and put it at six. It is exactly what I am preaching. I believe in England we are ripe for a six-hour day in many industries. I have had experience of eight hours for twenty-five years. The same type of people who say that six hours is impossible, said eight hours was impossible, said that ten hours was impossible, and that twelve hours was impossible, and so on at each stage of reduction from a fourteen-hour to the eight-hour day, so that I am not made despondent by the fact that I am told it is impossible.

" Work two shifts if you please, or work your machinery all round the twenty-four hours if you like, with three shifts, and we will agree, but we insist on the normal working day, with full physical effort. We will not agree to that over-work, producing the effect of over-fatigue, which destroys the maximum of production, undermines the health of the individual worker, and destroys his capacity for full industrial effort." That is almost word for word what I have said, except for the eight instead of six. We want higher wages, shorter hours, a larger production of everything, so that we can get a cheaper cost. Without that cheaper cost we have no funds to pay higher wages. Higher wages are merely a shadow unless you have lower costs giving increased purchasing power with the higher wages ; and I believe with that and with shorter hours we can realize all that we are striving for. I am told that at Ford's works they employ 40,000 persons. A boy worker can get £1 per day, and all employees are paid double Trade Union rates ; and there I am told that it is the exception for the workman not to have his own motor-car. Why should not the workmen have their own motor-cars ? They will not get motor-cars under a system of restricted output ; there won't be enough to go round. Every time we increase the output and reduce the cost we have a fund out of which we can increase the wages. It ought to be possible for men to have more leisure than they have to-day, when they commence work at six, or seven, or eight in the morning and work on until five or five-thirty in the evening. More leisure than that is an absolute essential if we are to live a complete, full life of citizenship. I say without hesitation, and I say it is within reach, now that we have got the wages up, we can afford automatic machinery, and so by means of automatic machinery we can produce more goods.

Everybody should be given an interest in the results of their work, and then they can have more satisfaction in it. And there could be more relief for the employer, so that employers also could devote themselves to a realization of shorter hours, with harder work during the time they are at work without fatigue, cheaper production and more leisure.

Well, now, that is what we want, but what are we drifting to ? I will show you. Gompers said : "It is thirty years since we had limitation of output," and so I will go back thirty years, when they dropped it and we began it. It is sometimes said that a dog returns to its own vomit. It seems to me we were a dog that returned to another dog's vomit. In 1886 the output of a certain class of worker in the United Kingdom was 312 units ; in 1906 (twenty years after) this output had been reduced to 275, and in 1912 (that is the last recorded year before the war) it had dropped to 244—from 312 to 244 in twenty-six years in the United Kingdom. In the United States, whilst in 1886 the output per worker was at 400, it went up to 596 in 1906, and in 1912 to 600, so that whilst we went down the United States have gone up 50 per cent. But we have Englishmen in other parts of the world—we have them in Australia. Do you mean to tell me that the Australians are not as strong trade unionists as any others ? And the same applies to the New Zealander and the Canadian. We all know they are strong trade unionists. In Australia in 1886 the output per head was 333, in 1906 462, in 1912 542, more than double per man what the workers are producing in the United Kingdom. Yes, but the wages are double. I want to tell you as the output goes up the wages go up ; as the output goes down, if the wages go up, the purchasing power goes down. In New Zealand the output per worker increased from 359 in 1886 to 470 in 1906, and 503 in 1912, and in Canada from 341 to 472. Of all the English-speaking races all over the world, we, in the United Kingdom, are the only ones who have fallen behind in our production per head of the workers. And is our condition improved under this policy ? Are we satisfied, and happy with it ?

I think if any of you have gone, as I have, to Australia, and seen the homes of the workers—seen them having their summer holidays on their beaches with their wives and families—you would see that their wages are not improperly used. Well, but for it all, they would tell us that increased output is the road to betterment and prosperity. Australia settled with the I.W.W., put a number of them in gaol, and this under a Labour Government. "Ca' canny" is a canker. I want to say how sincerely and earnestly I am, and have been all my life, with every master and worker in this room, although I cannot say whether there are more masters or more workers. I cannot say, but I do think this, that Lancashire men and Yorkshire men have very similar views, and very similar aspirations.

What I want is that we shall just inquire, if any change is to be made, whether it is right, and the first step to lead in the right direction. I do not want to claim that what I have said this afternoon represents the whole Alpha and Omega of this great question. I have only touched the fringe of it, but, believe me, the truth I started with is an absolute truth—that we shall not get our clothes, and boots and shoes, and houses dropping down from the sky, or jumping up from the ground like mushrooms. We will have to work for them, and in working for them, it is our business to consider how we can produce them with the least fatigue, the utmost leisure, the greatest cheapness, with the largest volume, so that out of the things created in this way there shall be an ever-increasing demand, so that however great this output, it shall all be absorbed ; a demand for all the necessaries, comforts, and luxuries of life as much from the workers as from those who are so-called masters, with such a fair and right system of graduated taxation, that those who have the ability to make money may utilize their creative powers or their opportunities to bear a strong man's burden of taxation, and so each in proportion to his strength will bear the taxation of the country. Working on these lines, I see an England where we can work a reasonable number of hours, where our children shall receive the fullest and most complete education—the children of the workman just as good an education as the children of the employer—so that there shall be every opportunity for all of us ; that there shall be a ladder for every man, and he shall be left to climb it if he wishes.

NATIONAL POSSIBILITIES

LONDON, *July* 10, 1917.

[As the guest of the Aldwych Club, Lord Leverhulme began a
speech on after-war problems by referring to his happy business relations, extending over many years, with the Chairman,
Sir Thomas Dewar. He told a story of a Lancashire man
who, when dining at a restaurant, was served with a lobster
which had only one claw. The waiter's explanation was:
" Well, sir, lobsters are very pugnacious animals, sir, and
when they fight, sir, they sometimes lose a claw." " That's
all right," replied the customer; " take this chap away, and
bring me the winner." Their Chairman was a winner. He
had nabbed the picture of " The Macnab "—painted by an
artist of whom the whole British race was proud—and had
thus prevented it going out of the country. Lord Leverhulme
went on to say :]

WE have met here as business men, I take it, just to have
a short conversation upon the problems we shall have to
face when this war is over. And, perhaps, in order that we
may consider the problems the better, it would not be amiss
to note what has been our attitude in the past towards the
race with whom we are now at war, and whom, we know,
when this war of armaments is over, we shall have to meet
in a war of commerce. You know wa are very easygoing
people. Any one who represents " John Bull " portrays
him as a very genial and jovial fellow; but he always looks
prosperous. Our attitude has been to magnify and extol
the race with whom we are at war, and to consider them
patterns of industry and organization and of every commercial
virtue, and we have rather run down ourselves. We have
thought little of ourselves and a great deal of Germany. I
think this ought to be inquired into. The attributes of a

nation will continue after the war is over, and when we come into conflict on commerce, we shall then be helped by our natural attributes as they will be helped by their natural attributes.

Now, in the past, certain inventions have been discovered, and the whole of modern civilization is built up on those inventions. How many of those inventions have the Germans given to the world, and how many have the English-speaking races on this side of the Atlantic and the other side of the Atlantic given to the human race ? I am not sure whether you would like me to give you a list, but I think it has a bearing, from this point of view. We are going to carry our inventiveness into commerce after the war as we have done before the war. If you consider the implements of warfare the Germans are directing against us—the submarine, the aeroplane, the torpedo, the machine gun, breech-loaders, Dreadnoughts, and explosive mines—they are all the inventions of the English-speaking race, either on this side or on the other side of the Atlantic. The names of the inventors are British ; they have no Germanic sound about them.

Apart from these, the world owes a great deal to the English-speaking inventor in many other directions. In the peaceful fields of industry the list is still longer. Not only have we been inventing implements of destruction; the inventions by English-speaking races include such articles of construction as the steam-engine, the locomotive, the air brake, the steamship, cotton-spinning machines, telephones, the telegraph, the sewing-machine, the typewriter, the phonograph, photographic films, motor-cars, pneumatic tyres, bicycles, vulcanized rubber, modern dyes, electric lighting, incandescent lamps, electric storage batteries, electric tramcars, harvesting machinery, reapers and binders, disc ploughs, threshing-machines, washing-machines, anæsthetics, antiseptics, new kinds of steel, compressed-air tools, and a further long list of improvements which, if I attempted to go through, would wear out your patience. Even the German so-called Kultur is the philosophy of Machiavelli, an Italian of the fifteenth century. It is a philosophy long ago discarded by all civilized people. Far from being new, it is more than four hundred years old, and Germany has simply revived it.

What has been the German method ? Young Germans have been sent here, to learn our methods, accepting a low salary, or no salary at all, to get into our offices and works, spy out all they could, and then return to their own country, armed mentally with English methods, which they have turned to account in their export and home trade, thus reaping a rich harvest from the brains of the English-speaking race. The Germans have never considered it a crime to plunder the brains and steal the ideas of other people ; but that form of stealing is as much a larceny as if a person picked another person's pocket. We are a good-tempered race, and the German laughed up his sleeve at our over-trustfulness. When Bessemer, the English-born son of a Frenchman, invented his process of manufacturing steel, inquiries were made from Germany and representatives came over to inquire into the system. They returned with drawings, but never paid one penny for a licence to use them. Recently I saw in the paper the case of a man who, long before this war, invented a machine of great utility. He received an inquiry from Germany, together with an offer to become his agents. When he supplied them with drawings and all the necessary information, they began straight away to dispute his patents, and gave him the choice of either a costly lawsuit or a free hand for them to benefit by the product of his brains. This is a sample of their methods.

All the great inventions of the past are the children of our brain, and these are only the elder brothers of the family of similar inventions which will succeed them after the war. And all we ask from our Government is reasonable protection for the brains of the country—not protection in any other sense. I am an ardent believer in Free Trade, but our brains have not been protected. When we are taunted with the story of aniline dyes and how the Germans exploited them, the whole tale ought to be told. It was not the fault of English manufacturers. It was the fault of the taxation of spirits for industrial purposes, which made it impossible for us to use those spirits in the production of aniline dyes. The German Government gave their manufacturers cheap spirits for industrial purposes, free of duty. The British Government only within the last few years, whilst the present Prime Minister was Chancellor of the Exchequer, made it possible for British industries requiring industrial alcohol to obtain the same free of duty. Such conditions as that to which I have referred no British manufacturer should be obliged to suffer under.

Again, foreigners have enjoyed exceptional terms from our Government for foreign shipping, and even as late as last July the British Chambers of Commerce had to pass resolutions asking that British shipping should receive the same privileges as foreign shipping. I am not going further into that. I only want to emphasize this fact, that we have the right brains and the right intelligence, and desire only the right opportunity, and, after all, this inventiveness owes its origin to the principle of government by the people. The liberty-loving English-speaking race, living under free institutions and free government, by encouraging individuality produces inventive genius. We are not willing to be dragooned and stifled. If we were to submit to that, our inventiveness would leave us and we would sink to the level of our enemies.

This is the position—how are we to make the best of this fine material we have here? Which way are we going to make the best use of it on both sides of the Atlantic? I say emphatically that the present antagonism between Capital and Labour ought not to exist. Labour and Capital must be fused into one. If Capital and Labour are wise, they will abolish all distrust and antagonism between each other. Capital wants the largest possible return on capital, and is not reluctant to receive it with the least possible exertion. Workmen want the biggest wages and the shortest hours, and are not averse to these being realized with a minimum of exertion. These twin brothers in wants have got to recognize they cannot, either of them, achieve their aims by the methods adopted in the past. The highest return on capital cannot be obtained by means of the longest hours and the lowest wages for labour, nor can the highest wages and the best returns for labour be obtained by any policy of " ca' canny."

The relations of Capital and Labour have been wrangled over until all arguments are threadbare. Why should not the worker be also a Capitalist in joint partnership with the so-called employer? The division of profits between the two in the past has not been on such a basis as could make Labour feel that it genuinely shared in the undertaking. We want to do away with that. Profit-sharing is liable to misconception. Co-Partnership is the one basis of commercialism under which we can have that comradeship between all classes in commerce that we have seen displayed between all classes and all ranks in the trenches. That is the spirit, and if that spirit could be evoked in fighting the enemies of the Empire on the field of battle, surely it would be equally forthcoming in fighting the enemies of trade and commerce in this country—men who tried to combat us in trade and commerce by unfair means. It only wants us to recognize the great fact that we are every one of us—so-called employers and workmen—born with the same hopes and ambitions and imbued with the same aspirations. Some of us may have been stifled by wrong surroundings when we were young; some may never have been given an opportunity to grow; but wherever there has been the opportunity of growth and development amongst the English-speaking races, whether at home or overseas, you find what has been termed the building of castles in the air and the attempted realization of ideals.

Modern industrialism is not very old—not two centuries old, and that is a short time in the history of the world. Prior to that man and master worked side by side. The master knew his Jack and Tom and Joe, and Maggie and Jane and Mary—in fact, every employee in his place. And they all knew him; they all came to him in their troubles. He knew their domestic worries and anxieties, and he helped and encouraged them. That worked well until, by the introduction of machinery, the business became so great as to render a continuance of the position impossible. The office might be in London and the factory in the Midlands, or even overseas. You could not to-day produce things in any other way. With enormous factories and machinery came of necessity a huge organization in which men working in the factory hardly ever saw the so-called employer.

The only thing that can restore to any degree that condition of two centuries ago is Co-Partnership.

[Here Lord Leverhulme dealt with essential conditions of Co-Partnership (see under that heading, p. 95) and with the Six-hour Day on lines similar to those of the article under that heading, pp. 14 to 35.   He concluded as follows :]

That is the outline, the very feeble outline, of the vision I have of meeting industrial conditions after the war.   We shall need to develop the inventiveness of our race.   Do you know how we got many of our great inventions ?   From the operatives themselves.   The safety-valve on the boiler was invented by a youth who was set to watch a gauge, and whose instructions were that when the indicator rose to a certain height he was to open the valve, let off the steam, and so reduce the pressure.   He got impatient—he wanted to be doing something else besides just *watching*, and he found that by the arrangement of certain weights in a certain fashion the valve would automatically open itself at the precise moment necessary, and he could go away and attend to something else.   He experimented until he had ascertained the exact weight required to do this successfully, and from that youth's idea was evolved the safety-valve as we know it to-day.   Many similar valuable inventions are continually being made by the men who can see and appreciate most keenly the assistance they will give—*the men who are constantly in touch with the actual machinery.*

Now, the greatest stimulus to the production of this inventiveness we wish to develop is a share in the profits. It would humanize our industries, it would make for brotherhood, and, above all, it would make the working man no longer antagonistic to Capital, because he would be a capitalist himself.

CO-PARTNERSHIP

CO-PARTNERSHIP

WOOLWICH, *November* 30, 1909.

["With regard to the great question of Co-Partnership, it is
doubtful whether any one in the world, in this or any other
age, has done so much as Sir William Lever has in this direction." Such was the testimony of Sir John Cockburn, speaking
as Chairman at one of the addresses reproduced in the present
volume. That address will be found in its place immediately following the one here presented, which was delivered
to the Woolwich Chamber of Commerce at the New Town
Hall, Woolwich.]

THE subject of "Co-Partnership or Profit-Sharing?" is
one that has always had the greatest interest for myself.
Looking backward, I find it will be twenty-two years next
March since I first made public utterance on this subject;
and therefore, before I come to describe the particular method
that has been adopted by myself, I would like, with your
permission, to take you over the ground that I travelled
during those twenty-two years before arriving at our present
basis, just as one wishing to travel to a far country would
desire first to spread out a map and see which routes were
possible, what rivers had to be crossed, mountains to be
scaled, torrents to be forded, and so on. So I will endeavour
to go with you to-night through some of the aspects of this
great question as they presented themselves to me; for,
believe me, the margin of safety, viewing safety as the stability
of industries of this country and the well-being of the workers
in them, is a very narrow one. Indeed, it would be very
easy to make the position of the workers infinitely worse
under Profit-Sharing or Partnership schemes than under
the present usual wages arrangement, if one did not exercise
the utmost care.

At present, Labour is in the position of Debenture Holder on all industries. Placed in that position by the law, if any firm becomes bankrupt, even before the Debenture Holder receives his money, wages must be paid in full, and, therefore, Labour stands in the position of Debenture Holder.

The three forces that go for production are : Capital, Labour, and Management. I know sometimes these are separated and made into two forces, called Labour and Capital, but this is not a true division. There are really three forces, Capital, Labour and Management, notwithstanding the fact that very often Capital and Management are comprised in the same person.

Now, the position is this, that Labour receives a fixed rate of wages ; Capital receives its fixed rate of interest ; and the product is a product of varying value, according to market conditions, and affected by the harvests of raw materials all over the world. Consequently, when you have two fixed factors and a variable product, it is obvious that the reward of Management, called profit, must be a variable quantity—sometimes it may be great, sometimes it may be small, and very often it must disappear entirely, only showing loss. Now, that is the position to-day, and practically the position of Labour is this—it comes to the employer and says, " I can't store my labour ; my labour has to be sold each day, and must be turned to account each day. If I do not make use of to-day's labour to-day, I cannot do so to-morrow. I cannot store it until a favourable opportunity for selling it occurs. I must sell each day's labour to-day—the day in which I exist. Now, with Capital, and with commodities, you may be able to stand the fluctuating markets ; I cannot —my commodity won't keep. In addition to that, I have a wife and family to keep, besides myself, and I must be assured every week of my weekly wage. Whether the product I produce for you realizes profit or loss for you, I have nothing to do with that ; I cannot have anything to do with it. I must be assured of my weekly wage, and if there is a profit, you are welcome to it. If there is a loss, I cannot help you to share it." Now, this is the attitude Labour takes up, and rightly takes up. It practically becomes a Debenture Holder. Remember that is also the position of the Debenture Holder. The Debenture Holder says, " I do not want big profits; I want an assured rate of interest with absolute security. I would rather have a sure 4 per cent. or 4½ per cent. on this business than I would have the Ordinary Shares, with a possible 10 per cent. or a possible nothing; therefore give me Debentures." Therefore Labour and the Debenture Holder stand side by side. Labour and the Debenture Holder, in asking for no share in losses, are placed in that position, relinquishing voluntarily, or of necessity, in order to maintain their security, any prospective share of profits. Now if we, therefore, approach this subject, we might find— if we approach it in the wrong way, we should certainly find —all we had done was to change the position. On any attempt to restrict Management from the receipt of profits, jointly created, Management becoming a fixed charge, Capital remaining a fixed charge, but with the produce still variable in value, then Labour would have to be the one that had to take the variable remainder. So that this is manifestly one of those propositions which one has to handle with the utmost care in order to be perfectly sure that in our intention to benefit Labour we have not unintentionally made the position worse.

And I would remind you that Trade Unions have, rightly, set no value upon Profit-Sharing schemes. They have never been interested in them at any time. They have never seen in Profit-Sharing schemes anything worth exchanging for the right to bargain for Labour at the highest market price that Labour can obtain; and I say they are right in that, for through the influence of Trade Unions Labour has been able to make better terms and better arrangements financially, in the form of increased wages without risks of loss, than could have been made under any system of Profit-Sharing or Partnership.

Now, I will tell you how this operates. Industries are started in this country, and in the early days of these industries there is practically very little competition amongst the holders of these industries, and profits are inflated, with the result that a rush takes place of money into such industries, and a rush of capital means that more men are employed in them. The wages remain a fixed charge, and in consequence of the inrush of capital and the greatly increased output, the value of the product, represented by the price it will fetch on the market, has a serious fall ; but the result of that new industry has been to employ more capital, and every additional workman put on in that new industry has relieved the labour market, and enabled Trade Unions the better to bargain for an advance in wages for all labour in that industry and out of it. When you turn to the cotton industry (I come from a cotton manufacturing county—Lancashire), in my younger days a cotton-spinner was called a "cotton-lord," and he was, relatively, getting a very much higher return on his capital than could possibly be obtained to-day. I know of cases in those days when a man could build a new mill out of the profits of the old one in three years, and so on ; but that has completely passed away with the organization of the industry, and with its becoming more stable and more settled. Such a state of affairs as that could not exist long. It was sure to attract fresh capital, and it was sure to produce a cutting down of profits ; but the very conditions that operated adversely for the Management, reducing the profits, operated in the direction of raising the wages of the workmen. If you take the cotton mills of Oldham, the balance-sheets of which are public property, you will find this extraordinary result, that in the last thirty years the payment of Management—because most of these mills got the bulk of their capital in Preference Shares and Debentures—the payment of Management represented by the rate of dividends on Ordinary Shares has decreased by 50 per cent., and wages to Labour, as shown by the Trade Union rate of wages, has during the same period increased by 40 per cent. Now, that is without any Profit-Sharing at all. That is the ordinary economic working of supply and demand, what is called the competitive forces that go on in all our industries ; and therefore we have got to be extremely careful in approaching this subject, because I am convinced of this, that anything which tends to complicate the basis on which Labour is paid makes it more difficult for Labour to obtain the highest price for itself, and everything which tends to simplify the arrangement enables Labour to obtain the highest possible price ; and if we introduce a complication of any kind, we might, so far from producing any benefits to those we desire to benefit, produce exactly the opposite result.

Now, when we come to examine Profit-Sharing schemes, I want to point out this ominous fact. They have been commenced in the commercial world and have been in active operation for over seventy years, yet the Board of Trade Return issued on this very subject shows that the average life of Profit-Sharing schemes with firms is only five years ; that whilst there may be some that have existed for twenty years or longer, the average duration is only five years ; and the last return of all, issued in February of this year, shows that at the present moment only forty-nine firms in the United Kingdom, employing some 64,000 workpeople—only 64,000 out of millions of workpeople represented by the Trade Unions —only forty-nine firms were dividing profits with their workmen. Now, that is a fact that you have got to bear in mind. And another point I want to mention (and it has been the cause of the break-up of many Profit-Sharing arrangements) is, that Profit-Sharing does not prevent strikes. I know it was hoped that under a Profit-Sharing arrangement strikes would cease, but how could it have that effect ? If a workman hears that in an adjoining colliery, as has often been the case with a Profit-Sharing colliery, a rise in wages has taken place, while he in the colliery where he shares the profits gets no such advance in wages, surely he is bound to resent what must appear to him nothing other than some arrangement under which he is asked to take less wages than he is entitled to, and must resort to strikes, which he consequently does. It is absolutely certain that no one will accept a Profit-Sharing arrangement in exchange for some abatement from the highest rate of wages he is entitled to receive. Well, now, there is another advantage in having wages fixed by Trade Unions. It is that in competition amongst masters it is of great importance, in my opinion, that masters amongst each other should not have the opportunity of competing in the rate of wages ; that the wage fund should be fixed, and that any man giving a tender in competition with another tender should not have any advantage out of a lower wage fund. The only effect that could have would be gradually to bear down the wage fund. " A " takes a contract to-day because he can get labour for less than " B." " B," not content with that, makes a corresponding arrangement and takes something next time out of the wages fund. There would be no end to it. Therefore, there is a great advantage in the wages being fixed. Any Profit-Sharing arrangement, therefore, that was based upon what you might call pooling the profits, Labour getting an uncertain share, would be sure to be disastrous in every way.

Well, now, I want to point out that sometimes employers are treated in the Press to a very great deal of what I may call "cheap morality." Hard employers are railed against, employers that are working on uncertain conditions are held up to public odium. Now, I say this without hesitation, and I think I can afford to say it because you know what I believe. There could be no worse friend to Labour than the benevolent, philanthropic employer who carries his business on in a loose, lax manner, showing "kindness" to his employees ; because, as certain as that man exists, because of his looseness and laxness, and because of his so-called kindness, benevolence, and lack of business principles, sooner or later he will be compelled to close. On the other hand, although it sounds hard, that man who adheres strictly to business principles, who pays, of course, the highest rate of wages, because to-day it is not possible to pay less, and carries on his business on so-called "hard" lines, will not be the worst friend of Labour at all. This man who is employing labour on strictly business principles is not the least respected by Labour in any way, and ought not to be.

To take another point, the incapable employer does not make profits, the capable employer does make profits ; so therefore we find in different businesses not only the profits vary, but in the same business you have varying profits because of the varying capacity of the employer. Now, the incapable employer making small profits may not excite the envy, criticism, and remarks that are hurled at the man of more capacity who earns larger profits, but he is doing his workmen a great injury. Supposing he has 100 workmen and fails to make profits. He gradually ceases to be able to employ 100 ; he cannot keep up renewals of machinery and upkeep out of the profits, so in time he has to discharge 50 of his men. He is now employing 50. It is true that the loss falls on him, but it equally falls on the 100. It is true it only appears to fall on 50 out of the 100, because only 50 were discharged, but that 50 discharged have to the extent of 50 depressed the labour market, and lowered the demand for labour by competing with men in occupation for labour. On the other hand, the more capable employer, employing 100, makes profits, and because he is making profits desires to increase his business. He doubles his plant, puts more money into the business, and employs 200 men, and is still making money. That man is not only benefiting himself and the 200 men he employs, but the whole body of workmen, by his taking 100 workmen off the market and finding them occupation, so benefiting the whole of them.

Now, I do not want you to think that in any case labour can be paid out of capital. It is not, and we find this curious fact, which has to be explained by those who rail against the position of Capital, that wages are always highest in those countries where not only is capital most plentiful and where capital earns the highest rate of dividends, but wages are always lowest in those countries where there is the least capital employed, and where capital earns the lowest return. In England, wages are high and the return on capital is high. If you go to Spain, there is less capital employed than in England, and the return on capital is lower and the wages to labourers are lower. If you go across to India, you will find there is less money again available in industries, and there is less return on money in industries, and you find labour pay at the lowest ebb of all, a fact which you can prove for yourself. In all countries where capital is plentiful and receives the highest return, there wages are highest. Therefore, we come to see clearly that it is intelligence and wealth that raise profits and wages, and ignorance and poverty that lower profits and wages. Therefore there can be no antagonism between Capital and Labour, and if we want to raise the position of the workers we cannot do that by lessening the wealth of any other class. Now, there are laws in the business world just as rigid and just as inviolable as laws in the physical world, and therefore we come to this axiom, that the only way in which wages can be increased is to increase the efficiency of Labour, and therefore the quality and quantity of the product. Wages can only be paid out of the fund that is created by Labour, and therefore, if we adopted Profit-Sharing under the idea that we should get a short-cut that would clear us of all our troubles—if Profit-Sharing meant inducing

6

a number of men to lean on each other, and to lean on the man at the top, and to think that he by his magic wand called Profit-Sharing could distribute a share of profits every year to improve their position—this would be an enormous mistake: it could not last long.   Therefore we find the average duration of life of Profit-Sharing schemes is only five years, and we find that those men who try to mix philanthropy and benevolence with business find it a mixture that is no more possible than oil and water—that you cannot mix them.   The business has to be conducted on sound business principles, just as mills and factories must be equipped with the most modern machinery.

Yes, but then, when you have got all your business methods and all your modern machinery and modern science, there still does enter into the calculation the human factor; and I say that the employer who merely guards machinery so as to prevent accidents in his factory that he would have to pay for, has entirely mistaken the true position. The true position is this, that if the hazardous nature of any occupation is reduced, if businesses that are unhealthy are made healthy, they become attractive to a greater body of workmen, a more intelligent class of workmen, and that industry carried on by a more intelligent class of workmen is much more likely to succeed than if carried on by a class that is less intelligent and less businesslike, so that the Compensation Act has another side to it than the payment under the Act.   Well, now, I would say, referring to that illustration, that there is the human factor in every works, and for the employer to merely consider the driving of the hardest bargain with his labour, and to get his labour at the lowest price, and to endeavour to force out of his labour the maximum amount of work that he can, is not to proceed in a manner which will favour his own ends.   He will not do it, he cannot do it; and I say this to the workmen: that the workmen who think that by reducing the output—what is called in the North the " ca' canny " policy—they will increase wages to Labour, and do well to make a job for two men spin out for three, are equally mistaken, and that they will not improve Labour by that method.   The only way these two, Management and Labour, can create a fund to increase profits—out of which wages and profits are paid, out of which,

it is possible to pay the highest rate of dividends and wages—
is to increase the quality of the product and increase the
quantity of the product ; that can only be done by becoming
more efficient. It cannot be done by working a greater
or less number of hours ; it can only be done by making men
in every way more efficient.

We find, then, that all the forces of production—Capital,
Labour, and Management—must work together ; must work
to one common end, must work on lines of enlightened self-
interest, and not on the lines of narrow personal selfishness, if
any good is to be done. Now, what feasible method have
we of drawing those forces together ? Well, let us carry
our minds back to examine the stages the industry of this
country has passed through, and see whether we have any
greater step to make to-day than our forefathers had at various
periods. In the first period of all, we were savages, we were
controlled by a chief, and if we met any other group of men
who did not belong to our section or tribe, we promptly killed
them if we could. And it was considered a businesslike arrangement, I have no doubt, in those days, for the very simple
reason that if we did not succeed in killing them they would
have killed us, and that was the whole basis of the state of
savagery. No working together was possible. The most
you could say was that the members of one tribe or little
settlement would work together, but the next tribe or settlement would be their deadly enemies, and we have that, of
course, existing in every uncivilized part of the world to this
day. After the state of savagery we developed into a state
of slavery ; that was the next step forward ; and there is no
doubt that under slavery life was protected, which was one
great gain, and consequently more effective work was done
for the community under a state of slavery than was possible
under a state of savagery. I have not the slightest doubt
that slave owners of those days considered it was perfectly
businesslike to drive their slaves to work with the lash and the
whip, and they would have thought kindness and consideration perfectly unbusinesslike and impossible to carry on ;
in fact, if in buying and selling their slaves they had considered them any other than cattle, if they had hesitated
for a moment to drag them to where they could get a good
price, it would have been considered totally unbusinesslike

and maudlin sentiment. In the present days of wages it is very nearly considered unbusinesslike and bordering on philanthropy to do anything more for workmen than is absolutely necessary, and strict business to get out of the workmen the largest amount of work by driving and by forcing methods rather than reasonable and proper methods. Well, I say this: we living to-day have not to make anything like so great a stride to take the workman from the wage-drawer—I use the word "drawer" because you cannot say under the wage system that it is always earned: a great section of men earn more than they draw, and the other section earn less than they draw—I say it is nothing like as big a jump from the position of wage-drawer to that of co-partner as there was from savagery to slavery and from slavery to wage payment. But, whilst it may be difficult to do so, and whilst, in addition, I may make a great many mistakes—for, as I said at the beginning, the margin of safety is extremely small—still, during the last twenty years I have tried first one method and then another working in that direction. I have always preferred to call my previous methods Prosperity-Sharing, and not Profit-Sharing, because I feel that Prosperity-Sharing best describes my ideals. I feel that when a business prospers it means that all the factors have entered into that success. It is perfectly certain that no one man could be responsible for all the success, and therefore, if the business prospers, I like to take the illustration of the family. If a father prospers in life he moves into a better house, his children get a better education, get better clothes, more holidays in summer, and so on; that is, without touching his profits at all. If that father said to his children, " I have made so much more this year, and will divide so much more with you," in my opinion the effect of that on the children would be that the next year, when the father had reverses in business and had losses, the children would begin to criticize him and say, " How is it that father is so much more a fool this year than last—why did he open that new office in London and lose his money ? " On the other hand, if he does not say anything about his income, but gradually betters his family, he can tide over those bad years and carry on without them knowing anything about it. Therefore, I commenced building houses, gradually improving the conditions without touching profits, which I did not wish to do. I felt I might make a very serious mistake, because steps taken in that way could not be retraced.

Now, another point comes up for our consideration when we go beyond Prosperity-Sharing, namely, the control of the business. Who is going to have control in a universal partnership? Now, here we come, in my opinion, to what may form a way out of the difficulty. Just as taxation and representation must go together, so it seems to me loss-bearing and control must go together. The man or body of men who say they will bear all the losses have the right, because they say they are going to bear the losses, to say they will have the control, and it is for them to say to what extent they would like to have the assistance in the control of those associated with them; and just as Labour cannot say that it will take any losses, so Labour, wanting to be in the position of Debenture Holder, has no right to say, " I will fix the policy of this business." If Labour claims it is right for Labour to fix the policy, it is quite obvious that such policy might result in losses, and as Labour could not bear such losses, it is clear that Management, forced to adopt a policy fixed by Labour, would have to bear the losses alone, whereas if there were profits they would have to share them. It would be a perfectly unfair arrangement that would not be right. To merely give out profits as sort of doles, in my opinion, would be equally wrong. We must cultivate the self respect of everybody we work with. There is not a man but must be able to look you in the face and say he owes you nothing, that he does not want cheques if he does not earn them; if he does not earn them as much as you have earned them, he does not want them. Therefore, we now come to consider on what possible basis we can work in Profit-Sharing.

In my opinion, ordinary Profit-Sharing has been proved and found wanting. Prosperity-Sharing is very good, but does not go far enough. Now, then, we come to a possible adoption of Co-Partnership. Now, in this Co-Partnership arrangement it must be fixed, as I have said, that those who alone bear the losses must take the control. For those who do not bear losses, whilst their help in Management would be welcomed, control is not a right that they can demand until they share' in the losses. Not until Labour can share in losses as well as

in profits can Labour assume control.   It is quite clear that
in all well-organized industries some must work with their
heads and others with their hands.   If food, clothing, and
homes are to be won for the whole body of workers, there
must be a head prepared to control.   I firmly believe that
the more we recognize each other as brothers, within the proper
limits of control, the more we shall raise ourselves as well
as those who work with us.   The whole body, employers
and employees, will be raised together.   Now, the employer
has, by force of circumstances, learned his lesson already
He has been taught that the best way for him to conduct
his business is to improve the quality and, as far as possible,
reduce the cost of his output, and that that is the only way in
which he can extend his business and increase his profits.
The workman has not learned that lesson because he has
never had a chance of learning it ; he has never been able
to have such a connection with the business as would bring
that lesson home to him, and therefore it is by admission to
Co-Partnership that he will learn it, and being in Co-Partnership he will see that it is only out of the fund created in the
business itself that any improvement or advancement is to
be made in the position of Labour.   Certainly, Co-Partnership, if not viewed in this light, if it has not the effect of
increasing products in value and quantity, cannot result in
increasing the wages, and cannot lead to any betterment to
the workers.   Co-Partnership, therefore, must first ask—
I am not giving these points in order of priority and not in
order of importance, as they are practically all equal—how
can we increase the output, improve the quality, reduce
cost, lead to greater care of tools and machinery, greater
economy of materials, and greatly reduce what is at present
an inseparable burden on all industries, the cost of supervision ?   I know supervision is at present, and always will
be to a certain extent, an absolute necessity, but I often think
if we could be Co-Partners we should greatly reduce that cost,
and we should have gone a long way in reducing the cost
of production.   Just as a slave worked better than a man-
eating savage, and a wage-drawer worked better than a slave,
I am convinced that a Co-Partner will do better work and more
of it, with less personal fatigue, under better social conditions
for himself, wife, and family, because his efficiency will

be increased, than the wage-drawer ; and it is only in that direction that we can uphold and maintain our system of Co-Partnership as better infinitely than any system of Profit-Sharing.

Now, what I want to say to the employer is : " Here is our system.[1] It means well, and we are going to give it a fair trial. I believe it promises well because it gives to the employee freer scope for the exercise of his abilities, it raises him and makes him a better man. This it is bound to do. The tendency is that the worry and cares of Management ought to be relieved by it. Working with a body of Partners must be infinitely better than working with a body of wage-drawers, and assuredly I believe, as certain as we are here, the wage fund and profit fund will not be reduced if we all understand it and work together ; but even supposing the profit were reduced, but that those at the head of the firm, the Managers, have lost the worry and the anxious time, even then I say that it is worth more than any amount of money."

To the employee I would say : " You are now offered an opportunity of sharing profits with Capital and Management, and have now the opportunity to show the kind of man you are ; join hands with your Co-Partners in a manly agreement to do your part in the Co-Partnership. You will continue to receive the highest rate of wages and will work the regulation hours, with all overtime rates that are provided on the fullest scale that has ever been paid or arranged. Join hands with me to make the profits of this business sure and increasing. Let it not be a one-sided Co-Partnership. There must be a fund created out of which you can benefit. There cannot be any one-sided arrangement that can be of benefit to either of us. Live up to our motto, ' Waste not, want not.' Fill your business hours with work for the business, increasing the quantity of the product, increasing the quality of the product. Take care of the machinery and tools, help me to weed out the chronic idlers and grumblers from this business. If we come on to years when dividends cannot .be paid you will suffer, but you will not be the only sufferer. Your Co-Partners will suffer, and I will suffer with you, and you will have learned what business means and what the

[1] See Appendix, p. 135.

risks of business are, a lesson that you ought to learn just as much as myself. Here is the Co-Partnership. I find you a ladder to raise yourself to the heights out of your present troubles and difficulties. I place it against the wall for you, but it is out of my power, or the power of any man, to push another man up the ladder—man and ladder both fall. I offer you the Co-Partnership : it is for you to make it a success."

II

CO-PARTNERSHIP AND BUSINESS MANAGEMENT

LONDON, *June 17, 1913.*

[Lord Leverhulme (then Sir William Lever, Bart.) addressed the Institute of Directors at its premises in Gracechurch Street. The Hon. Sir John A. Cockburn, K.C.M.G., M.D., F.I.D., who presided, spoke of the successful establishment of Co-Partnership at Port Sunlight. He envied the members of the staff and employees whom he had met ; they seemed to have everything that wealth could bring—all the advantages of social life and the benefits of travel—and they seemed to be a most happy family. He thought the secret of success in business was that, where service was rendered willingly and with a certain amount of joy in the work, it was always much more efficient. Lord Leverhulme said :]

IT was with very great pleasure that I accepted your invitation to be here this afternoon, because of all subjects, the one of the greatest interest to myself, and the one to which I have probably given the closest study outside my own business, is that of Co-Partnership. I believe that all manufacturers to-day are exposed to more criticism than probably any other class of the community. We are expected to adopt every method of every faddist in connection with our industry, while each one of us knows that if a manufacturer adopts any method that does not tend to produce more goods of a superior quality in less time, and at the same time pay labour higher wages, and give labour shorter hours, and simultaneously give goods to the consumer at a reduced cost, that manufacturer is led away from the ordinary commercial channels into by-paths of dalliance that can lead nowhere, and he is bound to come to ruin.

Well, the ordinary commercial relationship between each

of us, employer and employee, and one that has stood the test
of time, is that of the payment of wages, and it is being found
to-day that that bargain has a good deal of justice to recommend it. It is just this: a man says to the employer, " I
will let you have my labour for a certain sum ; if you make
money out of it, it shall be yours ; if you make a loss out of
it, you shall bear it ; guarantee me my wages, and make
your own arrangements after that." That man is practically
a debenture holder in the industry, and it is a perfectly
practical and sensible basis to, work upon. But it is not
found, as time goes on, to go quite far enough, because we
want more than the mere. desultory performance of duty ;
we want the whole-hearted interest of the man, and the
keener competition becomes, the more necessary it is that
we should have, throughout our whole staff, a personal interest
in the whole of the undertaking, which personal interest can
never be supplied by a mere wage-drawer.

Now we are in this difficulty. It is impossible to mix
different things with each other. It is impossible to mix
debenture holder and shareholder, for instance. There is
a sphere for each, and you cannot mix those spheres in any
way. You cannot let a man be a debenture holder and at
the same time take a share in the final profits of the business.
You cannot easily have a man a wage-drawer and also interested in the final profits of the business. And we have got
this problem to solve. Every manufacturer has ideals for
himself, in which he sees that his mills and factories are of
the very finest description, equipped with the latest machinery,
and in which he adopts the most modern methods. And there
we stop. As soon as we come to consider the question of
extending further and more modern methods to the labour
we employ, we are in this difficulty of mixing, or of trying
to mix, things that differ from each other. It is said, you
know, that it takes two to make a bargain ; and I believe
it is equally true that only one gets it.

Now, in former times the whole history of the world has
been a history of conflict. Conflict has been the rule of life.
It has been the question that has settled the stability of
nations ; conquest by war, and one perpetual conflict. And we
see the modern survival of this idea of conflict in competition.
The very antipathy of the public to anything partaking of

the nature of monopoly shows that they believe that war, or competition, is for the good of the public, and probably for the good of mankind. And we do know this—that competition does keep us alert, and does keep us strenuous in our business. It is more important, however, that we give good service to the public than that we waste our energies in competing strenuously with each other. Any method that we can adopt in our business that will improve our efficiency and the efficiency of those we employ, is a much more important matter for the public than that we should be engaged in keen competition with each other. And I say also that, however much the faddist may like to see a manufacturer who is also called a philanthropist, it is even more important for the workman that his employer should be a strict business man than that he should be a philanthropist. Capital is all-powerful to-day, and I think that, carrying our minds back to the time of conflict, it behoves Capital to remember that any conflict that may come between Capital and Labour is much better settled by an adjustment of rights, and a recognition of the rights of each side, than by a continuance of conflict. The recognition of rights does not mean that the manufacturer can be a philanthropist, because he cannot ; but each day Labour is demanding, and rightly and properly demanding, a greater share in the profits of industry—and to-morrow, in all probability, the positions may be reversed, and as the demand for labour increases and money becomes more plentiful, Capital may become the suppliant for employment, and Labour may be all-powerful and able to dictate the terms on which it is to be employed. That is, of course, an exact reversal of the position which we have to-day. Supposing even that that came about, the employer could not even then be a philanthropist, and the hardest employer who could possibly be imagined, who succeeds in keeping his people in full work at full wages, whatever that rate of wages may be, would be better, even under those conditions, for the workman himself than a so-called philanthropist.

Well, now, in Labour wars, of course, the weapon which has been used, and effectively used—and I think rightly used —has been that of strikes. But, like all methods of war— like all weapons of war—it is costly and extravagant, and I believe it is equally true in industrial warfare as in warfare between nations—and this has been proved by Mr. Norman Angell—that no practical profit has ever come out of war unless it has been a fight for liberty. And I believe that in this question of the adjustment of wages there is no question of liberty involved, and that all questions of this kind could be infinitely better settled by mutual forbearance and conciliation than by any question of strikes. In my opinion, all these strikes, and all this unrest in the Labour world, are a healthy sign. And it is still more healthy that no advantage at the present moment has resulted, or can result, from this warfare that will give either element a preponderance over the other. The tendency will be, as I have said, as money becomes more plentiful, for money to be the suppliant for employment, and for Labour to be able to dictate more closely its own terms. But even then, extravagant and costly production would ruin industries, would ruin the cause of Labour, and would bring Labour back to a situation of unemployment.

For a number of years past we have seen various Acts of Parliament passed to regulate the employment of labour. Now, I am not one of those who think that this has come about merely because the workman has the vote; I rather think it is because the community recognizes that the workman has certain rights, and because the regulation of labour in a proper manner has been recognized as being just and fair; and the very fact that it has resulted in giving advantage to the employer as well as to the workman proves that it is founded on sound lines. We have to be regulated. I know there was an idea in the middle of the last century that each of us had liberties which we could exercise at our own sweet will. But it is found that organized society cannot live in that way, and that we have to recognize the rights of others as well as our own rights. This is no new idea, I know, but we are beginning to recognize more and more that in this matter of the employment of labour it is right that the State should make certain regulations, so that one manufacturer, who is inclined to adopt proper safeguards of machinery and proper regulations of labour, shall not be handicapped in competition with another manufacturer who would prefer to disregard such safeguards and regulations. We are all of us the better for regulation in this direction.

But this again does not take us very far. It still leaves us very nearly where we were with regard to the wage question, and the situation is pretty much in this respect left as it was at the beginning of last century. Well, now, the question of capital comes in, and may I mention this, which I am sure is apparent to every one of us—that the shareholder in the large aggregations of capital that are known to-day, is no longer a partner ; he is merely an investor—a money-lender. Capital has become dependent on Management and Labour, and this result has produced a condition where, if you alienate the interest of Management and alienate the interest of Labour, so that the whole of the benefits resulting from the whole-hearted service of Management and Labour are merely to go to the financier, the money-lender, or the investor, then you have produced circumstances in a very large number of industries which did not exist a decade ago—where you have divorced Management and Labour from the fruits of the industry owned by these large aggregations of capital. That is going on slowly and gradually. It may be possible in certain industries, but in other industries such a condition of affairs is entirely opposed to their success. Now the conflict that has resulted from this changed position is rather considerable. The condition is now one in which Management, as such, is on the side of, or is in the same position as, Labour ; and in interesting both Management and Labour in rendering efficient service, I claim that the best interests of shareholders, who want a solid investment with security, and the best interests of the consumers, who want articles of uniform good quality at the lowest possible cost of production, would alike be realized. It is not easy at any time to evolve a scheme that will realize the possibility of interesting Management (which is not a shareholder) and Labour (which is also not a shareholder) in the products that they, jointly with Capital, create. The result is that very often complicated positions occur, and systems are evolved which are more or less temporary. The average life of such schemes, as I say, is about five years. Now, there must be a reason for this, and I cannot help thinking that the reason is the one which I have already mentioned, namely, the attempt to mix things that differ. As I stated before, the employer who shares his profits with his workpeople is

not entitled on that account to receive his workmen's labour
for less than the current rate. Some of the `Profit-Sharing
schemes have fallen to the ground because, after sharing in
the profits for a number of years, the workmen have struck
against a reduction of wages when no profits were accruing,
or have struck for an advance of wages when an advance has
been given in other industries, with the result that the Management has said, " Well, of course, if you won't take bad times
with good, if you are only going to take your share of the profits
when these accrue, and leave us to bear all the losses, we will
withdraw the Profit-Sharing arrangement altogether." Now,
it seems to me that that is an unreasonable position to place
Labour in. Labour must have its fixed rate of wages, which
in turn must be the Trade Union rate of wages, or the current
rate of wages in trades where there is no union. Labour must
have that rate of wages assured to it, and if the employer,
in prosperous years, shares profits with his workpeople, he
has a right to expect that whilst he is not interfering with
the rate of wages, he is, by adopting that system, increasing
the personal interest of his staff in their work, and that the
staff themselves will make the surplus profits which they
themselves are going to share. And on that basis, and only
on that basis, does it seem to me to be possible to introduce
a system of sharing profits with employees. Because, if it is
going to be a system merely of taking the profits made by the
employer and dividing a share of those among the employees,
then it is philanthropy, which is not required, and for which
there is no place in business ; and in a very small number of
years an employer adopting that course would inevitably find
himself handicapped by competitors who, instead of dealing
with surplus profits in that way, carried them to a reserve
fund and left them to fructify in the business. And in that
way the profit-sharing philanthropist would find himself
suffering a very serious handicap. If the workman, on the
other hand, felt that he was not assured of his full rate of
wages, the same as he would receive in any other workshop,
he would naturally feel aggrieved, because it is a matter of
life and death to him, with his family to maintain, that he
should have his full rate of wages, and he cannot do without
that full rate of wages.

Now I will tell you, if you will allow me, something of my

own little personal experience. I have endeavoured to indicate to yon the difficulties of the case, which are very real, and now I would like to tell you of the various means which I have adopted, during the last five-and-twenty years, to produce this personal interest of which I have been speaking, and of what has brought me to my present system.

The first and obvious course for a man to take is to allow those associated with him in his business to acquire some of the ordinary capital. It has been done very largely in a great many industries. Well, I tried that, and I invariably found that as a result of that, the holding of these shares produced a state of mind which was nervous, to say the least of it. So that if a new development was contemplated—for instance, the opening of works in Australia or in some other part of the world—then the holders of a small number of the ordinary shares were inclined to consider that the position of these ordinary shares was going to be jeopardized, and that the opening of those works was going to be risky, more or less, and that the risk ought not to be taken. And in many cases the argument was used, " We are doing well, and why should not we be satisfied with going on as we are ? " Well, of course, the number of ordinary shares held in this way, as compared with those held by myself, was not of sufficient moment to be powerful enough to alter the policy—if it had been, I think it would have been fatal to our progress—and the result that generally came about was that I had to buy back myself, at a premium, shares which I had either given for no payment at all or had issued at par. I never got them back at par in any single case ; I always had to buy them back at a premium. Invariably, as I say, there was a state of nervousness created in the minds of those who held these shares. They might be worth £40,000, £50,000, or £60,000 if realized at a particular time, and when there was any question of a new departure, such as the establishment of a new undertaking, the holders of these shares felt that they did not know where they were going to be landed, or how their value was going to be affected. This is the natural attitude of the small shareholder, and I respect it. I do not think I have any right to say that he ought not to take that view. A man who finds that if he goes out of the business at a certain moment he will go out without the necessity of any worry as regards the future

will naturally hesitate to go into a new branch of the enterprise and face unknown risks of which he does not, and in
the nature of things cannot, foresee the finality. Therefore,
as I say, the only result I got from letting these ordinary
shares go was that I had invariably to buy them back at a
premium, and generally before five years had passed. So
that, after having a strong desire to get rid of my ordinary
shares to those who worked with me, I ultimately found myself,
until two years ago, the holder of all the ordinary shares. I
should mention that then I let my son have some of them,
but he, of course, is on a somewhat different footing, and I
suppose that in all human probability he will have the lot
at some time or other. But leaving his shares out of the
question, all the others came back to me in the way I have
described.

Now, I had to give that idea up. It was leading me
nowhere. It was costing me a great many hundreds of thousands of pounds, so I had to give it up. Next I thought I
would try my hand at the creation of some preference shares,
the dividend on which would be restricted to 5 per cent. My
idea was to allow these to be applied for, and when the appli-
cants obtained them, they would receive the same rate of
dividend as the ordinary shares, the difference being *ex gratia.*
Now, I consulted our solicitor, and he pointed out to me that
that scheme had already been tried and had failed. So I
was saved from that particular pitfall. He said he knew
several firms who had tried the scheme, and that the result
had been that the employees had been able to borrow money,
say, at 5 per cent. on the security of the shares themselves,
and if they were paying say, 15 per cent., the borrower drew
10 per cent. and the lender took the other 5 per cent. So that
the employee could always get money on these shares, which
he looked upon as a mere monetary transaction, quite
apart from his own occupation. Therefore I never adopted
that plan.

Still I was not satisfied, because in a business such as ours,
with over fifty branches scattered all over the world, you
must have the personal interest of your staff. You cannot
ignore it. It is a thing which you must get. And then I
thought that perhaps by issuing what I call certificates—
certificates representing no money at all, and which could

not be negotiated—I might solve the problem. . I thought I would pay on these certificates the same rate of dividend as on the ordinary shares, less, say, 5 per cent., which would represent interest on the money if money had been paid for them in the same way as in the ordinary course it would be paid for ordinary shares. So I started the system of issuing these certificates, such certificates receiving 5 per cent. less than the ordinary shares. As you know, there are many profit-earning schemes (I do not need to mention names) where the endeavour is made to guarantee the workman $4\frac{1}{2}$, or 4, or 5 per cent. on whatever money he puts in, and then, after that, sharing the profits with him. Well, I saved all that guarantee by dispensing with his putting in any money at all, and merely calling these things certificates, representing, as I say, no money at all, though to the holder they represent dividends of the same value as the ordinary shares receive, minus 5 per cent. I created this scheme, and finally, after a great many years' work, got it into shape, I think, some four years ago. We created at that time £500,000 nominal value of these certificates, and this year we propose to create a further £500,000, raising the amount of these certificates to £1,000,000 nominal value. Then I began with the rank and file. I gave these certificates to all what I may call rank-and-file workers, to the extent of 10 per cent. of their wages. If any report came in with regard to any man having committed an act of insubordination, any neglect of duty, or any of the minor offences, he forfeited any allotment he would otherwise have received during that year. If, on the other hand, an excellent report came in concerning any man, he received more than 10 per cent. ; and if any man rendered the Company exceptional service, he received still more, perhaps many times 10 per cent. So that there was always elasticity, and the whole scheme was founded perfectly legally by the shareholders, the only shareholder who was required to vote being the ordinary shareholder. The scheme is upon the basis that the majority of the ordinary shareholders shall have the right to decide how many of these certificates are to be issued. So that the matter is entirely in the hands of the majority of the ordinary shareholders for the time being. Well, we worked on this footing and we created a savings bank, and the dividends, as they accrued, were credited to

each man's account.   If he chose, he could go to the savings
bank the same day that his account was credited and draw
the money then and there—the whole of it, if he pleased.   If
he left the money in the bank for three months, he received
interest on it at the rate of, say, 3 per cent. ; if he left it six
months, he received interest at the rate of, say, 4 per cent. ;
and if he left it twelve months, he received interest at the rate
of, say, 5 per cent.   He could draw the money out at any time,
and the interest was made up in accordance with the time
the money had been deposited in the bank.   So that if "he
left his money in the savings bank twelve months or longer,
he got, say, 5 per cent. ; if less than twelve months and over
six months, say, 4 per cent. ; between three months and six
months, say, 3 per cent. ; and if drawn out under three months
there would be no interest.

   Well, I found that a great many of the workmen drew their
money out to buy our Preference shares.   That was reported
to me, and I found that they had to buy our Preference shares
at a premium.   Then I saw what seemed to me a solution
of one of the schemes which I had discussed with our solicitor,
namely, the creation of 5 per cent. Preferred Ordinary shares,
the acquisition of which should not entail or permit of the
men borrowing any money at all ; and I created these 5 per
cent. Preferred Ordinary shares, which rank immediately
before the ordinary shares, and after all other classes of shares.
If the man chooses to retain these shares, he does so.   If he
wishes to realize on them, he can walk into the savings bank
at any time, and there is a market for them at par.   So that
although he draws what he may be entitled to in the shape
of shares, he can change them into money just as readily as
he could obtain the money originally when it was credited
in his bank-book ; while if he prefers to hold the shares, he
receives the same dividends as are paid on the ordinary shares.
Now, this has overcome the difficulty of the man applying
for shares out of all proportion to his available money.   Practically the money for these shares is found out of the dividends
he receives on his certificates, and the certificates, in turn,
represent no cash value at all.   So that now I have a medium
through which the man can come into the ordinary shareholder class by saving all his dividends on his certificates.   I
have only had this in operation for twelve months, and it

is too early yet to say any more than that I have started it. But you will see that my effort has been to interest a large number of people, by a convenient method, in the profits of the business, and to do it in such a way that a man could have no fear about his capital. I have thus overcome that original fear that a man had, that if we took over some fresh undertaking his ordinary dividends would be at stake, because these depend on the certificates, which certificates he has not paid for, and which certificates, not having paid for, he is very anxious should receive as high a rate of dividend as possible, because this is their only value to him, and he not having put any money in them, and the certificates representing, as they do, a perfectly unsaleable commodity, he cannot sell them at a premium at all. He therefore takes a different view with regard to the progress and development of the Company; he becomes anxious that the business should progress and develop, because it is only by such progress and development that he is able to obtain dividends on his certificates, which dividends, in their turn, he can invest, if he likes, in Preferred Ordinary shares during his employment in the business, and thereby receive, during his active employment in the business, the same dividends as are paid on the ordinary shares. If a man dies, or if he retires from the business, the shares then revert to merely 5' per cent. Preferred Ordinary shares, which is the only right conferred on them by the Articles of Association. The additional rights are equally binding so long as the holder remains with our firm—we have altered the Articles of Association accordingly—but what we have undertaken is merely to pay him the same rate of dividend as is received by the ordinary shares during the time he is actively engaged in the business. And in this way we hope that we have solved the problem of interesting our staff in the profits of the business and in the losses of the business.

But I want to impress upon every one present that no Profit-Sharing scheme will be of any use if the man is not made to feel that he is interested in the losses just as much as in the profits of the business. A Profit-Sharing scheme which merely mentions profits, and takes no account of possible losses, tells only half the commercial tale. We all of us here know —it is unnecessary to mention it in such a gathering as this

—that any business may have profits, and it may have losses and every one of us who has put his money, time, and energy into any business must necessarily be prepared to face either. And it is the fact that we realize that there may be losses which makes us, in all probability, so alert in guarding our interests, and safeguarding them, and endeavouring to ensure, by the stability of the business, that the capital embarked in it shall be perfectly safe.

Now, therefore, by means of these certificates, a man may have accumulated, as several in fact have, some thousands of pounds. If there is no dividend for the ordinary shareholder, or if there is only 5 per cent. for the ordinary shareholder, he knows that there is nothing for him, and he knows, when he goes upstairs and looks into the drawer where he keeps his certificates, that it is only during his lifetime, and during the lifetime of the profit-earning capacity of the business, that they are worth any more than the paper they are printed on ; and he knows that directly the business ceases to be profitable, the value of these certificates will have disappeared, since they are only entitled to receive dividends when such dividends have been earned. Now, I have endeavoured in this way to give him an interest without mixing things which differ. I have recognized the fact that whether the man concerned be the highest manager I have got, or whether he be the youngest worker in the factory or office, his wages must be proportionate to his services ; that those wages must be at the fullest rate which he could get in any other establishment for those services ; and that anything done by him beyond that must be done in the spirit of Co-Partnership, in which spirit he himself, with me and with all the others engaged in the business, endeavours to earn the profits which are to be shared by all of us ; and if we cannot enter into the spirit of Co-Partnership, if we feel that these profits will either jump from the ground or fall from the heavens without any exertion of ours, we know perfectly well we are all on one platform—we are all in the same boat, if I may use the expression—and that none of us will receive any dividends. I have had to link together similar conditions to what every investor feels, and every capitalist feels, with regard to his investments —I have had to endeavour to link those conditions together in giving these certificates to our workpeople ; and I want to tell you that as far as I know, the workman does realize this. But there are critics of the scheme, opponents of the scheme, who have the idea that the profits of a business are made, in some way or other, by the workmen, and by the workmen alone. I have had to meet that attitude, and if I may digress for a few moments I will tell you how I met it. The people who take that view have urged as a criticism of my scheme that the workmen themselves have to make all the profits of which they only take a share. On the other hand, they don't want philanthropy—in which I quite agree. I would not do anything with regard to our workmen that savoured of philanthropy in the slightest degree. But if profits are to be made, I am not going to make surplus profits for our staff to divide amongst themselves, and equally, I am not going to ask them to make surplus profits for me. I say, let us each in our own different positions jointly make the profits, and after they have received their wages, and after I have received 5 per cent.—which is the equivalent—then for any services beyond that, if there is any surplus, let us share it in a perfectly reasonable way.

Now I will make a digression, as I said, and try and tell you how I have met these criticisms of those who have attacked me, namely, Socialists, some of whom were my own workmen. I thought the best way would be to give them a paper, so I gave a paper at Port Sunlight, which I called *Day-Work or Piece-Work—Which ?* [1] Well, it attracted a great audience, because some of the men thought there was going to be a system of piece-work all through the works. But I have always looked upon day-work as representing Socialism and upon piece-work as representing Individualism, and I have never seen any other interpretation of the two things. Now, this paper of mine created some little commotion, and my audience did not feel quite ready to criticize it on the same evening that it was presented to them. So I said, " All right ; let us meet again and discuss this paper." Well, first one man got up and said he did not see but what the workmen made all the profits ; and another man made the same claim, and said that if there was to be any Profit-Sharing scheme which pretended to give the workman what he earned, he ought to have it all. When I came to reply, I said, " I

[1] See p. 309.

suppose I am talking to a number of sensible men, but according to what you have said just now, you seem to me very foolish indeed. Because you are saying that you make the profits of this business. Now, you certainly know a great many soap businesses which are not making any profits at all. Why not go, as a body, to these men who are making no profits on their soap, and say, ' Look here ; we work for that scallywag Lever ; he pays us the full rate of wages, it is true, and he gives us some share of the profits ; but he does not give us enough. How much will you give us ? ' " And I told them, " If you go in that way to these other people in the soap trade who are not making dividends, the very first thing they will say to you will be, ' What do you want ? ' Because whatever they get out of you will be to the good, inasmuch as they are making nothing now, and however little, or however much, you let them have will be to the good. You may tell them you want it all. Well, perhaps they will not listen to that. Well, then you can say, ' We want nine-tenths, and you can have one-tenth ' ; and, seeing that they are getting nothing now, they will no doubt take it. And then you can all leave me, giving me the usual week's notice, and go to the other man in the same trade, and put the case to him : ' This scallywag Lever only gives us a share ; you give us a bigger one.' Now go and try it ! " Well, of course they were looking at each other, and had no answer. They had never seen it in that light before. I am perfectly certain these people are sincere and I am perfectly certain their leaders are sincere. I have never seen any reason to doubt their sincerity, and I have come into very close and frequent personal contact with them. But they have been so fed up on the idea that when a man has done something with his hands he has produced something that is of value, that they cannot see the other side of the question. We, who have to sell that article, know that although it may have been of value yesterday, and may be of value to-day, yet next week, or at any particular moment, the market conditions may be different, and it may not have any value at all ; in fact, there may be a loss on its very production. Now, the men I refer to cannot realize that. You know the tale of the Socialist who came into a village and began to talk about the land question. He said the land ought to be divided up, and nobody ought to pay for it. His

,views were very popular among the villagers, and they all adjourned to the village " pub " to talk the matter over ; and they began dividing up the land of the village among themselves. One man said he would have this field, another that. And one man said he would have a certain field of the squire's, " because it was best for growin' 'taties in." When they had divided it all up, they had time to notice a quiet old codger who had been sitting in a corner all the time, smoking, and taking no part in the talk. So one of the other men, the one who had chosen the potato field, said to him, " Tom, why don't you speak up, lad ? Didn't tha' goa to t' lecture ? " " Ay." " An' dostna believe in't ? " " Oh yes, A' b'lieve in't." " Then why dost tha' not speak oop for thy share ? " " Oh," said the old fellow, " A'm not goin' t' work ma Socialism that road." " How then ? " " Dick," said he, " didstna say tha'd ha' that field o' t' squire's 'cos it growed t' best 'taties ? " " Ah." " And didn't tha say tha'd pay t' squire nowt fur it ? " " Ah." " Weel, I'll come and gather t' 'taties and pay thee nowt for 'em."

There is a necessity upon each of us, in my opinion, to recognize the changes of the times, the changes in the aspirations of those who work for us. It is not only a question to-day, believe me, gentlemen, of the increased cost of living, although that is great, but it is the cost of higher living. The workman wants to live better, and in order to live better he wants to live in a better house, he wants his wife and children to be better fed and clothed. And these are things that he ought to have. So that there are two factors in operation. The same living that a man was content with ten years ago is dearer to-day. But he is not content with having the same living as he had ten years ago ; he wants better living, and rightly wants better living. And the increased cost of the same living, coupled with the desire for better living, is producing an unrest which in my view is the most healthy sign we have got. Now, it is a question whether we can, in ordinary competition, go beyond a certain amount with safety. In a business in which there are debentures, we are all agreed that you can have debentures with perfect safety up to a certain point. Beyond that point you must have ordinary shareholders who have taken the risks of the business. And is it not so in regard to labour—that we can advance wages up to a certain point in competition with the whole world—advance them to a point a little higher than the whole world? Because I believe that we have the best available raw material of labour in this country. I do not believe that there is any labour material anywhere in the world superior to what we have in England, Scotland, Ireland, and Wales—in the United Kingdom. But if we are to make the enormous strides such as are demanded to-day, in my opinion it can only be done by increasing the interest of the workman in the article he is producing, and so making him a more efficient instrument of production by a personal element being introduced—that personal element which is the great stimulus behind each of us in this room to-day. We have got to share that stimulus with our workpeople, and if we do this, I believe the profits to be divided will be greater, and that everybody's share, including the workman's, will be greater. And side by side with the sharing of these greater profits, these increasing profits, there will go on at the same time a reduction of anxiety to us as managers. The anxiety of Management is greater with a number of wage-drawers than it is with partners. Many of us in business are working with partners, whom we have selected with care. Sometimes we may have been unfortunate, but you will recognize with me, I am sure, that ninety-nine times out of every hundred the partners work together in harmony for the good of the business in an entirely different way from what they would if they were wage-drawers merely. We want to produce that state of affairs right throughout our industries in order to get the greatest efficiency in our workmen, by giving them a personal interest in the article which they are pro-ducing. But in doing this—here I want to sound one warning note—there is to be no delegation of supreme authority from the Management; and in my opinion all attempts that would mean the introduction of working men upon Boards of Directors, unless coupled with giving them a training in the higher branches of work, will be futile. It is utterly impossible to take an ordinary rank-and-file worker and make a Director out of him. It is not reasonable to expect to be able to do so. He has to be trained, as all of us have had to be trained, for the position; and to expect that a man can be selected out of the works by his mates to sit straightway on a Board of

Directors is, in my opinion, an utterly futile expectation. It may be that one man can sit with six or seven other men, and, not having the supreme power of voting, may be of assistance to the Board of Directors (who have the supreme management) from time to time. But the supreme management must always be in the hands of trained men—men trained for their posts ; and the training which I am suggesting should go right through the staff is a training by means of which we can gradually develop their powers, through committees, to qualify them ultimately for a seat on the Board of Directors.

Now, having said this, I want to tell you that all our Directors have graduated as Directors through the works, the office, or the salesmen's department ; but in addition to this I have always taken such a man through the committees I have mentioned before finally making him a Director. As I have already said, I consider that the idea of a workman being appointed by his fellow-workmen to sit on a Board of Directors is futile. I do not think I need labour the idea, in such a company as the present, that real Co-Partnership means not only sharing in the profits, but also sharing in certain duties which a mere workman could not possibly properly understand. I might just as well say that I would go over to the pan side, where I should no doubt only succeed in making much worse soap than would be made by some of my lowest-waged workmen. On the other hand, a workman might come to the Board of Directors and might conceivably make more mistakes than even I do. But because I say that, it does not mean that we cannot work towards wider and wider improvements in our service, with the goal always before us that the profits to be divided will be divided equally in proportion to the amount of interest we take in the business and in proportion to the services we are capable of rendering.

III

RIGHT CONSTITUTION OF CO-PARTNERSHIP

[Extract from "Industrial Evolution and Co-Partnership," Cambridge, August 6, 1914.]

THERE is one great principle governing the world, which is that of self-interest. We find nowhere this principle more strongly developed nor finding more general acceptance than in business. It is the basis of the axiom, " To buy in the cheapest market and sell in the dearest.". It shows itself in competition, sometimes healthy, sometimes unhealthy ; but there are two kinds of self-interest, one the narrow, selfish self-interest, which is so short-sighted as to be blindly selfish to the exclusion of all other considerations ; and there is that broad, intelligent, enlightened self-interest, which says that it can only find its own best interests of self in regarding the welfare and interests of others. By the practice of this spirit of enlightened self-interest in the struggle for supremacy, and the practice of emulation and competition, mankind is made more and more intelligent, and is better able to obtain an advanced position. When the spirit of enlightened self-interest ceases to exist, mankind must of necessity fade out of existence also. This is just as certain as it is true that the practice of the narrow, blind, selfish self-interest can only result in the demoralization of society, and in constant struggle and warfare and in the decline of civilization.

The truest and best form of enlightened self-interest is when we pay the highest regard to those associated with us in business, and whose improved efficiency we must seek to obtain by binding them and making them, equally with ourselves, interested in, and dependent upon, the success of the business. If Capital desires Management and Labour to be efficient, then Capital must be fair in its division of profits with Management and Labour. If Capital wishes Management and Labour to make profits, then Capital must share profits with Management and Labour. If Capital thinks of nothing but its own narrowest and most selfish self-interest, without a single thought for Management and Labour, then Capital will never succeed in getting the highest possible amount of efficiency from Management and Labour. In fact, if Capital is justified in taking the most narrow and selfish view, then equally Management and Labour must be considered as entitled to consider how to obtain the highest possible salaries and wages for the least equivalent in skill, efficiency, and labour. And, equally, if Management and Labour consider nothing but their own narrowest and most selfish self-interest, if their thought is solely how to render the smallest possible amount of work—inefficient and, therefore, profitless—in the shortest possible number of hours and for the highest possible salary or wages, then Management and Labour will of necessity retrograde and suffer; but if Management and Labour adopt a system of enlightened self-interest, and Capital does the same, and each recognize the principle that by looking after the interests of all they are taking the surest way of achieving their own individual self-interest, then the undertaking must be healthier, profits are bound to be greater, the resulting happiness will be more complete, and the prosperity and advancement of civilization the world over will be assured.

It is claimed for Co-Partnership that by adopting Co-Partnership a recognition is made of this great fact, that justice demands for each of us equal rights in the products of our labour. This is the very basis of Co-Partnership, and it is claimed for it that it stimulates efficiency and produces economy and avoidance of waste, and it is only by so doing that Co-Partnership can increase well-being and prosperity and justify its adoption.

Before we proceed further, it would probably be advantageous to give a definition of what is meant by Profit-Sharing and Co-Partnership. There are so many systems of Profit-Sharing, some amounting to little other than gratuities or Christmas-boxes, that this definition becomes all the more important and necessary. In the Board of Trade

Report dealing with Profit-Sharing and Co-Partnership, Profit-Sharing was defined as " An agreement between an employer and his workpeople that the latter shall receive in addition to their ordinary wages a share fixed beforehand in the profits of the undertaking." Under this definition all bonus schemes are excluded. The Board of Trade Report stated that there must be a previous agreement, that the share of the profits must be fixed beforehand, and Co-Partnership was defined as an extension of Profit-Sharing whereby the employee gained, in some degree, the rights and responsibilities of the shareholder.

To enable us to judge the anticipated effects of the adoption of Co-Partnership, it is not unreasonable that we draw a parallel from what has been the effect of improving the condition of the workers in those industries that have been able to achieve this. It is a well-known fact that every reduction in the hazardous nature of an occupation has resulted in a wider selection and better workmen being available in that occupation. Businesses that were dangerous and hazardous, and that have been made safe and free from risk, have become attractive to a greater body of workmen, and, at the same time, attractive to a more intelligent class of workmen. There is the human element—the man behind the process and operation —to be considered in every undertaking. The only way in which to maintain an increased success in any industry is to maintain an increased efficiency, and thus by increased efficiency to increase the quantity and quality of the output, and so augment the fund out of which the wages and profits have to come.

I venture to state that our modern industrial system in this great United Kingdom stands self-condemned, when the income tax returns show that it rests on a basis whereby one-ninth of the population enjoy one-half the total income, and more than nine-tenths of the accumulated wealth, whilst the remaining eight-ninths of the population have only one-half of the total income, and possess less than one-tenth of the accumulated wealth. It is true that the one-ninth have full legal claim to half the total income, and the nine-tenths of the total wealth. Not one word can be raised against the legal right upon which this rests, but notwithstanding these circumstances let us ask ourselves, Is this great disproportion expedient and in the interests of the community as a whole, and the nation and Empire of which we all profess to be so proud?

.But hidden and buried amongst the above mass of figures and income tax returns are also the unrecorded losses and failures, the despair and madness of many a so-called capitalist who has seen the ruin of his industry, sometimes from his own errors and mistakes, but, it is equally true, often from changed economic conditions which render his industry obsolete, and have swept away his capital and profits; so that before we join in the general outcry of rights of Labour to share in the profits we must consider the proposition of Loss-Sharing as well as Profit-Sharing. Whole volumes have been written, and eloquent speeches have been delivered, on the subject of the rights of Labour to share in the profits. Men wax eloquent on these rights, but not one single line has been written, so far as I have been able to discover, to point out that if Management and Labour would share in the profits, Management and Labour must equally share in the losses. It has not even been claimed that Labour should share in the losses in those quite numerous undertakings where the ruin of the undertaking has been the direct result of the action of Labour. Therefore, there is one essential element of expediency and justice, when we are considering the application of Profit-Sharing to modern industrial conditions, and that is, that Loss-Sharing must of necessity go with Profit-Sharing, and cannot possibly be detached from it.

This Loss-Sharing must be so arranged that the employee is not under the necessity of sacrificing the security of his position with regard to salary or wages. Therefore, Profit-Sharing must be in addition to, and not in substitution of, the salary and wages system. Profit-Sharing must mean the giving to the employee the opportunity each year by increased efficiency of acquiring an enlarging personal share in the profits of the business. Therefore, Profit - Sharing and Co-Partnership must result in increasing the volume of profits. Salary and wages must first be paid under the old system to Management and Labour, and a reasonable rate of interest, say 5 or 6 per cent., must be paid to Capital as the equivalent of the salary and wages of Management and Labour. The employee is at present placed in a position of personal indifference, so far as his own financial responsibility is concerned, in the success or failure of the business. The employee sharing in the profits of the business, in addition to receiving salary or wages, would ever have in his mind that the failure of the business would sweep away his annually increasing share in the profits of the undertaking, which share, equally as is the case with the Capitalist, has taken him a lifetime of unremitting application and patient effort to acquire. Therefore, Co-Partnership, rightly constituted, must of necessity bring the employee into close contact with Capital in Loss-Sharing as well as in Profit-Sharing, which would lift both Management and Labour into the stimulating, developing, and elevating heights of profit-earner and profit-sharer in addition to that of the salary or wage-drawer.

IV

ESSENTIALS OF CO-PARTNERSHIP

[Extract from address on " National Possibilities." See Section IV., " The Six-hour Day," pp. 50–55.]

Do not let us think when we are considering Co-Partnership that we can treat it other than on the strictest business lines. I have just jotted down some nine headings that always appear to me to be essential to the success of any Co-Partnership scheme.

(1) Co-Partnership must not degenerate into charity or philanthropy. It would be an insult to the workers if it did.

(2) The object must be to increase efficiency, resulting in increased prosperity for all—not for the man on the top only, but for all.

(3) It must maintain the supremacy of Management. Just as in the Army we must have corporals and sergeants and so on up to generals, so in industrial organization there must be various stages of management arrangement to ensure efficiency, and these must be maintained.

(4) Co-Partnership must not result in the weakening of Management, but, on the other hand, Labour must be free to work out its own ideals—free from the tyrannies of victimization if it expresses its views.

(5) There must be a greater stability in these arrangements than a mere cash bonus.

(6) The benefits of Co-Partnership must extend to the wives and children. I attach the utmost importance to that. A man must know that his share in Co-Partnership, at his death, will go to his widow during her widowhood.

(7) It must elevate Management and Labour equally in the social scale.

(8) It must not be antagonistic to the legitimate rights of the workers nor of the managers, and

(9) The control must rest with those who find the capital.

When we have Co-Partnership founded on these lines there will still have to continue the underlying wages system, and the wages system must be maintained on the highest scale practicable in the particular industry. In other words, those firms who adopt Co-Partnership must lead the way in advances of wages as well as in the benefits of Co-Partnership. I was pleased to note in the recent Board of Trade Returns on Co-Partnership that it is there stated that the firms which have adopted this system were firms which had given the greatest betterment conditions and the highest wages—that is essential. If it were not essential there would be no benefit in Co-Partnership ; it would be the mere attachment of workmen to works for an elusive advantage. The conditions must not only be better, but the wage itself must be slightly higher than that paid in other establishments. It cannot be greatly higher, because the cost of production is a factor that has to be taken into account.

V

CO-PARTNERSHIP AND EFFICIENCY

BIRMINGHAM, *November* 8, 1912.

[A meeting was convened by the Consultative Council of the Labour Co-Partnership Association to hear an address by Sir William H. Lever, Bart.—as he then was—in the Mason College of Birmingham University. The Pro Vice-Chancellor (Mr. Alderman F. C. Clayton, J.P.) presided. The address is here subjoined :]

THE question that we have to discuss to-night is " Co-Partnership and Efficiency," with a great accent on the word " Efficiency." In approaching the subject, What is the cause of Labour Unrest ? there is a strong desire on the part of every one to try to arrive at a basis which will be something like finality. If there ever is, or ever has been, an age that was or is worth living in, it is this present one. There is no age where Progress has planted so strongly and firmly a determination to advance to higher ideals, and there is no country in the whole world where the conditions are so favourable to attain the highest possible well-being of the mass of the country as Great Britain.

The nineteenth century saw the triumphant entry of steam, electricity, machinery, transportation with economy and efficiency in productive enterprise, and the creation of enormous wealth. More wealth was produced in the nineteenth century, in consequence of the introduction of the above forces, than in all the centuries that have preceded it by man's unaided handiwork alone. Manufactures and shipping were almost in the same condition in the eighteenth century as they were in the time of the Romans, and if Napoleon the Great had attempted to invade this country, he would have done so practically under the same conditions as Julius Cæsar, both being dependent on wind and tide.

If the nineteenth century was responsible for the triumphant introduction of new methods for the creation of wealth, the twentieth century must see the triumph of the introduction of new methods or the more equal distribution of wealth. But in realizing, or attempting to realize, the better distribution of wealth, we must not fall behind in our power or efficiency to produce wealth. Therefore, modern developments must progress along the well-defined lines of efficiency.

Now, in the production of wealth and the more equal distribution of it, I do claim that, however great the progress already made has been, we have now arrived at a stage in the development of social well-being when, owing to the changed conditions of modern industrial activity—men and women being employed in large masses in industrial concerns, resulting in the obliteration of the individual and the loss of individual self-interest in industrial activity—we may fairly inquire what has been the foundation of our progress. Now, I claim that this has been the persistent, consistent, and uninterrupted effort of every right-thinking man to better his condition. This has laid the basis of all the progress we have made. This principle is as unvarying as the law, of gravitation, and it is from the operation of this universal law of self-interest of the individual that all progress has sprung and is maintained. It is like the great principle of life, which is ever operating to maintain healthy development ; and if Co-Partnership does not improve the conditions under which we are living, it will not appeal to us as other than a modern craze which will have its day and die out.

We have to consider what can be done by a change in our relationship with each other in productive enterprises. No system can supply the place of individual effort, yet in modern productive enterprise, collective action, as in a sound army, is the greatest force. We have to consider whether the connection between each of us shall be one of wages alone, or wages *plus* shares in the profits of the products of our collective labour. The wages system was a great advance on all other previous systems. The first system was slavery, and that was succeeded by serfdom, and then by the wages system, the last-named having developed the principle of self-interest, which is one of the greatest forces behind it. By Co-Partnership, we recognize the great fact that the Co-

Partnership system is founded on justice and on equal rights, for each of us, to the products of our labour. Such is the very basis of Co-Partnership, as distinguished from the wages system alone, and it is bound to stimulate efficiency and economy of products, for only by so doing can it increase our well-being and prosperity.

If Co-Partnership fails to increase the quantity of the products, or fails to improve the quality, or fails to ensure economy of material, tools, or implements, or fails in the better organization of production, or fails to reduce the waste consequent on strikes and lock-outs, then it is perfectly obvious that Co-Partnership is an absolutely useless implement of production. Any short-cuts to progress will fail, and any false methods will only mislead us. In the future, as in the past, the prizes in commerce, as in all other human activities, will always go to the strong, and we cannot alter that law, but it is equally true that such prizes cannot be held by the cunning. Only the strong can hold them, and the mere conflict of private interests in producing wealth will not enable us to hold the prize that has been won as a result of indefatigable labour and struggle. Business productive enterprise, as in all other activities, must end where it begins, namely, with the workers of all ranks and positions who are producing wealth. The way we work together under the wage system is, in my opinion, always against the modern spirit of the times—selfish Capital and selfish Labour cannot live together as efficient and economical producers of commodities. The Golden Rule, brotherhood and confidence, so often despised, must be introduced into business, as into all other affairs of life. The business world is quivering with an impulse at the present time, and with a strong desire, to get workers into more intimate connection with each other and to cease the continual warfare that exists. The elevation of the workers to the front rank is an ideal worth living for, and, in the end, there is very little else in business after the mere productive enterprise has been developed—there is very little else worth living for.

There can be no successful development of business that does not carry the employees along with it. Consciously or unconsciously, we must all aim at the common good of all engaged in any productive enterprise. Well-being first of all,

as I have already mentioned, consists in the increase of the
power of production and the consequent increase of wages,
and also a decrease in the hours of labour, without which
there can be no increase in social well-being. Now, this
increase can only be secured by increasing the producing
power of labour with less expenditure of vital force, and this
will be followed by a reduction of the proportion of cost which
labour bears to the total cost of any product, and which, in
turn, will lead to a reduction in the cost of the product, and,
consequently, to its increased consumption, and this, in turn,
will allow an increased margin in the wages to be paid to
Labour, and a reduction in the hours of labour. In fact, the
whole progress of civilization in the last century under the
wages system has followed along those lines—there may have
been ebbs and flows in the tide, but the tide of social betterment has flowed along this channel.

Now, we have to consider, when we approach the subject of
Co-Partnership, to what extent, and by what means, can the
productiveness of labour be improved and the expenditure of
the vital force of labour be lessened, and this has to be our
first step if we would make any advancement. If we consider
the question of farming, we find that, where the productiveness of labour on the land results in the lowest return, wages
are the lowest. When, from eight bushels of wheat from the
acre, we have by better cultivation increased the yield to over
thirty bushels per acre—practically quadrupled the production
—we find that with the quadruplication of the product the
wages are two-and-a-half times what they were, the hours of
labour are shorter, and that the product is consequently cheaper,
all because the production is four times greater. You will
find to-day in our own country, as in all other countries, that
where the quantity produced at any stage of manufacture is
greatest, with the lowest cost of labour in proportion to the
total cost of the product, then wages are the highest; and
that, where the total cost of labour is the highest in proportion to the total cost of the product, wages are the lowest.
Now, with the lessened proportion of labour to the total cost,
there will have developed, to a very marked degree, the
cheapening of the product, and only on these well-defined
and well-tested lines can there be an increase in the earning
power of labour.

There is one essential fact which is overlooked by most working-men when they approach this subject,' namely, that, simultaneously with the increase of average wages there has been a correspondingly steady decrease in the average earnings of capital invested in industrial enterprise. This is a solid fact that ought not to be overlooked. Interest on capital is highest in all countries where the productive power of labour is the lowest, and also wages are the lowest; and in all countries where the productive power of labour is the highest, there wages are also the highest, and interest on capital the lowest. Of course, there may have been periods when, the demand for Capital having exceeded the supply—for short periods—Capital may have had an advantage; but we can trace without possibility of error that, to increase the productive power of labour and the wages to Labour, has the tendency to decrease the interest earned by Capital.

The reason for this is obvious. Capital invested in industry has always to| be engaged in seeking to meet its liabilities for interest, and, therefore, must employ Labour, and when Capital invested in industry ceases to employ Labour to meet its obligations for interest—this great fact has to be borne in mind —Capital then has ceased to exist. It is entirely apparent that the larger the prospective return on Capital invested in industries, and the more Capital competes to obtain Labour, this must result ultimately in less interest being received by Capital itself. Every period of extreme industrial activity must, of course, see some slight modification in this. Now, whilst at the same time that Capital has been receiving less, Labour of all kinds, including salary to Management, has received more, not only have the nominal wages increased, but the actual wages, calculated in the purchasing power, have increased also.

Now, we therefore see, in view of the progress we have made in the nineteenth century, that the wages system and the so-called capitalist system have no reason to be apological for themselves, and it behoves any one who, like myself, believes in Co-Partnership, to have full regard to this solid fact in considering new methods for betterment and advancement of social well-being. The present wages and so-called capitalist system is in operation all over the world, and it has given us more and better food, more and better clothing, more and better houses, more and better education, more and better wages, shorter hours, lower cost of commodities, lower cost of travelling, better health, more rapid transit, and better means of recreation. But, the so-called capital and wages system has only succeeded to the extent that it has moved along the lines of the principle of enlightened self-interest. Now, I claim that still greater development can be made in our system of employment of labour in industrial activities by directly increasing the personal interest of labour engaged in industries, and, if this is so, then Co-Partnership, as I understand it, must depend for its power to increase our rate of progress on improving the social conditions, and on increasing our economical producing powers. Co-Partnership cannot reverse the law that has operated during the last century in giving us more and better food and clothing, higher wages, etc., by means of our power to produce more of those products at a cheaper cost, in fewer hours of labour. If Co-Partnership does not operate on those lines that have been so well tested, and are the proved basis of our success in the past, then it is a useless and silly fad.

Co-Partnership must, as the very charter of its existence, so operate that it can produce more and better food, clothing, houses, and social requirements, in fewer hours and with less unhealthy strain and stress, and with ability to meet the problem of increased demands in wages by giving Labour, in addition to wages, a share in the profits of the enterprise. How does Co-Partnership propose to achieve success? Co-Partnership does not propose to abolish the wages system. It does not propose to abolish payment of interest on Capital; but it does propose a modification of the wages system, and a modification in the relation of that portion of Capital engaged in industrial products which is at risk, which is taking the risk of the enterprise, but no change in the relation of that portion of Capital which seeks a more secure position at a fixed rate of interest. Co-Partnership proposes to retain Management in its present position, and it proposes to retain the wages system and also interest on Capital, and to ask that portion of Capital which is at risk to join in partnership with Labour.

Now, there is one distinct fact in connection with modern

productive activity under the co-operative system. It has been a wonder to many people why co-operative production has not progressed at a greater rate. In my opinion, the cause of this partial failure of co-operative production has been that the co-operative system ignores Management, and lowers Management into the position of a fixed wage-drawer ; whereas, under the ordinary system of production, Management, as owner, has had a direct interest in the profits of the undertaking. The Co-Partnership system we advocate would remove Labour from its present position of wage-drawer or salary-drawer to the higher position of a partner in the success or failure of the business, and, to that extent, it is an advance which moves the whole of those engaged in industrial production on to a higher platform, whilst the co-operative system lowers those engaged in direct management to the ranks of the wage or salary worker.

In agriculture, Co-Partnership, as you all know, is the oldest system of any. In the fishing industry, Co-Partnership is the practice, and always has been, from time immemorial. The owner finds the ship and takes his share of the catch ; the captain finds the skill and ability in navigation, and his labour, and he takes his share of the catch ; and the crew, in their turn, take their share of the catch. Now this is, I think, the most concrete example of Co-Partnership we have, and we may depend upon it that fishing on those lines will have the effect on all in the fishing-boat that Co-Partnership will have, namely, a direct interest in the profits of their joint combined efforts, so that in alertness to discover the whereabouts of the fish, and in lowering and hauling in the nets, every faculty shall be exerted in order that the catch be as large as possible.

We are all servants of the public engaged in industrial occupations, and there is no distinction between us, and that is why I do not agree with the terms " master " and " servant," as we are all servants of the public—the so-called master just as much as the merest office-boy. Neither so-called master nor servant is satisfied with the present system ; the employer has to adopt many makeshifts, such as piece-work, bonuses, and such-like, to increase the interest of Labour in the product of Labour ; but, in my opinion, the only solid means of realizing such ideals is by giving the workman a direct interest in the product of his own handiwork, and I claim that the only effective way in which that can be done is by means of Co-Partnership. No one considers that the wages system is ideal ; employers, by their actions, if not by their words, admit that it is a wrong basis, and the best we can say of it is, that it is an advance on all previous systems.

I claim that the next advance we have to make to a higher level must be by means of Co-Partnership, and I will tell you, apart from the points I have referred to, one great gain this will be over the wages system, namely, the reducing of the strain and responsibility thrown upon the employer or proprietor of the business. The man who draws wages cannot reasonably be expected to worry about production and profits when he goes home at nights, but the man whose capital and whose very livelihood is involved is bound to worry about these. When we are all Co-Partners, this worry, now pressing with crushing force on the heads and backs of a few men, will rest on the backs, the brains, and the heart of the whole body of those who are engaged in the industry. Co-Partnership will give equal interest, and is, therefore, bound to give equal responsibility to each by substituting a partner for a wage-drawer, whether the profits have increased or not. I do not see any reason why profits should not be increased, but whether profits are increased or not, the enjoyments and the pleasures in business, and the relief from worry and strain in working with Co-Partners rather than with wage-drawers, will more than compensate.

Modern industrialism has deprived us of the ability to produce goods individually. One man, for instance, has no power to produce one hundred pins as a commercial proposition successfully, but one hundred men, taking the various stages of the production of pins, going hand-in-hand, can produce hundreds of millions of pins as a successful commercial proposition. Now, there is only one elevation possible for the worker, as for all others ; he must preserve his individualistic faculties, and must cultivate their extension and his higher powers, and if our system of Co-Partnership does not inspire a man with the idea of raising himself, then it is futile. You cannot push a man up a ladder—there is no other means of elevating a man than by letting him climb up the ladder by himself, and that is equally true of the master and of the man. There are not two different ladders—and I want to emphasize this—one for the master and one for the workman ; but they have both to climb the same ladder, which ladder is—producing more goods with less labour in fewer hours, so as to allow for larger wages and a bigger margin for profit. The idea that the workman's interest is opposed to the master's is entirely wrong, as they are both bound together, and it must not be forgotten that the workman—the human machine—if he is a " hand," is human. I always resent the phrase that we have, when we speak of so many " hands," as if we were dealing with a mere hand without the brain or heart of a man. I believe that, if we appeal to a man's sense of justice and right, we may take him into our confidence and elevate his character, and, in that way, we shall have assistance in our business, which will not only make our business run more smoothly, but will also assist us from the point of view of cheaper methods of production, by the high efficiency this will bring out. Just as machinery, electricity, steam, and all other mechanical appliances of productive power have enormously increased wealth, so I believe that if we take the workman more into our confidence, so as to develop his highest powers by making him a Co-Partner, he will become a better producer of the products he turns out, because we shall have fostered a spirit of comradeship and brotherhood.

I always resent the maudlin sentiment that is often talked in reference to Co-Partnership. Sometimes it is described as extremely " generous," and the man at the back of it is spoken of as a " philanthropist " ; that is all nonsense, and probably this is the reason why Co-Partnership schemes in the past have not lasted for more than five years on an average. If a man thinks Co-Partnership is a system which is " generous " or " philanthropic," he is approaching it on lines which will, sooner or later, bring it to decay. We do not consider it generous to buoy channels of rivers, nor do we consider it philanthropic to put lighthouses round our coast to mark sunken rocks, but we consider all that good, sound business ; and I say that, to enable the individual to avoid shipwreck on rocks of wrong methods, to enable us to raise our fellow-workers to the height which inspires ourselves, is bound to cheapen production. Then let us dismiss all vague, maudlin, wrong ideas on the subject of Co-Partnership. Co-Partnership can only be a means of better, fairer, and more just relationship of so-called employer and employee, resulting in better productive activities.

With regard to the question of management, I want you to understand that the progress of Co-Partnership must, essentially, be one of education ; for instance, you could not take a man from the ranks, as a navvy or labourer; and suddenly make him a Director of a Company with ideals and standards of high management ; it is not reasonable to expect it.

In conclusion, and with your permission, I would just like to quote from Robert Browning a few lines which, slightly adapted, seem appropriate to such an occasion as this :—

> The common problem, yours, mine, every one's,
> Is—not to fancy what were fair in life
> Provided it could be—but, finding first
> What may be, then find how to make it fair
> Up to our means : a very different thing !
>
>   * * * * *
>
> Our business is not to remake ourselves,
> But make the absolute best of what God made.

VI

CO-PARTNERSHIP AND HIGH WAGES

[From an Address by Lord Leverhulme to the Co-Partners' Club, Port Sunlight, April 17, 1914.]

I BELIEVE that wages are going steadily to rise, and I believe that the firms who are giving Co-Partnership can always rise with them and always continue to pay the highest rate of wages. Of course, as I have always explained, we have ourselves to make the profits, and I want to point out what is the difference between an article priced by the manufacturer on a high scale of wages, as in some countries I have visited, and the benefit to the man who produces articles and receives wages and also a share in the profits. The complaint in all high-waged countries is the high cost of living. It does not matter what country you go to, where the wages are high the cost of living is proportionately high, and when the English Government made their Board of Trade Report, they found that although the wages were lower in England, the amount paid for house accommodation, the quantity of clothing and food which could be purchased by those wages was greater than the amount which could be purchased with the higher wages in other countries. In other words, the conditions of the workers in this country, taking the cost of living, clothing, and food in proportion to their wages, was better in the United Kingdom than in any other country in the world. But I want this country to have the highest wages possible without the cost of living being increased. If the cost of living goes up here, as I have seen it go up in other countries, a Board of Trade Report would come along and say we are no better off in 1930 than in 1910. The wages in 1930, I am sure, are going to be very much higher than now, but in my opinion real betterment can only be obtained by

Co-Partnership. Now, this is a business proposition, and I notice Mr. Greenhalgh transfixing me with his accountancy eye, and I hope he will tell me if I am wrong in my next remark. If any statement of cost is prepared for me with regard to any article we produce, Mr. Greenhalgh will put down in that statement the wages of the men who are working in that department. Whatever wages they receive will go as a charge against that article. In addition, there will be the interest and depreciation on the machine they are working. Then there will be the cost of power, interest and depreciation on buildings, which in turn will be made up on the basis of the amount paid to the men who made the bricks and the mortar ; the joiners who made the doors, windows, and flooring, and so on. Mr. Greenhalgh never inserts in that statement any provision for cost of Co-Partnership share of profits or any dividends to Shareholders at all. We see that there is a margin of profit which, in our opinion, will be possible of achievement. We might ask a profit which would result in not being able to sell our article at the price, or which would result in the article being sold at a loss. But the prime cost, whatever it is, is made up of wages, interest and depreciation on buildings, plant, and machinery, and all fixed charges. You all know that. If we work, therefore, on a Co-Partnership basis, and divide the profits, the profits come without increasing the prime cost of the product. I want you to see that. The profits come without increasing the cost of the article produced. The employer always takes into account the cost of materials, wages, etc., but he never takes into his cost the profit he desires to make on the contract. He *allows* for a profit, and therefore if we divide the profits with the workers, we are sharing in the reservoir of profits, which have not been added to the cost of the article, but have been produced by the business ability, by the foresight, by the knowledge of the markets, etc., of the employer. In hardly any industry can you see a profit on an article if you eliminate foresight in buying your supplies, skill in managing your business, and knowledge of trade conditions in selling your article. There never is a profit if you are not possessed of these, and the reason why some firms collapse, and why some men are never able to carry on a business, is because they never see beyond the end of their nose. They can only think of the immediate job in hand, and can only buy to-day if they can sell to-day. They cannot see into the long and distant future. They cannot think what the effect of this or that will be ten years hence and so on. In our business we are to-day only getting profits, or at any rate only for the last few years, practically to-day, from undertakings which we started in 1901, 1902 and 1903, and to-day we are spending money in many directions which cannot bring us profits until five years hence.

That is the way profits are made. In the open market of competition between two firms there never will be a profit, never could be a profit. It is only this business acumen and foresight that will ever produce profits. Therefore profits are not added to the cost, they are the reward of efficiency of the staff, and the reward of efficiency of the employer, and if we enter into a system of Co-Partnership we can produce profits by our ability, "Waste not, want not," and by our efficiency, without increasing the cost of the goods. Therefore, the betterment of the workers in this country will be increased in the same way as the betterment of the masters has been—not by salaries. I can tell you of private firms where partners may be drawing £10,000 a year in profits and only £500 a year as salary, the salary being put down as all they would be worth as ordinary managers of the business. What the profits are after they have charged that salary they take as partners. That is the common rule under all partnership arrangements. That profit has been made by their business acumen and foresight, but is not added to the cost of the article. If it had been added to the cost, the article, perhaps, could not have been sold. They have been able to make a profit by their application to business, by their keenness and alertness, and by their acquaintance with the markets, and so *we* can, and why should not *that* spirit permeate through all the staff and animate every one if we are going to share in the profits? If this system is right we can increase the well-being and betterment of the members of the staff without increasing the cost of living. There is no other system in the world by which this may be done.

Wages Boards may sit and decide that the cost of living has gone up and that another 2s. a week, or whatever it may be, must be added to the wages of labour. The cost of the article is then increased, and this goes on all round till the effect produced is that the cost of living has again gone up all round, and the labourer says, " I am no better off for the 2s." How can he be ? It is an impossibility. If you are going to put 2s. more on, say, to the price of soap, soap will be dearer—there is no other way.   But if we join in partnership and by business acumen and foresight can produce our goods with skill and ability, and market them with skill and ability, we can produce our profits without adding to the cost of the goods.   We can divide these profits amongst us, increasing the benefit to every one, actually, really, and tangibly, not artificially and nominally.   In one of the countries I visited, I saw a house of the type in which you would care to live, and the rent was 22s. 6d. a week, and for very poor houses the rent was 14s. a week.   But there is no mystery about it. The builder has to consider the cost of wages for the bricklayers, etc., and the cost of materials.   The house costs a certain sum, and that fixes the rent, and if he cannot get the rent he does not build the house.   So, therefore, the supply of houses is just in proportion to what people will pay, and what the house costs.   It cannot be any other way.   The same applies to a tailor.   He has to pay certain wages, and the coat must cost so much.   The point is, we are all consumers as well as producers.

I want wages to go up.   They will go up, but I want better conditions to go up in advance of wages.   I do not want the rise to be an artificial one, but a real one, so that as wages go up, better conditions may go up with them.   It is not a real increase when a man receives more wages and has to pay all the advance away in higher cost of living.

In one country a number of people called upon me and asked me to help them with their passage home.   I also received a pathetic letter from one woman in which she told me a tale of great hardship, of how her husband and herself managed to live.   It must be so in these countries.   It could be no other way, because we are all workers and all consumers.   It may be all right for persons who draw their money from some other source, but the workers of a country are the consumers of a country.   When they draw higher wages articles must be dearer, but if you work together as Co-Partners with fairness, and with determination to conduct our business properly, the same will not occur. A man who becomes a builder on his own account knows perfectly well that his success or otherwise depends entirely on his skill. It depends on that skill whether or not he makes a profit on a contract. Are not we all Co-Partners and therefore can all be profit earners ? I have tried to show you Co-Partnership is real. I have tried to show you that those firms mentioned in the official report of the French Government who have Co-Partnership are paying the highest rate of wages, working the shortest hours, have the best sick benefits and best holiday arrangements. Therefore, those advantages are not at the expense of the, wages. Those benefits come out of the increased efficiency of the employer and the increased efficiency of the workers.

VII

HARMONIZING CAPITAL AND LABOUR

MANCHESTER, *October* 20, 1916.

[The difficult problem of the relationship between Co-Partnership and Trade Unionism was faced by Lord Leverhulme in a speech delivered at the Manchester Athenæum. He said :]

I FIND from old records that it was nearly forty years ago—in the year 1877—that I began to experiment on lines which, eleven years later, namely in 1888, led me to adopt a system of what, for want of a better name, I called Prosperity-Sharing. But it was not until twenty-one years after that, namely in 1909, that I adopted Co-Partnership completely and fully, as a practical business relationship between so-called employer and employee—so you will see I have not " rushed in where angels fear to tread," but gone cautiously, and not too hurriedly, forward to full development, as becomes a Lancashire man whose father was born in Bolton and whose mother was born in Manchester—and not even north of the Tweed can more prudent, cautious forbears be found. If you asked me where I first met with the idea of Co-Partnership, I should have to answer with the Lancashire man who was asked where he first met his wife, and who replied : " I did not meet her, she overtook me."

Before launching myself fully on the tempestuous ocean of Capital and Labour, I would like, with your permission, to change the title, which was " Mutuality of Capital and Labour," to " Harmonizing Capital and Labour." The dictionary meaning of " harmonizing " is " adjusting in fit proportion," and, really, this meaning seems to define my address much more accurately than any other.

The very idea of an attempt at harmonizing may upset many deep-rooted eighteenth- and nineteenth-century false ideas, founded on " master and man " theories that Labour is merely the paid tool of Capital. These false ideas have got to go " bag and baggage," for the solution of our problem can only be found by frankly admitting that no individual, or body of individuals, representing either Capital or Labour, can disregard the rights of others or their own duties. What these rights and duties of each to the other are we must endeavour to find out, but the' solution can only be found on sound economic lines. Mere desire for harmony will not suffice, however earnest and sincere it may be. Business is not only the science of the production and distribution of goods, it is also a social science. But the human elements combined in Capital and Labour are neither social scientists nor political economists nor philanthropists ; yet to be able to meet the modern twentieth-century outlook they ought to be acquainted with certain general basic principles.

We must admit that in spite of better conditions of employment and higher wages the present position occupied by Labour is not acceptable to the workers.

The so-called practical business man, ostrich-like, buries his head in his ledger and ignores the writing on the wall. We must not let this attitude influence ourselves, for, after all, has it not been truly said that the so-called practical business man is one who continues to practise the mistakes of his predecessors ? Our duty is to search out certain basic principles that must serve Capital and Labour somewhat in the same way as the compass serves the mariner in navigating the trackless sea, or as the calculations of the astronomer make clear the mysteries of the starry heavens, or as the investigations of the chemist have laid bare the secrets of organic and inorganic matter. For in this relation between Capital and Labour, which must be acknowledged to be the greatest and most intricate problem of all, no attempt has yet been made to get down to first principles. As regards Capital alone, and solely as Capital, this remark does not apply ; for in respect of the science of banking, compilation of statistics on currency, bank reserves, rates of exchange, and so on *ad infinitum*, business men representative of Capital have taken care to be fully equipped for every emergency. But no corresponding statistics dealing with the human element in Labour have been prepared.

9

Of course, I do not say that statistics of wages, hours of employment, strikes, lock-outs, are not available, because these can be obtained to the finest detail ; but Labour as a human element in production and distribution has not been scientifically analysed as Capital has been for the guidance of Capital. The workman called ".Labour" is no longer a "hand" ; Labour to-day is an educated man, and his wants are growing and his outlook is extending. He is to-day the hope of the optimist and the despair of the pessimist. Labour to-day is ambitious, and has created for himself and his wife and family new and better standards of living than his father, and still more than his grandfather, ever dreamt of.

In our first consideration of the new conditions, let us remember that in dealing with them sound methods are more important than the attainment of immediate results ; unfortunately, as between Capital and Labour, it is too often only the immediate spot-view that prevails. Present relationships and present conditions are causing profound dissatisfaction to both Capital and Labour. This great war has forced upon us a better and closer relationship between all classes in the British Empire and has aroused our industrial conscience. This war has revealed to us that, bedded in each and every stratum of society, we can find the highest ideals of truest patriotic service ; that for the cause of right, life itself is as freely given up by the lord as by the labourer ; and that the British Empire possesses the finest material in men and women, bred both in mansion and cottage, that the world can produce.

We only require to recognize the rights of others and our own duties by adapting our industrial system to these high ideals to do away for all time with the bogey of clash of interests between Capital and Labour. Cannot Capital and Labour, after having fought and died side by side in the trenches of Flanders and France, regardless of wealth or station, be won over to fight for the success of our Empire industrially after the final war victory on the sanguinary field of battle? Too long has there existed a wide gulf between Capital and Labour ; for too long have suspicion and distrust produced active opposition between these twin brothers in productive enterprise. Not until Capital and

Labour have solved their difficulties in working frankly and whole-heartedly together can the Empire be as well equipped for the coming war of commerce as she has been rapidly and efficiently equipped for the war of armaments, or be able to devote all her energies to expansion and betterment.

It is merely a question of harmonizing interests and forces. It is not a question altogether of higher wages, shorter hours, or better welfare conditions of employment. The profound dissatisfaction with present conditions goes much deeper than this. This dissatisfaction has its root and spring in the fact that no attempt has been made by Capital to study the human element to be dealt with and handled. The cause of disagreement between Capital and Labour is quite as much psychological as it is material. Human nature called Labour has two very strongly marked characteristics— it is at one and the same time gregarious and individualistic. To the Socialist, man is purely a gregarious being, and Socialists find that they preach in vain the doctrine that every man ought to contribute to the Commonwealth according to his abilities and to share out of the Commonwealth according to his necessities. But apart from the impracticability of this theory, in that it provides no solution as to who shall be the fair just judge, possessed of superhuman insight, to decide as to claims in contribution according to abilities or to award benefits according to necessities, it has failed hopelessly to interest Labour, because it has ignored the other equally marked characteristic of our common humanity, namely, that in addition to being gregarious, man is also strongly and intensely individualistic.

These being two very strongly marked characteristics of human nature, we are not surprised to find that, whilst the greatly preponderating majority of mankind prefer to live in communities, such as cities and towns, rather than in villages or on the scattered country-side, mankind demands, and insists upon having, his own individual house and home ; and that when housed in barracks or huge tenements piled floor upon floor, one on top of another, with common staircases, he rapidly degenerates. Give mankind homes free from overcrowding, where each can enjoy his own individualistic garden in addition to the public park, then, with such a combination of the communal life with individualistic environment, they improve in bodily health and in mental and moral strength. Equally, mankind prefer to follow their daily occupation in groups and masses, as in workshop and factory. But the individual still insists on retaining his individualism, and looks for his own individualistic recognition and reward for his labour. The joiner or mechanic will not be willing, as the Socialist would wish, to contribute according to his trained skill and ability and receive as reward exactly the equal, provided his necessities were the same, as the unskilled labourer. He would not do so whether working at the State Dockyard, or Woolwich Arsenal, or in Government Postal Service, any more than for the capitalist. And he is right, because the socialistic system would make parasites and paupers of one-half the human race.

Now, this is the situation we have to face. Each of us contains in his own mental outlook the elements of an oligarchy and of a democracy; and as our present industrial system is founded on these attributes, it is scarcely surprising that it has been described, and correctly so, as an oligarchy existing in a democratic country. This position of our British industrial system is the result of the haphazard way in which industries have grown up from the small workshop of two or three centuries ago, when the capitalist was also a workman, and master and man met on terms of equality. But modern industrial conditions, with thousands and tens of thousands of workmen, and in at least one industry a quarter of a million workmen, under one oligarchical rule, are intensely anti-democratic, and as such violate the gregarious instincts of humanity. And just as it is true that the position of British industries to-day is the result of yesterday, so their position to-morrow will depend on our actions of to-day. Capitalists have now the task set them to democratize their system, and to create conditions that will enable Labour to take some democratic share in management, and some responsibility for the success of the undertaking. Productive and distributive business must in the future be carried on under less oligarchic and under more democratic conditions. Labour will not be brought to work side by side with and to harmonize with Capital merely by ever higher and higher wages, shorter and shorter hours, combined with better and better welfare conditions.

The wages system has broken down as a sole and only solution. As huge businesses have sprung into existence, the difficulties of the wages system as such have increased. It is impossible under the wages system alone to make Labour realize that the true interests of Labour and Capital are identical. There is a story told of a Lancashire farmer who, on his wedding-day, after the return from church, took his wife into the orchard, where he had arranged a long rope hanging over the fork of a big tree. He asked his wife to get hold of one end of the rope, and he himself took hold of the other. He then gave the signal for them both to pull their strongest, and he soon convinced his wife that, pulling against each other, neither could pull the rope over to his or her side. Having taught this lesson, he asked that they should both pull together at one and the same end, when, of course, the rope was pulled over almost without an effort. Let us hope that pulling against each other during the centuries past has taught this lesson to both Capital and Labour : that no progress can be made in that way, as compared with the progress to be made by both pulling together.

Productive and distributive business must be so organized as to harmonize the relative positions of Capital and Labour. The claim of Capital for as big an output as possible at as low a cost as possible has hitherto had to pull against the claims and aims of Labour for as high wages as possible with as restricted an output as possible. The capitalist has a deep-rooted belief in the fallacy that the lower the wages and the longer the hours worked by Labour are, the lower the cost of production must be—the falsehood of which has been proved, over and over again, by the low wages and long hours of Hindoos and Chinamen, as compared with the lower cost obtained by the extremely high wages and shorter hours of the United States. Labour has a deep-rooted belief in the fallacy that there is only a certain limited amount of work to be divided amongst an ever-increasing number of workmen, and that, consequently, restriction of output is the most sure and certain way to provide work for all ; the falsehood of which has been proved by the fact that restriction of output has been shown always to act as a deterrent to consumption and to demand for labour, whilst the increased output ' per man in the United States has stimulated and increased demand and resulting employment and wages. The lesson of this for the capitalist is that high wages, short hours, and good healthy conditions, by increasing intelligence and efficiency, increase output, and actually reduce costs. And the lesson for Labour is that increased output stimulates consumption, and, consequently, demand for production and distributive labour, the fact being that consumers of all classes supply themselves where they can be best and most economically served.

These are such well-known and simple truths that it is almost necessary to apologize for calling attention to them. We thus see that Capital and Labour, by faith in these fallacies, are merely pulling against each other. How can we harmonize these conflicting elements? Only by Capital identifying itself with Labour, and creating for Labour the same economic environment and conditions as Capital itself enjoys. Only by entrance into Co-Partnership together can Capital and Labour be brought to pull together, and only by Co-Partnership can they be harmonized.

We are agreed that the elements in production and distribution are Capital and Labour—I prefer myself to make it a three-legged stool by including Management as apart from both Capital and Labour. But sometimes Management is part of the activities of Capital, and at other times must be included with Labour. We British have always been well supplied with all three. We acquired the capital because we had Management and Labour, and good Management always accumulates capital. The accumulation of capital that we may look forward to during the twentieth century is bound to be greater than was the case during the nineteenth century, and still more so than during preceding centuries. But whilst we had no difficulty under the existing system in the acquisition of capital, we have not been equally successful in its distribution, and this is the root and cause of all the antagonism between Capital and Labour. This system, under which all the profits or losses go to Capital, ignores entirely the psychology of the workman. He is not a mere machine to be kept well oiled with good wages, well tended by not being worked for too long hours, and kept in good going repair by welfare systems, canteens, and good housing conditions. He is a complex human being, with all the ambitions, ideals, and mental outlook possessed by the capitalist in an equal and sometimes superior degree.

If high wages, short hours, good housing meant finality to Labour Unrest, then Labour would not be a man but a vegetable. Labour has economic interests that also require satisfying, and that press on Capital for their solution. We have heard it said of our educational system, that to make it complete a ladder must be provided by which a boy or girl can climb from Board School to University; so that an apt pupil might have the opportunity of living its full life without limitations from the environment in which it was born. To harmonize Capital and Labour similarly, a ladder must be provided from the humblest position in industrial organization to a seat on the Board of Directors. Capital must provide a broader outlook for Labour.

Has not the political orator speechified, has not the eloquent preacher sermonized, and the profound philosopher theorized, on the necessity for harmonizing Capital and Labour? And yet it is all so very easy and simple. The only possible way of harmonizing Capital and Labour is to provide both with the same outlook by dividing the profits their joint labour has created fairly and squarely between them. On this system, each will also automatically share and suffer from losses when they have to be faced. Step by step the lesson is being taught and learned that the Co-Partnership system is the only possible system for harmonizing Capital and Labour; and, fortunately, it is capable of application in principle, by varying methods, to all but a very limited few occupations; and when applied honestly and faithfully, it has invariably produced improved relations, with better commercial results. With Co-Partnership comes less anxiety and reduced responsibility for Capital, for with division of profits must also be included division of responsibility and sharing of control. Co-Partners become more and more interested in the policy of the business as a whole, and associate themselves more and more with Management. There is no conflict in these Co-Partnership results; and they satisfy the gregarious and democratic instincts of Labour and the equally strong individualistic instincts. Whilst Co-Partnership satisfies the aspirations of the civic and democratic spirit of Labour, the wages system (varied as to rates to meet varying skill, strength, or ability, or combined with piece-work rates or bonus or premium scales) still continues as a necessary basis of remuneration to satisfy the aspirations of our individualistic instincts.

If Co-Partnership resulted in exclusion of individual reward for individual effort, then Co-Partnership would be foredoomed to failure in harmonizing Capital and Labour. Co-Partnership is required, and indeed is essential to success, as a means of equalization in the final division of profits, and as the preventer of the intrusion of a spirit of greed between Capital and Labour. But there is no reason why Co-Partnership, to meet the civic and democratic nature of humanity, should not be combined with salaries or wages varied to fit abilities and efficiency, and plus bonus, or premium, or piece-work, to supply the need of the individualistic spirit. And there is no reason why this combination, by meeting the civic and democratic wants of humanity and satisfying individualistic aspirations, should not prove as successful a harmonizer as is possible in the present stage of advancement and development of industrial relationships.

But Co-Partnership must be more than a mere division of profits. It must have its base resting firmly on the deep solid rock of human nature. It must be the means of enabling men under modern conditions, wherein thousands of workmen are operating together in factories, mines, and workshops, to do so as real Co-Partners. Labour must be Co-Partner with Capital in fact as well as in name. But this Co-Partnership must not extinguish or crush the strong spirit of individualism which is such a pronounced element in human nature. It must give to each man the stimulus and security of the man in business for himself. The British workman has a profound distrust and dislike of paternalism. Co-Partnership can only fail when Capital or Labour expect too much as a result of it, and where Labour, after being taken into Co-Partnership, is not treated as a partner. Capital must not expect that Labour, after Co-Partnership, will cease to make demands for higher wages, or relinquish its right to combine in Trade Unions, or will not show disaffection if other conditions irritate or create a feeling of oppression; and, equally, Co-Partnership must not be shipwrecked by Labour expecting that Capital shall cease to fill its function of control and to maintain discipline.

At the same time, Trade Unionism ought not to be a barrier. Trade Unions are as essential under Co-Partnership as under the present existing system. Trade Unions are, for both Capital and Labour, indispensable as a means of collective bargaining. There is no reason why Trade Unions should be either apathetic, or, as is most often the case, openly hostile to Co-Partnership. Such hostility on the part of Trade Unions can only exist so long as they ignore the obvious fact that to make Labour Co-Partner with Capital is a democratic step tending in the right direction, by putting Labour on the road to share in Management and to enjoy increased welfare. For by Co-Partnership the total earnings will be increased by Profit-Sharing, and the total earnings must always include the payment of full wages on the Trade Union scale and for the Trade Union working hours. And it is obvious that if the total earnings are larger in Co-Partnership workshops, then this improvement is bound to react on all other workshops, and so Co-Partnership must inevitably tend to the improvement of backward industries. An intelligent Co-Partner, working under the above conditions, receiving full Trade Union wages and working Trade Union hours (including, when such is the rule, either bonus, premium, or piece-work additions), is bound to realize the value of his efforts to the business as a whole, as well as to himself as an individual. And so the outlook of the Co-Partner becomes broader and he becomes keen to adopt new methods calculated to produce a larger output with lessened cost of production, with the result of adding to the profits in which he himself and all Co-Partners share. High wages, bonuses, premiums, or piece-work, apart from a system of Co-Partnership, can alone bring no solution of Labour difficulties. Only the true spirit of Co-Partnership can tend in this direction, and, by combining the democratic with the individualistic attributes of human nature, will result not only in higher total earnings, but greater efficiency, happier life, and improved mental condition. Therefore, the opposition of Trade Unions can only be based on some fundamental misconception which assumes that the interests of Capital and Labour are diametrically opposed to each other.

Time, and the steady growth of the Co-Partnership movement, alone can correct this.

Co-Partnership can do no more than produce the right environment and create conditions for Capital and Labour that are mutually healthy and stimulating. Thanks to our various Education Acts, from 1870 up to the present time, Labour to-day is alert and intelligent, and has imbibed ambitions and aspirations, and in addition Labour is gaining experience every day by service on local government bodies and on Trade Union committees, and is the better prepared and equipped to take greater responsibilities, but Labour must move gradually and somewhat slowly to the higher sphere of Directorships.

But throughout it all, in seeking to harmonize Capital and Labour we must never lose sight of the fact that what is called the present Labour Unrest is healthy and encouraging, for it discloses a psychological problem just as large as one of wages and of hours of employment. And in this aspect, Co-Partnership means much more than sharing profits as an addition to wages. It means the spirit of comradeship—the spirit that recognizes equality and brotherhood ; and it is working on these lines that the harmonizing of Capital and Labour best promises to dispel the present atmosphere of suspicion and distrust.

VIII

TRADERS' PARTNERS

BOLTON, *October* 11, 1917.

[Addressing the Bolton Combined Traders' Association, Lord
Leverhulme referred to the early days of his business career,
when he was a grocer in Bolton and Wigan. His experiences
in that business, combined with what he had learnt from his
father, who was apprenticed to the same trade as long ago
as 1824, had left upon his mind certain impressions to which
he owed whatever success he had since attained. He thought
the grocery trade afforded the best education a business man
could possibly have. He said :]

THERE are many ways besides sharing profits in which you
can make those associated with you in business into partners.
I' know many businesses where Profit-Sharing and Co-Partnership in profits are quite impossible. Take the great business
of domestic service. There are no profits appearing in the
balance-sheet of servants of a household and the duties they
perform, and yet we all know that a kind and encouraging
word will do far more in making life comfortable to the
servant and happy for the mistress; and in making the home
bright and cheerful, than any mercenary bond there may be
between them. And so, also, the trader, however small his
staff may be, however impossible it may be to have a Profit-
Sharing scheme of an elaborate nature, can, by consideration
of his staff, make them just as enthusiastically his partners
as by any sharing of profits whatever. Why, every trader
must, if his business is to succeed, enthuse and put energy
into his staff, and, believe me, enthusiasm and energy are
synonymous terms. By consideration of their hours of
work, by cheerfulness towards them, by courtesy to them,
by the payment of the highest wage the business will afford,

the employer may energize his staff, and stimulate them in a way that would not be possible in a larger business, even with the most complicated, elaborate, complete, and generous scheme of Co-Partnership. There must be personal contact on these lines.

You know, business is business ; and good business demands enthusiastic workers ; and you can't get energetic, efficient work without some bond of sympathy between employer and employee. Sympathy with the staff—why, look how it would clear away the cobwebs ! It would not only increase a trader's business, but would decrease the loss and expense, and it would not only increase his own happiness, but his popularity with his customers as well as his own staff ; and, further, it would enable a trader of mere mediocre ability to accomplish more in his business than a trader of great brilliance and genius could accomplish without it. It will bring up a mediocre man far in advance of the talent o a brilliant man. But I would like continually to repeat, f in whatever I have to say, that there is no philanthropy in business, and a trader cannot allow sympathy with his staff to fill his business with pensioners and inefficients. No matter how much an employer may idealize as to running his business for purposes other than mere money-making, he will find he must run his business for money-making if he wishes, to make a perfect and ideal organization for his employees as well as for the customers he serves. He must work on ideal conditions for all his employees and his customers if he wishes to safeguard the capital he has in the business— to build up a solid, successful, money-making business.

The trader must so balance his ideals with practical business as to neglect neither. At an Agricultural College a discussion was taking place as to what slopes of land were best suited to give the biggest crops, and an old farmer, who knew nothing probably about scientific methods of farming and slopes of land, and so on, got up at the end of the discussion and said that in his experience it did not matter so much about the slope of the land as the slope of the man. And so I would say of every one of us in business, whatever systems we adopt, and whether we are able or unable to adopt some plan of Profit-Sharing or Co-Partnership, far more will depend upon our own inclinations and leanings towards our ideals than any particular method we may adopt. The slope of a man can make success or failure, and it can make a mediocre man into a superman.

Let us examine into the question of Co-Partnership on ordinary lines of Profit-Sharing in any business. There are three active partners, generally speaking, in every business. Whether we acknowledge Co-Partnership or not—whether we do anything to recognize it or not, there are three partners joined together—the employee, the public, and the proprietor. Each of these three partners has within himself three sleeping partners. I will call the Employees, the Public, and the Proprietors the active partners. The three sleeping partners are Habit, Inertia, and Imitation.

One of the hard business facts of life that has an immense power on success is habit. It is by habit that we think and act most efficiently. We do very little efficient thinking until we do it by habit. If you watch the child first beginning to toddle, its footsteps falter ; but when it has learned to walk, and walks by habit, then it becomes a perfect walker. Habit means that condition of body and mind, or both, which has become established by constant repetition. The successful trader is the man who has acquired the best habits for his own particular business, and that is all that success means. Mediocrity, by constant repetition, can surpass brilliancy that has not acquired habits by constant repetition. We have had that experience, each of us, in our schooldays. We saw the less brilliant scholar, by constantly repeating and learning his lesson, able to pass examinations and take prizes that a more brilliant scholar, who would not go through the drudgery of repetition, failed to secure. The best way to acquire good habits is to make the mind lead off in the right direction, and the best business habit to be acquired first is system, a good system which leads to success. Success does not depend on the head of the business, the captain of the ship, being on the bridge all the time. With system, a man could multiply his powers a hundred-fold. A man with the aid of system can enable his shop assistants to get through ten times the work that they are capable of without system. Compare the shop or any business where no system prevails, where the master has no daily or hourly programme and where all is confusion, with the shop where system and order prevail, and you will at once see the difference. So that habit in business means, first of all, acquiring system.

The second of these sleeping partners is Inertia. In acquiring habits we have to overcome Inertia. You see it when a horse is drawing a load. It takes many times the strain to start the movement, to overcome Inertia, than it does to maintain the movement; and that is equally true of the effort to stop the movement. You can't stop an express train in a moment any more than you can start it off at full speed. This principle applies equally, or more, to the beginning of new habits and to the stopping of old habits. The strong, progressive habit cannot at once overcome the Inertia of old habits. It is actually easier for some to do their work in the hardest and most difficult way possible, when that way is an acquired habit, than it is to change to new and easier methods. Now, this Inertia of old habits is the sole reason why young men get ahead of the older ones in every and any business. This fact about Inertia teaches us, as business men, that improvement in our business involving radical changes should not be made too suddenly, just as you would not turn a corner at top speed in a motor-car. Were we considering the introduction of Co-Partnership, the greatest radical change we can make in our business, it behoves us to bear in mind this principle of Inertia. It is an element in the minds of our staff and in our own minds.

In overcoming Inertia we have the help of our third sleeping partner, Imitation. We all love to imitate what we see. If we wish to adopt Co-Partnership, our inclination is guided by our love of imitation, which helps us to overcome Inertia. A going concern has a goodwill. This goodwill is due to the effect of the increase in the volume of profits, proving that business is founded on right habits and on the firm basis of repetition and on the overthrow of Inertia. Before I pass to the active partners, let me just recapitulate these three sleeping partners. Habits, rightly founded, make for progress Inertia has to be overcome, but, at the same time, it does lend itself to stability. Imitation helps us to overcome Inertia, and Inertia is a natural tendency to continue without change. The only way to build a business and train a staff is to bear in mind these three principles. If we overlooked them we should get discouraged and give up our task, whatever we had set ourselves to do.

May I give you an instance of widespread Inertia we had through the country a few years ago? You remember when Willett introduced his Daylight Saving Bill he was ridiculed in the House of Commons, and at once came against that huge mass of Inertia which could not be moved. But, in a little while, we began to think about it, and, although Willett did not live to see his plan adopted, the Inertia was overcome, and who, to-day, would go back to the old-time calendar in the summer months? I mention that because it is such a recent and such a good illustration of the point I wish to bring out—that, in this huge problem of Co-Partnership, we have the same difficulty to face, and we must bear it in mind both for our own guidance and in the guidance of our staff, and in regard to the public we serve.

Now, let us consider the three active partners: the Employee, the Public, and the Proprietor. No proprietor, at any time, was independent of those about him, and he is more dependent upon them to-day than ever. He cannot succeed alone. Employers and employees must work together as partners with the public. Employers must recognize that their employees are an asset to the business. Hitherto, employers have simply looked upon the assistant as a liability that had to be cleared every week at pay-day. An enthusiastic Co-Partnership employer, in a distributive business, has stated that his employees, since they had been made Co-Partners, have reduced his changes in his staff, increased the permanency of his staff by 35 per cent., and their efficiency by over 50 per cent. Every employer in a retail business knows that his point of contact with his customers depends on his staff. The nearer he can bring his staff to himself in their interest in and enthusiasm for the business, the more successful is his business likely to be. In fact, employers and employed are like the strands in a rope. Spun into a cable, they can bear great strain, but unwound and unravelled they can bear none.

Now, we are told that a house divided against itself cannot stand, but modern business goes further than that. The position to-day in business is that a house must have unity

of aim and purpose, and enthusiasm and loyalty ; otherwise
it cannot stand.   As an illustration of enormous power
running to waste, take the Falls of Niagara. There is a
similar enormous waste of energy when employees are outside
the reach of a Co-Partnership, either in profit-sharing or in
sympathy, in kind acts and consideration. Hundreds of
millions of horse-power are running to waste at Niagara.
A few of them have been chained up, and light up Buffalo
and other cities, and drive many industries.   But only the
mere fringe of the power has been utilized, and I venture
to say that, in most businesses, from 50 per cent. upwards
of the ability of the staff is never developed at all. The
employer must make the employee feel that he is his best
friend, and that he is an inspiration to him ; that he is the
employees' instructor, adviser, and helper. All this means
confidence, trust, and leads up to Co-Partnership.

There is a subtle influence, an atmosphere that emanates
from the employer, and many a man in business has strangled
the spirit of his employees by his cold, fault-finding methods.
It is easy to judge the character and type of the employer
by studying the character and type of employee working
under him. If the employer is morose and gloomy, how can
you expect his employees to be bright and cheerful with
the customers in the shop ?   Employers are learning more
and more the value of creating a cheerful atmosphere in
their business, equally with a cheerful, bright, newly decorated
interior of their business premises.   The two go together.
None of us, I venture to say, would to-day consider it businesslike to have the interior of our business premises slovenly,
neglected, dirty, and requiring beautifying.   We must be
determined that the minds of our employees are just as free
from cobwebs, and as bright, cheerful, and happy, if they are
to be attractive to the customers who come into our shop.
If one were to sow nettles and thistles, one would never expect
to find a harvest of perfumed roses, sweet and fragrant ;
and if we sow morose words amongst our staff, they will
reach, through our staff, to our customers, and drive them
away.   We none of us can do our best work under any other
conditions than when we are at our happiest. It is, remember,
the warm sun that causes the buds to open and give forth
their perfume. You know what George Macdonald said :

" If I can put gladness into the heart of any man or woman, I shall feel I have worked with God."

If Co-Partnership were merely a matter of money-motive—a money stimulus—without the putting of gladness and happiness into the hearts of the staff, then, I say, Co-Partnership would be a gloomy failure. The employee has a right to happiness and freedom from anxiety. Remember, that whatever attitude is adopted towards the staff will react upon the employer himself, as well as on his business. We must begin to realize the fact that a large part of the employee's ability is never awakened because it has never been energized or utilized. We all of us know those who have been in business with us at various times and whom we considered of no special merit as long as they were our assistants, but who have developed by leaps and bounds when they have got into business for themselves. Why could not we develop these latent powers ?

Now, let us consider the second partner in business—the Public. Many think the only use of the public is to make profits out of them. You know the man who was boasting of his profits during the war in the smoke-room of his club. He said, " You know, I have made it all by sheer, downright pluck—every penny of it." The worried listener : " And whom did you pluck ? " Many a man of business thinks price is the only element of success. There are dozens of reasons for success besides prices. Customers will go past one shop to another, because gracious courtesy, civility, efforts to please, reliability on recommendations of quality, all count for far more than price cutting. Many customers would rather trust the trader's recommendation than their own power of selection. Remember, the satisfied customer not only comes himself but sends others. The assistant must be trained in habits of courtesy to the public. A multiple shopman spent a great deal of money in sending telegrams to every branch manager at each of his shops throughout the United Kingdom : " Did you say ' Thank you,' to every customer you served to-day ? " He sent those telegrams from time to time until he had burnt the importance of this fact into their minds. He spent over £1,000 on those telegrams, merely asking that question. He says it was the best £1,000 investment he ever made in his life.

10

There are hundreds of men who would scorn to tell a lie who would let their goods lie for them. They do not hesitate to sell shoddy, second-rate goods. None of them would dream of cheating or lying. They are conscientiously, and not hypocritically, above it. There is no hypocrisy; but in building up a business, if we are dealing in anything other than the quality that customers have a right to expect from the class of trade we do, then we are, in our business, living a lie. The grandest advertisement ever written is poor compared with the reputation for keeping high-class goods and giving a true description of them.

You know the story of the young man who started a fish shop, and fitted it up with marble slabs, and tiles on the wall; then he wrote a sign and put it up. There was his name on the sign, and then, " Fresh Fish Sold Here." A friend came along and admired the shop, and, after looking all round said, " Look at your sign." " What's the matter ? " he asked. " Why do you say ' Fresh Fish Sold Here ? ' You do not need to say ' here.' You are not selling them across the way." So the young man painted the word " Here " out, and the sign read " Fresh Fish Sold." Another friend came and admired the marble slabs and the tiles. When he had admired everything he said, " But look at your sign. Everybody will know your fish is fresh." He got his paint pot and painted out the word " Fresh." So now the sign read, " Fish Sold." Another friend came, and when *he* had admired the shop and the slabs and tiles, he too, said, " Look at your sign. Why say ' Sold ? ' Nobody will think you are giving the fish away." So he took out that word also, and now the sign simply read, " So-and-so, Fish." Still another friend came, and when he had looked all round he said, " Look at your sign." " What's the matter with the sign yet ? " asked the young man. " Why say ' Fish ? ' " was the reply; " I could smell fish as soon as I turned the corner."

There is a motto that runs, " The deceiver only deceives himself." If any of us think that we can make a second-rate quality of goods appear equal to the first-rate quality, we are only deceiving ourselves. Deceit is a boomerang, and if we put ourselves in our customers' place, we shall realize the whole position. Nothing will so quickly forfeit confidence as disappointment over quality. People do not like to deal with traders they have always to be watching. Millions upon millions of pounds sterling of turn-over are done entirely and solely on the character and reputation of traders for straightforwardness.

Well, now, what about the third partner, the Trader himself? Many men in business are unable to trust those associated with them with any power or authority whatever. These men can only think in inches, and have only an eye to petty cash items, and as long as they themselves can oversee everything and attend to all the details themselves, they get along all right, but the moment they have to delegate to others, they go all to pieces. That is because they do not know how to select their staff, and consequently can never trust them. With these men, every employee who does not exactly please them at the moment is cleared out. If the employee were to express an opinion upon the business, or make suggestions, he would be dismissed. With such an employer, the employee must not move hand or foot without the employer's approval. Such traders will not recognize the fact that no man can attend to all the details of his own business, and know every point about even his own one business.

Now, the trader, to be successful, must begin right away by trusting his staff, and until he can trust them—until he has trained and educated them so that he knows, whether he is there or not, that his business is going on as he would wish it, and that his customers are being courteously attended to, he is not ripe for the consideration of Co-Partnership, the spirit of which comes a long way after that stage. If we are suspicious and distrustful of our staff, then our staff become suspicious and distrustful of us, for distrust and suspicion breed distrust and suspicion. We have to encourage our staff. No employee can be at his or her best if always conscious that some one is watching in a fault-finding attitude of mind. The interest of the employee must be awakened ; it cannot be forced.

There is no doubt we all make errors in business : buy at the wrong time, and fail to sell at the right time ; and I always consider that the business man is more than a hero, braver than any man in the trenches, who dare freely acknowledge openly before his staff that he has made a mistake, and applies the ink eraser to his own mistakes rather than continue them. This is the state of mind we have got to cultivate, and once it has been cultivated and become a habit, there is nothing that will place an employer on a higher pedestal with his employee. It sounds a paradox to say our very mistakes and failings would raise us with our employees and, literally, it would not be so. The man who made three mistakes in five actions would never win the esteem and respect of his employee; but, equally, the employer who claimed to be able to do right all five times, and never acknowledged that now and then even he might make a mistake, as well as his staff, would fail to win the esteem and real support of his staff.

Now, the most dangerous period in the business career of any tradesman is the time when he begins to feel sure of his position. Over-confidence in any one of us is the first sign of decay, and we all of us do our best work when we are struggling for position. When a man says to himself, " Now, I can take things easier; I hold the field; I am head and shoulders over all my competitors, and I can afford to breathe more freely "—then he is in the greatest danger of his life. It is dangerous to run a business on its past reputation, for there are too many others pushing forward for supremacy all the time. It is astonishing how soon the best business goes to pieces when the proprietor begins to take it easy. Managing a business is like rolling a stone up a hill; take one's hands off, and down the stone rolls to the bottom again.

Now, I want just to come to the point that this fact brings us up to. I am sure you will agree with what I have said about the necessity of constant vigilance in business. If this were the final word in business, the prospect for our old age would be gloomy indeed. Business would mean hard labour for life and the agony of seeing our business fade away in our old age. But if we take time by the forelock, if those bright young fellows who pass through our hands at various stages of our career are attracted to us by sympathy, are trained and developed in our business by our watchful care, are made partners in our business at the particular moment when they have proved themselves worthy of it and of our confidence, then, as our own physical powers grow less their physical strength is growing greater, and the fair and just treatment we have dealt out to them wins their loyalty and support ; for all through their life they are able to say they could never have done better under any circumstances whatever, for even if they went away from the business in which they were trained and developed to start a business of their own, the increased competition, the heavy responsibilities, the difficulties for capital, would not make life so well worth living for them as a partnership in the firm they were with, a share in the profits that were made, and the opportunity to invest their money in the business each succeeding year. On this system the employer, as I have mentioned, need not be always at the helm. He can take his reasonable relief as years get on, and when, finally, it comes to the Indian summer of his life, as the sun is declining, it will leave a golden glow through the skies ; he will be surrounded by those whom he has trained and developed to look upon him more as a father than an employer. Whether they are single units, or tens, or hundreds, or thousands, however many they may be, their willing hands will go forth to build up the business. The business will become more than a mere machine to them. It will become a living being to be cared for and tended and cultivated as lovingly by them as ever by their master in his own young days. And so we can see our business extend and grow, and if there were nothing else in Co-Partnership than the relief it will give to a man when his physical strength declines, I say that argument alone—apart from the increased prosperity which Co-Partnership, in the experience of those who have adopted it, brings ; apart from the fact that when you have interested your staff with you in the profits you have applied the most just, fair, and powerful stimulus you can to their efforts—apart altogether from all that, this one factor alone ought to win it adherence.

Now, as to the particular form of Co-Partnership to be adopted It is utterly impossible for any man to decide this question other than the man who is going to apply it. As I have said, it may not be possible to share profits at all, or to have a partner. There are many occupations, such as domestic service, in which it is quite impossible ; but in one

form or another, either by kind actions and sympathy, consideration in sickness, and the joy of happiness in health,
the payment of high wages, or the sharing of profits, a human
bond of sympathy must go out from the head of the business,
from the proprietor, right down to the youngest office boy,
and, that secured, I do not care whether you call it Co-
Partnership, Profit-Sharing, or what you call it, you have
introduced into business the human element, which will not
only make the staff working for you happy, but will make
yourself happy. It is true that a business carried on for
mere money-grabbing objects, as I ventured to say at the
beginning, will, in my opinion, fail to realize even the narrow
ideal of making money ; but carried on upon the broad lines
of recognition of equal rights to a share of the fruits of the
industry of every one connected with the business, whoever
they may be, then the harvest is greater as it is shared with
others. Then, as the sunset comes along in the skies, the
owner, instead of shutting down in dark weariness with the
knowledge that the business must pass into the hands of
strangers or be closed entirely, and that the physical strength
of the proprietor is unable to keep up with the energetic
action of younger men, will see it stronger than ever, and
have in it an ever-increasing pride.

APPENDIX

THE CO-PARTNERSHIP TRUST IN LEVER BROTHERS LIMITED

FOUNDER—LORD LEVERHULME

Lever Brothers Limited began in 1909 to give workers a share in the profits.

Power was at first taken to issue Partnership Certificates up to £500,000 nominal value, and this was afterwards increased to £1,000,000.

These Certificates are issued to employees in proportion to wages or salary each year. The Management provisionally allot Certificates to the Staff, but Co-Partners have the right of appeal to a Committee composed jointly of Staff and Managers. The system of allotment is based on value of service. The very slacker and ne'er-do-weel receives *nil*, the apathetic from 5 per cent. to 10 per cent., and the enthusiastic, appreciative, and responsive above 10 per cent., with special allotment for special services and helpful suggestions.

The final appeal can be made to the Chairman of the Company should any Co-Partner or Employee feel that he has been overlooked or unfairly dealt with.

For the purpose of the Certificate distribution the Staff is divided into four classes—Directors, Managers and Foremen, Salesmen, General Staff.

The Co-Partnership extends to both male and female.

The original *minimum* age-limit for Co-Partnership was twenty-five years, but is now lowered to twenty-two years.

Originally the Co-Partnership Certificate was only given after five years' service ; now it is given after four years' service.

The Staff sign an application form, containing a pledge in the following terms :—

" To the Trustees of the Partnership Trust in Lever Brothers Limited.
   " GENTLEMEN,—I, the undersigned, request that a Partnership Certificate be issued to me under the above Trust,

and I undertake that if the issue is made I will in all respects abide by, and conform to, the provisions of the Trust Deed and the Scheme scheduled to it, and will not waste time, labour, materials, or money in the discharge of my duties, but will loyally and faithfully further the interests of Lever Brothers Limited, its Associated Companies, and my Co-Partners, to the best of my skill and ability, and I hand you herewith a statement in writing of the grounds upon which I base this application."

Once admitted, and so long as their record is clean, Co-Partners receive further Certificates each year on above basis in proportion to wages or salary, until they have reached their maximum holding, which ranges from £200 to £3,000, according to their annual earnings.

They receive dividends on the amounts of their accumulated Certificates like Ordinary Shareholders, but as the Certificates contribute no Capital to the business, they receive on that account 5 per cent. less than is paid on Ordinary Shares.

The dividends are paid in 5 per cent. Cumulative " A " Preferred Ordinary Shares, which the holder can sell at any time for cash at par value if he so desires ; but so long as the shares are held by the Co-Partner to whom they were originally allotted they also participate further in profits to the extent that they yield to him the same rate of interest as that enjoyed by the Ordinary Share-holder.

These 5 per cent. Cumulative " A " Preferred Ordinary Shares can only be allotted as dividends in lieu of cash.

Co-Partnership couples up Loss-Sharing with Profit-Sharing. If a man has acquired Co-Partnership Certificates, and if profits were to cease to be earned, he would suffer equally with Capital in loss of dividends.

When an employee retires from active work in the service of the firm, his Partnership Certificates are cancelled, but if his retire ment is due to ill-health or old-age, or if his services are dispensed with through no fault of his own, he receives in exchange Prefer-ential Certificates which bear interest at 5 per cent. on their nominal par value and are a charge on the profits ranking next after the first 5 per cent. taken by the Ordinary Shareholders.

The nominal amount of a Preferential Certificate is either ten times the average dividends paid in respect of the former Director's or Employee's Partnership Certificates during the three preceding years, or the same nominal amount as that of the Partnership Certificate so exchanged, whichever shall be the lesser.

The granting of these Certificates does not in any way interfere with the old age pensions under Lever Brothers' Employees Benefit Fund.

So long as an employee is in the active service of the firm he cannot (except for flagrant inefficiency or misconduct) be deprived of the Partnership Certificates already issued to him, and the annual interest which may be payable on those Certificates. The conditions can only be varied by the consent of the holders of not less than three-fourths of the total nominal amount of the Certificates issued.

Both Partnership and Preferential Certificates are cancelled by the death of the owner unless a widow is left. But a widow receives Preferential Certificates in exchange for her late husband's Partnership Certificates, or if he had retired and was holding Preferential Certificates, these are transferred to her, and she is entitled to hold them, subject to the conditions of the Trust, while she remains a widow.

On January 1, 1918, the nominal value of the Partnership Certificates, Ordinary and Preferential, issued and outstanding, was £751,536.

At the same date the number of Employee Partners, including employees of Associated Companies admitted to Co-Partnership, was 5,066.

In the nine completed years of the Co-Partnership there has been distributed, for the benefit of the employees, in Co-Partnership Dividends, and in Prosperity-Sharing generally, £487,353.

HOUSING AND SOCIAL WELFARE

UNDERCURRENTS OF HOUSING, CAPITAL, AND LABOUR

CARLISLE, *November* 5, 1917.

[In view of the important developments taking place at Carlisle —its transition from an old-world cathedral city•to a centre of industrial progress, the establishment of munition works expected to be the largest in the world, and the carrying-out of a valuable experiment in the control of the liquor traffic —Lord Leverhulme evidently felt that the topics on which he spoke at the invitation of the Carlisle Chamber of Commerce were appropriate to the place and the time. He recollected also that he was in the neighbourhood of Gretna—the scene of so many romantic marriages—and, thus prompted, he gave new expression to his hopes of social welfare : " What better love-match could there be than one between producer and consumer, both interdependent ? " He went on to say :]

OUR first great task is to win this war. We are winning. The final victory which is bound to come may be a little delayed from the events of the past few months, but it cannot be withheld. Victory is bound to come to the cause of right against the brute force of mere might.

It would be a world scandal if a democratic people who could organize to win victory on the battlefield found itself unable to organize for better conditions of life as the fruits of that complete victory. The great stumbling-block to our progress is our tendency here to follow precedent. The progress of the world has gone on in spite of our British reluctance to take new departures. I am sure you will agree with me that the progress in science and knowledge of the secrets of nature that we have gained from the days of Sir Isaac Newton to the present time is infinitely greater than it was from the time of Adam to Sir Isaac Newton.

So great and so rapid have been the changes in the last fifty years, that we may say we have gained more in that time than from the time of Adam to Sir Isaac Newton. All the immense possibilities of this progress have been achieved be persistent hard work on the lines of individualism, and in spite of the opposition of Governments. In fact, during the centuries we have spoken of, Governments have persecuted the men of science—have burned them at the stake, and applied the thumb-screws of the torture chamber to them; but, in spite of the opposition of Government, science has progressed.

The British Empire, as we know it now, has not been the product of the British Government, but exists as the product of individuals in spite of Government and Colonial and Foreign Offices. We should never get much out of Parliament. The reason is clear. The province of Government is not to do things for us, but to govern so as to ensure each citizen equality of rights, equality of opportunities, and equality of protection under the laws. Our limited monarchy is the best form of government in the world, and, compared with the United States or France or elsewhere, the best form of democratic control in the world to-day.

My strong faith in democracy is founded on the fact that the citizens will themselves feel the pinch when their own errors produce ill effects. But we must take heed now of undercurrents. Just as our airmen flying through the air encounter currents of which we did not know—pockets, I think, they call them, which they have to learn and study before they can conquer the means of flying—so it is in our ideals and dreams of betterment. When the Franchise Bill of 1869 was passed we were told we must educate our masters, and our education has resulted in teaching the people to look to Parliament to give them anything and everything—to be to them a sort of Universal Provider. We have, apparently, taught our citizens to expect to get from Parliament by vote what citizens ought to obtain for themselves by work. Everything is to be provided by Government

Now we come to touch the problem of the shortage—the alarming shortage—of houses. We know that something must be done, and it is natural that, by this process of education, people should look to Parliament to give them free or semi-free houses.   Now, this is not the democratic control of free men, but nursery rule. We must get rid of the idea that we can get something for nothing.   It is a delusion.

What are the reasons for the shortage of cottages ? There must be some reason.   Hitherto 98 per cent. of the cottages provided have been built by private enterprise.   The total number of cottages built by private enterprise in ten years, from 1900 to 1909, was 1,100,000.   As long as Great Britain has existed all cottage houses have been built by private enterprise.   The speculative builder may have his faults, but, on the whole, he has cheaply and well provided, at his own capital cost, for the housing of the people, the landlord financing the builder who leased his land.

Why has this private enterprise come to an end ? What is the cause of the present shortage of cottages ?   The cause is the shaking of confidence in the security of any invest-ment in cottage building, and in this form of business enter-prise.   The talk of Government providing houses on some basis of assistance out of the general taxes of the country to provide what has hitherto been provided by private enter-prise has shaken confidence.   The depreciation in the selling value of cottage property in the last eight years has approxi-mated to an aggregate of £200,000,000 sterling.

After shaking the confidence of those who previously provided the building of cottages by raising the expectation of Government help being given to others to build further cottages, there came the war, the calling-up of all men of military age and in fit condition to serve in the Army.   Then, after the outbreak of war, an Act was passed preventing the owners of cottages from raising their rents and the owners of mortgages from raising the interest on mortgages.   We all of us, myself included, allowed that this was the right step to take.   Then meetings were held in approval of the Act, and it was endorsed unanimously by those who attended the meetings.

But here, again, we have an undercurrent, because the Act promptly stopped all building of further cottages and the loan of money on cottage property.   The builders could not build because the rents of existing cottages were not advanced to meet the increased cost of repairs and renewals. Building of new houses could not proceed because it was not an attractive investment, apart from the difficulties of finance caused by the calling in of mortgages, and the impossibility of replacing them except on an increased margin. This has brought in its train loss and ruin to owners, who have been compelled to realize on forced sales at an enormous loss. Mortgages could not be raised on new cottage property, and banking facilities are extremely limited. Capital was attracted to other and more lucrative channels. This led to widespread loss, and many owners of cottage property and builders could not go on, and in a great many cases the owners of property were ruined. Every owner of cottages, notwithstanding the increased cost of building, is a keen seller at less than the present cost of building.

I do not think we have a corresponding case in the whole of the United Kingdom in any other form of investment. These cottages could not be replaced at anything like their pre-war value, and yet owners are keen sellers at less than the cost. No such conditions exist in any other investments. Small wonder that builders ceased to build cottages, or that landowners have ceased to develop their estates. There is less wonder that to-day we have a house famine.

The fact is that 80 per cent. of the houses in Great Britain are let at rentals of from 1s. to 7s. 9d. per week, including rates and taxes, and on these rentals, obviously, there is no margin for profitable investment. Long before the war the house famine existed, and cottage building had practically ceased. Taking the country as a whole, it is doubtful if more than half the number of these cottages were being built each year even before the war since 1909 as in or prior to 1909.

How has it been proposed to deal with this situation? Meetings are being held at which resolutions are being passed to the effect that " private enterprise cannot now be depended upon " to make good the shortage. So that fact has been grasped by all of us. Private enterprise can no longer be depended upon to make good the shortage.

Resolutions follow to the effect that " the local authority shall recognize and fulfil the duty of providing decent housing accommodation for those unable to pay an economic rent, and that the Government shall provide the difference between the rentals of such cottages and the rentals the proposed tenants can afford to pay."

These resolutions are very vague as to how this is to be carried out—whether a sum of money is to be paid to a public body, or private builder, to make up the difference in the rent proposed to be received and the rent which is actually required to pay interest and repairs and sinking fund. All is left perfectly vague. The very common form is to suggest that the Government should grant money for the building of cottages at the pre-war rate of 3 per cent., whilst it has to borrow at the present rate of $5\frac{1}{2}$ per cent.

But what group of citizens would be induced to provide the margin required to secure the Government advance, the rents being arbitrarily fixed on some assumed basis of cost that is certain to be exceeded ? The margin required would be at least 20 per cent., and that margin would disappear with bad trade in the country and the falling empty of the cottages built in a time of commercial prosperity. Would our Town Councils be justified in providing this margin and leaving the ratepayers to stand the loss ? Would private individuals be able to ask the banks to lend money on that margin ; or would a man be entitled to take the savings of his lifetime—what he intended to keep the hunger-wolf from his widow and children—into that margin which would be necessary to entitle him to the advance of the Government even after receiving money at 3 per cent. which has cost the Government $5\frac{1}{2}$ per cent. ?

I do not think the scheme would be attractive to individuals or municipalities, and it certainly would not be attractive to the Imperial taxpayer. I would suggest that all these methods ought to receive fuller and more serious consideration than they have received up to now. They are undercurrents, and one does not know whether they will draw us closer to our ideals or whether they may carry us on to rocks or shoals. They might easily make the housing conditions infinitely worse twenty years hence than they are to-day.

I would like to suggest one or two alternative methods, with your permission ; and, first of all, steps should be taken to restore public confidence in the building of cottages and in money invested in land and house property. Then let the towns and cities purchase the land on the fringe of their towns at agricultural value. They could do it wisely and

11

judiciously, awaiting the right opportunity when such land comes into the market. This can be done if taken in time. I have known land within seven miles of the Marble Arch, in London, to sell for £50 per acre. When that land came to be developed for building purposes, if the municipal authorities of the group of boroughs in the City had purchased that estate, they would have provided ample opportunity for housing the people.

The towns should secure the land on the fringe of the suburban area and prepare a comprehensive town-planning scheme, embracing not only the suburbs but the centre of the town, and so providing areas for industries, manufactories, garden villages for workmen, residential areas, and central shopping districts. Then let the land be valued on the basis of cost—the actual cost the municipality would have to pay with the sinking fund to provide for time occupied in development over a number of years—sixty or seventy would not be an unreasonably long period. Then sell this land on this basis of cost in various allotted areas, each area valued on its own, a lower price for garden village sites, a higher price for factory sites, and a higher price still for shop sites. The garden village sites should be on a basis of not more than eight to ten cottages per acre.

Having done that, the next step I want to suggest is much sounder, and likely to prove more profitable to the country as a permanent remedy for the shortage of houses than assistance out of the Imperial Exchequer. The towns and cities should, as I advocate, acquire the land on the fringe of the suburbs, and then they should get rid of all rates and taxes on improvements of land and cottage houses, and substitute a local income tax. The difference between such a tax and the incidence of taxation on improvements is this: You practically say to the builder of a cottage, " Whether it pays you or it does not pay you, we will take an annual sum from you in the form of rates and taxes." We agree, do we not, that you cannot tax except on income? However you make an income tax or a super-tax, it is a tax on the individual and his wealth in the shape of income.

If we substitute a local income tax and raise our revenue clear of rates from cottages, then you stimulate the building of more and better cottages. The man who builds the best type of house to-day knows that he is going to be penalized by being rated at a higher value.

.I have an instance in my mind which occurred only a few months ago. A farmer on some land I owned, when I went to see him, wanted some improvement made. His water supply was an old well. I said to him that I was willing to put all these matters right, to build additional shippons for extra cows, and better accommodation for his horses, · and I suggested that I should bring a supply of the town's water, which ran past on the main road, for use on the farm instead of relying on the old well. Both he and his wife talked it over. I told him it would mean an additional rental charge of 4 per cent. on the cost of the work. They thought they could well undertake and afford to give the increased rent for the increased accommodation to be provided. They were delighted at the idea of having the water supply, but within a week I got a letter in which the farmer wrote that he had thought over the matter, and had discovered that his rates would be increased by so much, and so much more for water, that he preferred to go on as he was doing.

The whole stumbling-block to the improvement of property has always been the rates. Even if you put up a little greenhouse, properly built with brick foundations, it is a subject for increased rates.

Abolish the rates and you would accomplish two objects. You would restore confidence and attract capital for building, provided there was cheap land. We do not want these advantages to go to the owners of the land. The land on the fringe of our towns should be purchased at agricultural value for the community.

Having gone so far, there should be an alteration in the building by-laws to cheapen the cost of road-making Sufficient land should be reserved for wide roads, but the actual roadway need not be so great until the building of houses had developed. It only burdens those who have to develop the land. Building by-laws require to be altered so that we can build what I call machine-made houses—machine-made cottages.

They can be made of reinforced concrete on many systems. Edison suggested moulds into which the cement is poured, and when it hardens the moulds are removed. There is a better system proposed to be adopted in many districts. It is a much sounder system of making cottages, and is known as the panel system. These panels can be prepared and set in any central factory where gravel and sand are available, and the panels can be transported, and can be assembled and erected perfectly dry, and in a week or ten days the cottage can be completed and ready for occupation.

The building by-laws are our obstacle—the greatest hindrance in addition to those others I have mentioned. Under existing by-laws the manufacture of machine-made cottages on the factory system is impossible.

These clothes I am wearing would, a few centuries ago, have been made by hand. We marvel at the cheapness of cloth and its varied patterns. Perhaps a whole factory may be running all the time on one pattern, but go where you will about the town, you never find dull repetition of the same pattern. The patterns are infinitely varied. So there can be in the building of cottages, on the panel system, an infinite variety of design, and the work done on the sites can be reduced to a minimum. The cottages could be let at very much lower rentals than at present without nursery rule or help from Governments; all of which would, I contend, produce a state of affairs twenty years hence infinitely more disastrous than what we are suffering from to-day.

There are other phases of this subject, but I would like, with your permission, to pass from the question of housing to the question of the relation between what is called Capital and Labour, or the employer and the employee.

Let us consider this most carefully, as there are undercurrents in connection therewith. Just as we have seen that the action of the Government in limiting rentals to be paid for cottages may be perfectly right in time of war, but may come back as a boomerang upon those who want cottages to live in, so let us be careful that we try to see, as far as human foresight will avail us, the effect of any proposal in reference to employer and employee.

A cynic has said that the keynote of all difficulties is imbecility. The greatest of our industrial imbecilities to-day are suspicion and distrust. Employers and employees both distrust each other. The trade unionist is suspicious and distrustful of his union and his leaders. Parliament and people distrust the Government, and so it goes on.

There are no fools in this world, believe me, like the shrewd fools. This so-called shrewdness is merely another word for suspicion and distrust. Suspicion and distrust bring the worst, not the best, out of us. We have seen the effect of the creation of a spirit of lack of confidence in producing a shortage of houses, and the consequent sufferings of the people. We are now on the brink of an equally serious industrial situation. The present war taxation is heavy, but war conditions justify it, and we are fortunate in being able to put on the statute book the taxation we have in operation to-day.

Napoleon said, when asked what was the greatest essential for war, " Money "; what was the next greatest essential ? " More money "; and what was the greatest essential of all ? " Most money."

We are very fortunate in having available this system of taxation, but when the war is over it is quite clear that much of the present high taxation must continue. Don't let us make an error and produce lack of confidence in putting capital into industries, or harass industry and drive capital away. We are tending rapidly in this direction by the excess-profits tax, which is a tax, not on the individual, but on the industry. It is thought to be a tax on the individual, but it is not. It is a tax on industries. Obviously, in war-time and for war necessities, we must have this whether it is a curse or a blessing. We have no alternative. We are forced to raise money to meet current expenses as far as we can out of income. But we shall be wise if we consider the effect of this so-called excess-profits tax in shaking the confidence of capital in industries, and especially its effect on the wage-earners.

Income tax and super-tax, however high they may be, are on the individual—on the income of the individual ; and so are the death duties, however high they may be graduated, on the wealth of individuals. But the excess-profits tax is not the same. The position is just as if the Government were to say to any one embarking in an industry, " Heads I win, tails you lose." It is true that in new industries the Government say they will allow 6 per cent. on capital for profits before they calculate excess profits. What has induced money to flow into new industries in the past has been the knowledge that if the money was lost it was a fair loss, because if money was made it went to the people who took the risk and put their capital into the business, and stood to make or lose money. It was a fair risk, whether it was in ship-building, without certainty as to the conditions which would prevail when the ships were launched, or in whatever form of industry capital flowed to.

But in the excess-profits tax the Government says, " You must take the risk. If you make a profit, we take 80 per cent. of it, and you can have 20 per cent. If you make a loss, you take the whole of the loss."

As soon as the war is over we shall require to have money flowing into new industries to provide employment for the men who return from the front, and to extend our export trade, and generally to bring us victory in the field of commerce, as we shall have won victory on the field of battle.

Do any of us realize how little the profits of capital in industry are, and how great is the gain to labour of attracting ample capital to industries? In countries such as the United States, where capital is more free and plentiful, wages are highest. Capital seeks investment in plant and machinery, and because of that investment pays higher wages. Where horse-power and machinery is the greatest, there wages are the highest per head of the people. Each machine we possess is a storage battery for brains and a producer of wealth. The pre-war figure of productive capital in the United Kingdom invested in plant and machinery was five times that of Italy and Spain, twelve times that of China and Japan, and two and a half times that of all Europe, including in that France, Germany, Russia, and all other European countries.

In the United Kingdom, however, labour was only 4 per cent. as compared with the productive power represented by both labour and machinery. That is to say, labour was 4 per cent. and machinery 96 per cent.; in Spain, labour was 24 per cent. and machinery 76 per cent.; in Italy, labour 34 per cent. and machinery 66 per cent., and in Portugal, labour 42 per cent. and machinery 58 per cent. And the wages paid the wage-earner were proportionately highest in the

United Kingdom. All wage-earners, and those receiving small salaries, are inclined to exaggerate the profits on capital.

Let us take the income tax returns for the last pre-war year, 1913-14, or one that includes a few months of the war. The returns for income tax show that the profits on business, professions, and salaries of same were £504½ millions sterling. Now we can with confidence deduct, say, one-third from this for professions and salaries, leaving, say, £330,000,000 as profits of trade. We can be certain we have not over deducted, because the return for the salaries of Government and Corporation and other officials amounts to £76,250,000, and we may reasonably have confidence that salaries paid in business and incomes of doctors, solicitors, architects, and all professional men added together cannot be less than £174,000,000. Now this £330,000,000 is equal to 4½d. per head per day for every man, woman, and child in the United Kingdom. The income derived from land and houses for the years 1913–14 was £165,500,000, which is 2¼d. per head per day. The excess profits were estimated to produce for 1916–17 about £75,000,000, but we will say £200,000,000, which is again 3d. per head per day for each man, woman, and child. The total is thus 9¾d. per head per day, and if we add retained by capital, say, £165,000,000 for the fullest excess-profit tax—the rate of taxation was 50, then 60, and then 80 per cent.—so we may take it at £165,000,000, or 2¼d. per head per day for every man, woman, and child in the United Kingdom. That makes a grand total of 1s. per head per day for every man, woman, and child in the United Kingdom.

But, in calculating, one must remember that only three out of every five are workers. Then, upon that calculation, it comes to 1s. 8d. per head per day for each worker.

During that same period wages have advanced over 2s. 6d. per worker per day on the average for the United Kingdom since the war ; in many industries 5s., and in certain industries by as much as 10s. per day. Profits, therefore, are not large when considered from the point of view of what would be available for distribution, if equal division were an ideal that would help the cause of progress.

If any system of conscription or exactly equal division would produce most goods, highest wages, and most houses, then I venture to think there is no right-thinking man in the United Kingdom who would not be out to advocate what would produce the greatest good to the greatest number.

Yes, but it is said, " Let us conscript all wealth."

Now, it may be thought by some that this is an ideal that would help. Let us see whose wealth we would conscript. I was speaking to a Trade Unionist on this subject, and he referred me to another man, with whom he had been arguing this question.

" Tom," he said, " you have never saved anything. You spend all you receive, and you have always made more thar I have. Here, I have managed to save £500. You would not save, and do you think it would be fair to take my £500 when you have no £500 to be taken ? "

The spendthrift workman and the prodigal son of the merchant would have no wealth to conscript. Do we want to penalize and discourage thrift, to encourage the spend-thrift and wastrel, or to encourage the workman or the son of the manufacturer who works hard to endeavour to main-tain the position of his father's industry in the world of commerce ? Some say that whilst it might be a mistake to conscript all wealth, we could conscript incomes by making the income tax so high that it would come to the same result. But if we conscript the total income, who will produce any income ? Where will there be found any incomes to conscript under such circumstances ?

I would point out that wages are highest and living most full where the accumulated wealth of the thrifty and the careful is the greatest. Discourage the production of wealth and you will make goods dearer, and wages lower, and employ-ment scarce. And if you do discourage it, what about the widow, the retired schoolmaster or tradesman ? Believe me, any idea of increasing the welfare of the workers or of the community in that direction is a delusion. You cannot improve the condition of any people by any scheme of con-fiscation of capital or income, or by any scheme of redistribu-tion. You can only increase wealth by increasing production. You can only increase wages by increased investment of capital in machinery, resulting in increased production and reduced cost. You can only increase production on the basis of increased consumption.

There would not be in the Congo, where I travelled some time ago, any increased production, because there is no increased consumption. The way to make people increase consumption is by increasing leisure. Increases of consumption also depend on increases in wages and reduced costs, so that wages are not only larger in coin, but in purchasing power. All this means the raising of the standard of living on sound and healthy lines. Therefore our raising of the standard of national life and of the whole British Empire depends upon better organization of our industries, resulting in the shortening of the hours of labour ; increased production by the employment of more capital in machinery ; cheapening of the cost of product, increased leisure, and resulting increased power of consumption. Therefore, I advocate one step in this direction—the Six-Hour Working Day.

The Six-Hour Working Day has an intimate bearing on these ideals. It does not mean a loafer's paradise. Its effect on the cost of continuous running of machinery is where we shall gain. Our machinery will run an increasing number of hours, even to the total of twenty-four hours, while the human being attending the machine is not running more than six-hour shifts. We shall largely increase our power of production and of employment.

And what must be our final aim to avoid all misunderstandings and secure the greatest well-being of all ? Co-Partnership. The user of the tools must own the tools. That must be our final ideal. We cannot take one spring toward that ideal. We can only move cautiously and slowly. You cannot take a man straight from the Liverpool Docks and put him on the Board of Directors of the Cunard Steamship Company ; but if we have the ideal, then in time, with the operation of the Six-Hour Day, we shall produce men and women in this country as a race who will not look upon manual labour as we have in the past been too apt to do, but will rather look down upon the man who does not work to support himself and his family, though he is able to live without working. The time will come when it will be a disgrace to be a non-worker.

Under this system the workers in industries of all kinds can take their proper and larger share in the business affairs of the nation, in improving the conditions of employment, in meeting new developments, and so on. In the looms in your chairman's factory you will see a number of coloured threads. With skill and dexterity you will see all those colours worked into the texture and united in a piece of cloth of beautiful pattern. If one single thread breaks, the pattern is marred. We can organize for service in the industrial life all elements in the United Kingdom—the professional man down to the errand boy—by proper apportionment of our time and proper education. And by all citizens working on these lines we can produce a pattern such as the world has never known. We can produce an empire which will endure for ever, and one that will be the pride of, and work for the betterment of, the whole civilized world.

II

LAND FOR HOUSES

BIRKENHEAD, *October* 4, 1898.

[In the following address (delivered to the North End Liberal
Club), Mr. Lever, as he then was, advocated a policy of " Free
land for housing," and defended it as neither unfair to any
one nor revolutionary.]

THE subject " Land for Houses " is one the importance of
which requires no words of mine to commend itself to your
earnest consideration.   The few thoughts I venture to place
before you on this great subject are very crude and incomplete,
and, consequently, are no doubt open to much adverse criticism.   But, happily, honest criticism can only lead in one
direction, that of further calling attention to the question
of housing the people, with a view to whatever may be the
best means of remedying the defects of our present system ;
a system under which the housing of the people has become
a scandal and disgrace, as well as a danger to the physical
and moral well-being of the nation.   It is impossible for us
to visit any of our thickly populated centres without feeling
that, however great strides we have made in political economy
during the present century, as far as housing of the people is
concerned we are probably in as bad a condition to-day as
at any period of our history ; and this notwithstanding the
fact that as far back as 1851 two Acts for dealing with this
question were passed by Parliament, and also that since
then, at constantly recurring intervals, right down to the
Act of 1890, succeeding Parliaments have repeatedly attempted
to deal with this subject.   Except in the way of police control,
we are bound to admit that none of these Acts have really
been effective in dealing with the evils they were intended
to remedy.

Before I proceed further, allow me to acknowledge the

assistance I have had in preparing this paper from reading
the book by Mr. Bowmaker on *Housing of the Working
Classes*, also the works by Mr. Charles Booth on the *Labour
and Life of the People*, and various other writers. All who
have carefully read the works of the leading writers on this
subject must be impressed with the extreme gravity of the
present situation, and the more one inquires into the question
of the housing of the people, the more one is impressed with
two things—the enormous amount of work required to be
done, and the great importance that it should be done with
as little delay as possible. As to the amount of work to be
done, it is not only the grosser forms of overcrowding—the
slums and alleys—that require to be dealt with, but almost
of equal importance is the question of the crowding of houses
side by side with only 12 feet or 15 feet frontage, small yards,
and 6 or 8 feet back roads. It is said that "God made
the country, and man made the towns." But there can be
no reason why man should not make towns livable and
healthy, and if towns are made livable and healthy they will
be just as much subject to the beneficent influence of bright
sunshine, fresh air, flowers, and plants, as the country. But
just as surely as the country is made by God, so surely is it
that man is made also by the same Creator—who constituted
him a social being, loving the fellowship of his fellow-man,
and therefore loving to live in towns and cities, where he
finds the greatest scope for his social instincts, and where his
genius and abilities have the fullest opportunities for development. Therefore, it is an established fact, and one that all
past history of the human race confirms, that men prefer
city life to country life; hence the great importance to the
well-being of the race that city life be carried on under proper
conditions as to housing, with a view to securing surroundings
the most favourable to health. It is for the citizens themselves as a body to control this matter through their municipal
organizations. It must not be left to individuals, as in the past.

We are too apt in this country to leave good work for
the benefit of one's fellow-men to the care of philanthropists,
but in this instance, owing to the very stupendous character
of the question of housing of the people, philanthropists have
practically been unable to effect anything, notwithstanding
the large sum of money devoted by men of the stamp of

Mr. Peabody, and others too numerous to mention. I venture to submit that it is not a matter to be dealt with by philanthropists at all. Philanthropy is only another name for charity, and charity can only mean pauperism. The housing of the people is not in any way connected with pauperism nor charity, and does not come within the scope of philanthropists.

We have experienced during the last forty or fifty years that mere Acts of Parliament can effect very little. In what direction, then, must we look for help to come? Before we can answer this question, it would be, perhaps, of advantage for us to inquire into the extent to which the grosser forms of overcrowding exist, and what are the effects on health and character of overcrowding. As to the extent of overcrowding, many who have not thought deeply on the subject would be surprised to hear that it exists to just as great an extent in villages as in large towns, and in the very smallest hamlets, proportionately, to as large an extent as in London ; that it exists in new towns and cities like Birkenhead, as well as in the oldest city in the United Kingdom. We find by the last census returns that throughout the whole of England and Wales, of the number of rooms composing tenement houses, 52 per cent. of the separate tenements included four rooms or less, of which about 5 per cent. were of one room only, 11 per cent. of two rooms, 12 per cent. of three rooms, and 24 per cent. of four rooms. Taking London separately, we find that, instead of 52 per cent. as in the case of England and Wales, tenements of four rooms and under are 67 per cent., and that the single-room tenements in London amount to 18 per cent., as compared with the 5 per cent. for the whole country. Now, if we consider for one moment the life a family must lead who have only one room in which to eat, to sleep, and to live, we cannot wonder at the social degradation produced in those who live under these conditions ; and yet, the rents paid for these single rooms are sufficient to pay a reasonable return on the capital required, if properly expended, to provide suitable accommodation. In the worst parts of Liverpool at the present day 1,000 people are huddled on the space of one acre. At an inquest in Spitalfields, London, concerning the death of a child four months old, the evidence showed that the child, with six other children and its parents, had lived in a room 12 feet

by 12 feet, for which 4s. 6d. a week rent was paid. Just
fancy nine human beings living under such conditions as
these! All such places must prove very hotbeds of vice
and misery. I could give thousands of other examples taken
from both town, city, and country, but I will give one instance
more only to prove that overcrowding is just as prevalent
in country districts as in towns. In a village, not many miles
from here, I was asked by a widow, shortly after the property
came into my possession, to provide another bedroom to her
cottage. On my asking why, she replied because her son
was growing up, and there was only one room for herself
and him to sleep in. I imagined, of course, that he would
be a little boy, say eight or nine years of age. I asked his
age, and found it was nearly twenty. This caused me to
make further inquiries, which revealed the fact that this was
only a specimen of the conditions under which many of the
inhabitants of that village were living. We drive or walk
past ivy-clad cottages in the country, admire their beauty,
and the thought that there can be fully-grown men and women,
not always even brothers and sisters, forced to occupy the
same bedroom from the lack of proper housing accommodation
never presents itself to us. The words used by the late Lord
Shaftesbury before the Royal Commission appointed to inquire
into the subject of overcrowding are just as true to-day as
they were at the time they were uttered. Lord Shaftesbury
then declared that, however great had been the improvement
in the condition of the poor in other respects, overcrowding
had become more serious than ever it was before. Evidence
produced before various Royal Commissions who have examined witnesses on the subject all proves that an enormous
proportion of our village populations know no other home
than such as provide one room for the whole family to live
in, and another room for the whole family to sleep in.

It is not necessary for me to occupy your time in proving further that overcrowding does exist. You know it
exists. I know it exists, we all know it exists, apart
from Government returns and population statistics or
Blue-books. We know it because we see it, and read
about it in the police reports every day of our lives. Such,
then, being admitted to be the state of affairs, let us next
inquire what are the results which overcrowding produces.

There is one result which it certainly ought not to produce in ourselves, and that is indifference on our part to the nameless misery and brutalization which overcrowding generates in the poor. And sometimes one is inclined to think that, whilst on all hands we have evident signs that the condition of the poor calls forth greater sympathy to-day than ever, and whilst we know that in the providing of hospitals and infirmaries, in temperance work, religious and social work, we have not been unmindful of our duty, yet in the very question which lies at the root of the uplifting of the people, and the elevation of them to a full enjoyment of all the possibilities of life, we have grossly neglected our duty. In dealing with the moral effect of overcrowding, it is not an easy task to collect statistics. We know that overcrowding and degradation go together, but we do not clearly see whether it is the degraded who prefer to herd together, or it is the overcrowding that produces the degradation; but whatever our individual views may be on this point, we shall all agree on one point, namely, that as to the degradation of the children there cannot be the slightest difference of opinion. Lord Shaftesbury, speaking of the effect of overcrowding on children, describes it as "totally destructive of all benefits from education"; and who can wonder that this is the effect produced? A child that knows nothing of God's earth, of green fields, or sparkling brooks, of breezy hill and springy heather, and whose mind is stored with none of the beauties of nature, but knows only the drunkenness prevalent in the hideous slum it is forced to live in, and whose walks abroad have never extended beyond the corner public-house and the pawnshop, cannot be benefited by education. Such children grow up depraved, and become a danger and terror to the State; wealth-destroyers instead of wealth-producers, compared to whom the South Sea Islander, the Maori, or Zulu is an educated, intelligent citizen.

That overcrowding produces drunkenness, vice, misery, and wretchedness, we know, notwithstanding we cannot easily collect statistics showing the exact extent to which the moral nature is affected by overcrowding. But if we cannot get statistics with regard to the effect of overcrowding on the moral nature, we can with regard to the effect of overcrowding on health; and in considering this side of the question, let us not lose sight of the truth that a nation's health is a nation's wealth. The population of England and Wales at the last census was—for the towns, about twenty-one millions ; for the rural districts, about eight millions. Calculating the death-rates in the towns for corresponding age and sex, and comparing them with the same for the rural districts, we find that whereas the death-rate for the town is 23·32 per thousand, the death-rate in the country is only 17·62 per thousand. In other words, that whereas in the towns death on an average would occur at the age of about forty-five, in the country it would occur at the age of about sixty. But if we look further into these figures, and subdivide the towns, we find that in the congested parts of cities the death-rates are double those of the suburbs. In London the death-rate of the outer, or suburban, districts is only 15·4 per thousand, as compared with between 30 and 40 per thousand in the most crowded parts. That is to say, that whilst a man in the crowded districts would, on an average, only live to be say about thirty, in the suburbs he would live to be about seventy. In Liverpool, also, the death-rate is double that of the rural districts surrounding.

But this bare statement of figures gives us but a very poor idea of the loss to the nation from overcrowding. We have to consider, in addition to the early death of the victims, the years of sickness, poverty, misery, and suffering that ill-health entails on them and their families, and the consequent loss of their ability to earn sufficient money to keep themselves, thus laying a heavy burden on the rates, and upon those relations who, whilst assisting them, are already heavily overburdened to maintain themselves. It is estimated that in overcrowded districts every workman loses, on an average, twenty days each year through ill-health, say, on an average of 4s. per day, equal to £4. This is not only a loss to the workman and his family, but to the whole nation. This loss to the workman is not represented by the £4 he has failed to earn ; he has lost something that he can never recover. For a rich man to be a few days away from business from ill-health may, perhaps, not be a serious consideration. His business in all probability will not suffer. It would be conducted by his staff, or by his partners, without interruption ; but not so the work of a poor man. Therefore, the question of good health, or ill-health, is of all questions the most important one to the workers of this country. Why overcrowding should have such serious effects on health, and increase so enormously the mortality returns, is a matter more for a doctor to deal with than myself, but when one considers the all-importance of ventilation and free circulation of air—which conditions can never be obtained where there is overcrowding—one sees one possible explanation, and that probably not the least. The importance of fresh air and ventilation upon health is shown when we examine the effect of overcrowding in large cities as compared with overcrowding in villages, and the statistics I have just given you, showing the death-rates of the two, prove that, as far as the effects on health are concerned, overcrowding in rural districts is nothing like so pernicious as overcrowding in cities.

We have now inquired into the extent of overcrowding and its effects. Let us now see if we can obtain any information as to the cause and remedy. I venture to submit to you that it is not sufficient to say that the cause lies with the growth of population. It may be claimed that the rapid growth of the population of this country has produced overcrowding ; but when we see that overcrowding exists just as much in the rural districts of England, where the population is decreasing, as in towns and cities where population is increasing, we are bound to look deeper for the real cause, and this we find in the difficulty—either from one reason or another—in obtaining land upon which to erect houses for accommodating the people. We find that as land becomes more valuable, houses formerly occupied by one family have been arranged so that each room in that house should accommodate a family, and in many cases even more than one family in each room. As land becomes still more valuable, what were formerly the gardens of these houses have been built upon, thus producing slums, courts, and rookeries. Every public improvement, such as the demolition of old property, widening of streets, etc., has increased the overcrowding. I venture, therefore, to submit to you that one of the principal causes, if not the sole cause, of overcrowding is the difficulty in obtaining land at such a price that houses for the accommodation of the working classes can be erected

12

thereon, and the remedy must, therefore, be to provide land on such a basis that houses for the accommodation of the people can be built thereon, to let at rentals within the means of those they are intended for.

This point of view opens up a very grave subject for our consideration. It is not my province to-night, however, to go into any consideration of land reform. The question I wish to go into is solely that of the providing of land for the erection of houses ; and, in doing so, I venture to submit to you that our municipalities have ample powers in the existing law to enable them—if they are so minded—to efficiently deal with this question. The overcrowding, as we have seen, is at the centre. The remedy for this must be in relieving the pressure that exists and which forces the people to live near the centre. Dispersion must be the remedy, but not forcible dispersion. Our past experience has proved that we have only aggravated the evil, when our ideas of dispersion have proceeded no further than the destruction of slums and rookeries. We must make it possible for the working classes to live at a distance from the centre, otherwise all our efforts will be in vain. Our efforts, therefore, must be directed to gradual dispersion from the centre to the suburban districts, so that, by relieving the pressure at the centre, we may lead not only to the result of the total abolition of overcrowding, but to the lowering of the rents to such an extent at the centre that those who are forced to remain there, near their occupation, will at least have the benefit of proper accommodation for themselves and families.

In making it possible for the working classes to live away from the centre, we must consider two matters— that of rent and that of transport. Already, overcrowded as they are, we find that 88 per cent. of the working classes pay more than one-fifth of their income in rent ; of these, 42 per cent. pay about one-quarter of their income, and 46 per cent. about one-third of their income. We shall all agree that rents should not bear a greater proportion to income than one-sixth to one-eighth. Therefore, it is manifest that present rents cannot be increased, they must be reduced. And, also, that if the working classes are to be drawn from the centre to the suburbs, the total cost of rent and transport at the suburbs must not exceed the cost of rent alone at the centre. I will go further than this, and say that the cost of rent and transport must be less at the suburbs than the cost of rent alone at the centre, if a tangible inducement is to be offered for removal. To produce these conditions, we must look to our municipalities to provide the land. It is impossible for working men to become owners —to any great extent—of their own houses, and, in my opinion, it would not be a good investment of their earnings for them to own their own houses. The shifting nature of their employment, and the uncertainty of the exact locality where it may be necessary for them to live from year to year, both render it practically impossible for them to become their own landlords. If it were not for this, then it is manifest that the working man could make no better investment of his savings than in purchasing his own house, and so becoming his own landlord ; for apart from the honourable ambition of every man to dwell under his own roof, there is the freedom this would secure him from arbitrary interference.

It being doubtful whether schemes for enabling working men to acquire their own houses are a remedy for the evils attending the present system of the housing of the people, municipalities must face the task of offering facilities for the erection of better houses in the suburban districts, the rents of which, together with the cost of transport of the occupiers to and from their daily work, should be less than the rental demanded for inferior houses in the congested districts. I know of no better way in which this can be done than by the municipality acquiring suburban land in large quantities, at reasonable prices, and offering this land absolutely free for the immediate erection thereon of cottages, in conformity with building by-laws specially drawn up for dealing with the same. I am aware that this will sound at first a very revolutionary proposal, and further, that it will appear to many as absolutely unfair to the remaining portion of the population. In reality it is neither. It is not revolutionary because we have ample precedent for the course proposed. Have we not fully admitted the nation's responsibility for the education of the nation's children, and have we not recognized that the only way in which we can ensure that all children shall be educated is to make education free ? We have seen that the millions we spend annually on education are to a certain extent wasted, owing to the improper housing of the poor. Therefore, to give free land to ensure the proper housing of the people is only an extension of a principle we have already accepted. As to the objection that it may be unjust to the remaining portion of the population, my endeavour must be to prove that the property built on this free land will not only pay for the land which is being given, but, in addition, result in a profit to the municipality adopting this policy. Therefore, the proposal is neither revolutionary nor unjust.

But, it may be asked, Is it absolutely necessary to provide free land? Cannot we leave this question of free land alone, and proceed in some other way? There is no other way than first dealing with the question of land for houses. All other methods are simply tinkering with the evil we would remedy. Corporations, and notably Liverpool, have built blocks of workmen's dwellings—so-called—and anything more hideous, more undesirable for the rearing of a family, or more wasteful of the public money it would be impossible to find. The most you can say of them is that they are better than the slums and rookeries they have replaced. Whenever I see these blocks of buildings in London and elsewhere, I ask myself what our nation will become after a few generations have been reared under such conditions, and the children's children of those bred and reared in these barracks have to take their place as the backbone of this country. No! this system will never do, apart altogether from consideration of its costliness and extravagance. But I can imagine some one asking, How will free land assist us in dealing with this question? I answer—in many ways; and, amongst others, by preventing speculation in land for houses. Now, I do not for one moment wish it to be thought that this in itself is an evil, although in many cases it is a very serious evil. To-day, land can be bought within reasonable reach of the centre of Birkenhead, and other towns, at from £100 to £200 per acre. Within the last three years, a plot of 300 acres on the Edgware Road, London, within seven miles of the Marble Arch, sold at £50 per acre. But, by the time the spread of population reaches such land, and it is coming into demand for cottages, the price will probably be 4s. to 5s. per yard, with the result that it can only be used for the erection of cottages by scheming and planning how many cottages can be squeezed on to as few yards of land as possible. Instead of which, if the municipality steps to our aid, and selects land with reasonable business forethought and acumen, they can secure the land at a less price than any private individual, and can afford to restrict the number of cottages to not exceeding twelve per acre.

With regard to the price of land, there should be no difficulty in buying such land as I have indicated at from £100 to £200 per acre, freehold. This is the price that land can be bought for in most districts before speculation in land has set in. It is many times above the agricultural value of the land, and on this basis, the proceeds of the sale, when invested, would produce many times the income previously being derived from the land. It is a fair price, and one that most landowners would be very glad to receive. At the same time, I do not suggest for one moment that an arbitrary fixed value should be put on the land to be acquired. The value in all cases would be in relation to the market value of the land in the district, and could, of course, be easily settled by arbitration. I merely take the figure of £100 to £200 per acre as the price at which in many localities such land could be bought, when purchased in large quantities and free from speculation. I have already stated that on this land not more than twelve houses per acre should be built. This would give each house about 400 square yards, including roads and streets. This will·be found to allow ample space for the free circulation of air, and for a small garden both at the front and back of the house.

I will now endeavour to prove that the giving of free land for houses is no injustice to existing ratepayers, but that in fact the scheme is self-supporting. Taking the acre of ground at the cost of £200, the interest on this, at say · 2¾ to 3 per cent., would be £6 per annum. The rateable value of the twelve houses we will take at only £10 per house, total £120. In most towns the total amount of the rates is rather over than under 5s. in the pound; thus the rates on this property would amount to £30 per annum, showing a surplus of £24 on the rates, after allowing for interest. Of course, I do not mean to say that the whole of the £24 would be profit. A very large sum out of it would necessarily represent the increased expenditure of the municipality incurred in consequence of the erection of this property. It is clear, however, that there is considerable income at once to be derived from the property, and I claim that out of this income the loss of interest, together with sinking fund for extinction of principal, could be met. No city could possibly be ruined by the adoption of this policy. The municipality, that is, the ratepayers, or citizens as a body, are the real owners of all property within the city boundaries. The so-called owner has in reality only a life interest in the property. The demand for payment of rates comes first of all, and must be satisfied before mortgagors or owners receive their interest or rents. This being so, it is clear that the adoption of this policy is nothing more than applying the ordinary rules of business to the management of municipalities. What business man is there in Birkenhead who would not willingly expend £200 on his property in order to enable some one else to expend £2,400 in further improving it ? Or, who would not willingly face an increase in his working expenses of £6 in order to increase his gross profits by £30 ?

But some may urge that they fail to see how the value of the city is to be affected, or the city itself be made more prosperous, merely by attracting people from the centre to the outskirts. To this I would reply, that drawing the people from the centre to the suburbs would not be the only effect of the adoption of the policy I have outlined. Such an enlightened policy, offering such facilities, would attract newcomers to reside in our midst. But even if it were true that the only effect were to draw from the centre to the suburbs, I say that this would not in any way affect the truth of the claim I have made as to the advantages this system offers. It is a well-known fact that overcrowded and wretched property, from which it is desirable to withdraw occupiers, does not yield anything like its fair share to the rates, and that such property is not rated on anything like the basis of the rents being paid by the occupiers. A family may pay 4s. 6d. a week for the occupation of a single room in a tenement house, but it would be extremely difficult to assess such a house on that basis, owing to the fluctuations of the occupancy. The house in most cases is rented as a whole to one man, who farms it out to the various sub-tenants. The rates are fixed upon the rental as a whole.

But there are other considerations than the mere balance of revenue actually in sight. The whole trade of the borough would be improved by the erection of these houses. Bricklayers, stone-masons, joiners, plumbers, plasterers, painters, etc., would find employment. And when the houses were completed the whole of the shopkeepers of the city would be benefited by the necessary expenditure for the maintenance of the occupiers. The amount of money required to be invested in land would relatively be small, compared to the benefits to be derived by the whole district. The cost of the land should not exceed one-tenth of the cost of the property erected upon it ; thus there would be ample margin for security. The cost of making the roads on the land would, as at present, be chargeable on the property they served. But it may be urged that the mere giving of the land would effect no reduction in rents, and that the cottages built on free land would not necessarily be let at such rentals as would be any inducement in attracting from the centre to the suburbs. This is not so. Dear land is the chief cause of high rents for cottage houses. The cheapening of the land will be the most powerful factor in reducing cottage rentals. Let municipalities use reasonable care and judgment in securing suitable positions for the erection of working men's houses, and builders will not be slow to avail themselves of the advantages offered. Competition will prevent any excess in rents being demanded. The law of supply and demand will govern the number of houses, and the whole tendency will be in the right direction. Therefore, seeing that although the land were given free, those who received the land would have sunk on twelve houses at least £2,400 per acre in building, and that this would improve the whole trade of the borough, we may safely claim that owners of the existing property would be more than compensated by these advantages, and by the stimulus the adoption of such a policy would give in drawing to the city an increased population.

What is it that is making Birkenhead prosperous at the present time ? We shall possibly be told that it is the magnificent docks she possesses, or the manufactories

.that have been established in her midst ; but I venture to assert that her real prosperity has sprung from her increase in population. It is true this population has been attracted to Birkenhead by the employment to be obtained at the docks, the manufactories, the shops, and elsewhere, but this does not affect the question that it is to the increase in population that Birkenhead owes her prosperity ; therefore, the adoption by Birkenhead of a policy which would still further increase her population must still further increase her prosperity. I know of no city in the United Kingdom that has such opportunities as Birkenhead for the adoption of such an enlightened policy as the one I have outlined. The real wealth of Birkenhead is her inhabitants, and the prosperity and capital which have been attracted to her. Stimulate the increase of population. Offer inducements for more capital to be spent in the erection of houses in the borough, and you apply the soundest and most powerful stimulus you could possibly apply for still increasing her prosperity. In the case of Birkenhead, two special benefits would accrue, namely, increased traffic on the ferries and increased traffic on the electric trams you will soon have running. Of course, it would be wise, and necessary, to allow on both of these special low rates for the convenience of workers at certain hours of the day. But experience has always shown that such low rates are really more remunerative than high ones. In addition, you have done a noble work in lessening the overcrowding of the centre ; for as the better class of workers are drawn away from the centre to the outside districts by the inducements you would be able to offer in reduced rents, by facilities of transport by your electric cars, so the overcrowding at the centre would cease.

I have occupied your time already too much on the financial aspect of the question. I feel confident that you will agree with me that if we were to confine ourselves solely to the financial point of view, we should be taking a very narrow one of our duty. Far greater than the financial aspect is the improvement that such a policy would bring about in the condition of the people. I speak from experience when I say that nothing elevates and raises the man, his wife, and family, so much as placing them under the most favourable conditions with regard to their homes. This is especially true with regard to the children who are growing up. It is, in my opinion, simply ludicrous for us to spend millions a year in educating the young, whilst at the same time a very considerable proportion of them are compelled to live in houses and under conditions which, as Lord Shaftesbury has pointed out, absolutely neutralize all the benefits to be derived from education. We hear it sometimes said that the result of our free education is not everything that we expected, or that we were justified in looking for. May not the cause be, not in our system of free education, not in the people themselves, but the method in which the majority of them are housed? To raise the tone of the mind by education, and to cultivate the intelligence by reading, then to force both body and mind to live amidst squalor and under the most wretched conditions, can only have one result—the neutralizing of any good effects that would otherwise have resulted from our well-intentioned but misdirected efforts. Until we have dealt with this great question of the housing of the people, evangelists, temperance reformers, social reformers may rest assured that they are simply attempting to clean out an Augean stable, and that, despite all their efforts, the state of those they are attempting to elevate will not be better, but worse, as each year rolls on.

I must apologize for having occupied your attention for so long a time, and taxed your patience in listening to this paper. My excuse must be the importance of the subject. For, believe me, it lies at the very root of the future prosperity and happiness of our country. Let us face this question boldly. The money is a mere bagatelle, as compared with the benefits that would accrue. We are the richest nation in the world. We require fresh outlets for our capital. Nothing that could possibly be suggested would give a greater return to the nation than the one I have indicated.

III

VISIT OF INTERNATIONAL HOUSING CONFERENCE

PORT SUNLIGHT, *August* 9, 1907.

[Lord Leverhulme welcomed the International Housing Conference to Port Sunlight, gave the visitors every facility for studying an object-lesson so valuable to them in their labours for reform, and delivered the subjoined address.]

THE cottage home is the unit of a nation, and therefore the more we can raise the comfort and happiness of home-life, the more we shall raise the standard of efficiency for the whole nation. In the earliest stages of man's civilization and development, the struggle for supremacy was between individuals, and the individual who excelled the most in the possession of health and strength had the greatest probability of long life and such happiness as the battle and the chase gave to him. Next, the struggle for supremacy was between towns, villages, and small communities ; but to-day the struggle for supremacy is between nations, not so much on the battle-field as in the field of manufactures and commerce. But still to-day, as of old, that nation will be declared to be the fittest to survive and enjoy the longest life and the utmost possible happiness and comfort whose individual citizens possess the greatest measure of health and physical fitness. The strain of modern life is ever increasing, but this need not necessarily tend to the deterioration of the race. Nay, on the contrary, the very struggle for existence, as in the past, will in the future, if proper attention be paid to healthy home-life and environment, tend to produce the greater efficiency of a healthier, stronger, and more virile race. Once let a nation become careless and indifferent on the question of the housing of her citizens, and the reasonable and proper enjoyment by those citizens of healthy relaxation from toil when strenuous work is done, and of the conditions favourable to healthy life, and that nation is bound to witness a gradual deterioration of physique and vigour. All nations, none more so than our own, have been far too long indifferent to this great question of Housing Reform and all that it means. Happily, all nations, and none more so than our own, are now awakening to a due appreciation of the importance of this matter. Proper housing conditions require not only proper air space and good planning within the home, but equally the provision of large open spaces and recreation grounds outside the home. Statistics have proved, beyond the shadow of doubt, that the more the homes of the people are spread over the land in proportions not exceeding ten to twelve houses to the acre, the lower the death-rate and the higher the birth-rate become. Statistics equally prove that where the homes of the people are packed like sardines in a box, from fifty to eighty houses to the acre in the slum areas, the death-rate is more than double the death-rate of those districts where the houses only average ten to twelve to the acre. Superior conditions for the cultivation of physical fitness have been proved to affect young children most of all: adults may stand for a time conditions of overcrowding, but not so children.

Dr. Arkle, of Liverpool, read a most valuable paper at the beginning of this year before the North of England Educational Conference held at Bradford. At the time of reading this paper the Royal Commissions on National Degeneration and the Underfeeding of School Children were holding their sittings. Dr. Arkle, at the request of the Liverpool Educational Committee, had examined all the children in various grades of schools in Liverpool. The careful method he followed ensured the absolute reliability of his information. Dr. Arkle arrived at the following startling conclusions :—

(a) That the difference of physique between the children in the Higher Grade Schools and the poorer Council Schools has reached an alarming proportion.

(b) That the deterioration appears to grow greater as life progresses.

(c) That, medically, there is nothing to account for the deterioration ; and

(d) That the Industrial School figures show that by care and attention this deterioration can be stopped, and to some extent, at any rate, the leeway made good.

Dr. Arkle classified the schools into four classes—

HIGHER GRADE SCHOOLS, where the sons of leading wealthy citizens are educated.

COUNCIL SCHOOLS (a) : Type of the best Council School, where the parents of the children are well-to-do and the children have mostly comfortable homes.

COUNCIL SCHOOLS (b) : Type of school where the children are mostly of the labouring classes. It was selected as a type for the children of the labouring classes whose parents have constant employment.

COUNCIL SCHOOLS (c), the last of the Council Schools, is a type of the poorest class, where the parents of the children belong almost entirely to the unemployed or casual labour sections.

To this list we will add a fifth class, viz.—

PORT SUNLIGHT SCHOOLS, which may be taken as equal to the type (b) of the Council Schools. The parents are mostly of the labouring classes, in constant employment, but with the difference that the houses in which the children mostly live are built with ample air space, not more than seven houses to the acre.

At seven years of age we find the average height and weight of boys to be as follows :—

	Height. In.	Weight. Lb.
Higher Grade Schools	47·4	49·3
Council Schools (a)	45·3	44·1
,, (b)	44·8	43·0
,, (c)	44·0	43·0
Port Sunlight Schools.. ..	45·7	50·3

At eleven years of age :—

	Height. In.	Weight. Lb.
Higher Grade Schools	55·5	70·3
Council Schools (a)	53·1	61·4
,, (b)	51·8	59·0
,, (c)	49·7	55·5
Port Sunlight Schools	52·4	65·9

At fourteen years of age :—

	Height. In.	Weight. ·In.
Higher Grade Schools.. ..	61·7	94·5
Council Schools (a)	58·2	75·8
,, (b)	56·2	75·9
,, (c)	55·2	71·1
Port Sunlight Schools.. ..	60·7	105·0

The measurements of Port Sunlight children were taken by Dr. J. Mackenzie, M.B., Ch.B., Resident Medical Officer, Port Sunlight, and he writes as follows :—

MESSRS. LEVER BROTHERS LIMITED.

I certify that I have taken the weight and height measurements of all the children from five years of age and upwards attending the Port Sunlight Schools. The results are given in the accompanying tabulation (see Appendix, pp. 174 and 175).

The height measurements were taken with boots off, and the weights in ordinary indoor clothing.

(Signed)   J. MACKENZIE, M.B., Ch.B.

Dr. Arkle comments, in comparing the boys in the Higher Grade Schools and the type (c) Council Schools, that the startling fact is disclosed that a boy of eleven in the Higher Grade School is practically as tall and as heavy as a boy of fourteen in the type (c) Council Schools. We may further add to this that Garden City life at Port Sunlight discloses the fact that the sons and daughters of our artisans and labouring population of Port Sunlight attain superior height and weight at equal ages than the statistics show in Council Schools in Liverpool at which the children of parents in similar positions are educated. I do not think we need be surprised at this— the development of the child must be affected by the food it eats and by its environment. However that may be, the figures relating to Port Sunlight conclusively prove that, given regularity and permanency of employment of the parents, and consequently also of feeding and clothing of the children, reasonable and proper housing conditions, plenty of surrounding land for healthy open-air recreation, provision of parks, swimming baths, gymnasia, football field, cricket field, clubs, and all that makes for healthy outdoor life, and the children of our artisans and labouring people become equal in physique to those of the better classes. Unhappily, the statistics relating to type (c) Council Schools equally clearly show that

		6 Years.	6½ Years.	7 Years.	7½ Years.	8 Years.	8½ Years.	9 Years.	9½ Years.
		Ft. In.	Ft. In.	Ft. In.	Ft. In.	Ft. In.	Ft. In.	Ft. In.	Ft. In.
lementary ..	Port Sunlight	3 6·91	3 8·04	3 9·74	3 10·70	3 11·51	4 0·50	4 1·19	4 2·67
condary ..	Liverpool	..	3 11·00	3 11·40	4 1·83	4 2·61	4 2·50	4 4·03	4 4·37
ouncil School "A"	do.	..	..	3 9·33	3 10·70	3 11·67	3 11·62	4 1·76	4 1·75
do. "B"	do.	3 7·25	3 6·75	3 8·80	3 8·17	3 10·00	3 11·33	4 0·80	4 1·61
do. "C"	do.	..	..	3 8·00	3 10·00	3 8·37	3 9·20	3 11·00	4 0·00
dustrial School	do.	3 3·00	..	3 9·25	..	3 10·30	..	3 10·80	..
		Lb.	Lb.	Lb.	Lb.	Lb.	Lb.	Lb.	Lb.
lementary ..	Port Sunlight	44·16	46·54	50·28	51·24	53·36	54·86	58·66	56·61
condary ..	Liverpool	..	48·00	49·30	56·70	56·70	52·50	59·52	61·40
ouncil School "A"	do.	..	..	44·10	48·77	46·44	47·00	53·33	57·35
do. "B"	do.	37·00	36·50	43·00	42·11	45·64	47·20	50·85	53·16
do. "C"	do.	..	..	43·00	46·00	43·87	45·30	48·38	51·50
dustrial School	do.	41·00	..	46·75	..	49·50	..	53·50	..

HEIGHT AND

		6 Years.	6½ Years.	7 Years.	7½ Years.	8 Years.	8½ Years.	9 Years.	9½ Years.
		Ft. In.	Ft. In.	Ft. In.	Ft. In.	Ft. In.	Ft. In.	Ft. In.	Ft. In.
lementary ..	Port Sunlight	3 6·13	3 8·02	3 8·81	3 9·61	3 9·31	4 0·09	3 11·41	4 0·37
ouncil School "A"	Liverpool	..	..	3 10·75	3 10·13	3 11·50	4 0·25	4 2·62	4 2·25
do. "B"	do.	..	3 8·00	3 8·25	3 9·77	3 10·73	3 10·57	4 0·25	4 1·20
do. "C"	do.	..	..	3 9·12	3 8·75	3 8·87	3 9·50	3 11·16	4 0·00
dustrial School	do.	..	..	3 7·70	..	3 6·25	..	3 8·25	..
		Lb.	Lb.	Lb.	Lb.	Lb.	Lb.	Lb.	Lb.
lementary ..	Port Sunlight	44·88	44·45	47·36	48·78	49·98	54·29	56·01	53·69
uncil School "A"	Liverpool	..	..	43·00	44·60	48·85	50·00	52·00	52·85
do. "B"	do.	..	45·30	41·10	45·00	45·90	47·50	49·90	52·50
do. "C"	do.	..	..	47·00	50·00	44·16	46·70	48·50	50·05
dustrial School	do.	..	..	40·00	..	38·30	..	42·40	..

MACKENZIE'S LETTER

WEIGHT OF BOYS.

10 Years.	10½ Years.	11 Years.	11½ Years.	12 Years.	12½ Years.	13 Years.	13½ Years.	14 Years.	14½ Years.	15 Years.
Ft. In.	Ft. In.	Ft. In.	Ft. In.	Ft. In.	Ft. In.	Ft. In.	Ft. In.	Ft. In.	Ft. In.	Ft. In.
4 2.41	4 4.75	4 4.36	4 5.00	4 6.24	4 6.84	4 8.46	4 7.47	5 0.75	5 2.75	5 2.50
4 6.41	4 6.83	4 7.50	4 8.87	4 10.00	4 9.40	5 0.55	4 11.77	5 1.75	5 3.60	5 5.43
4 3.30	4 3.70	4 5.11	4 6.25	4 6.90	4 7.50	4 9.05	4 8.62	4 10.20	4 8.80	5 2.75
4 1.70	4 3.04	4 3.80	4 4.53	4 5.60	4 6.34	4 5.90	4 7.23	4 8.25	..	4 7.25
4 0.50	4 0.75	4 1.75	4 2.30	4 3.60	4 4.16	4 5.60	4 6.55	4 7.25	..	..
4 1.12	..	4 4.04	..	4 5.00	..	4 6.51	..	..	..	..
Lb.	Lb.	Lb.	Lb.	Lb.	Lb.	Lb.	Lb.	Lb.	Lb.	Lb.
62.26	63.01	65.86	66.79	72.71	74.22	79.60	73.72	105.00	108.50	106.75
66.03	68.76	70.27	74.75	77.05	74.00	88.25	85.72	94.50	108.90	108.30
55.10	56.43	61.45	62.80	66.60	69.00	73.42	74.26	75.82	72.80	96.30
53.00	56.60	59.05	60.79	63.92	67.50	68.75	68.50	75.87	..	65.00
..	54.37	55.50	58.30	62.05	63.73	69.33	70.63	71.14	..	..
..	..	65.81	..	68.00	..	73.00	..	..	..	..

WEIGHT OF GIRLS.

10 Years.	10½ Years.	11 Years.	11½ Years.	12 Years.	12½ Years.	13 Years.	13½ Years.	14 Years.	14½ Years.	15 Years.
Ft. In.	Ft. In.	Ft. In.	Ft. In.	Ft. In.	Ft. In.	Ft. In.	Ft. In.	Ft. In.	Ft. In.	Ft. In.
4 2.36	4 4.31	4 3.97	4 5.32	4 6.90	4 8.37	4 9.63	4 11.32	5 0.25	5 0.25	..
4 3.25	4 2.75	4 5.00	4 4.75	4 7.25	4 9.00	4 8.30	4 10.75	5 0.50	5 1.25	5 0.25
4 1.76	4 3.35	4 4.12	4 4.25	4 5.70	4 6.14	4 7.30	4 8.87	4 5.70	4 10.00	..
4 0.17	4 0.30	4 1.06	4 2.70	4 4.16	4 5.16	4 7.50	4 7.00	4 8.50	..	..
4 0.30	..	4 1.05	..	..	..	..	..	..	..	..
Lb.	Lb.	Lb.	Lb.	Lb.	Lb.	Lb.	Lb.	Lb.	Lb.	Lb.
59.85	64.24	62.34	67.69	73.19	76.77	80.23	83.12	78.00	97.50	..
57.50	55.46	61.28	60.70	71.31	77.30	70.30	80.50	93.30	97.10	93.45
54.30	59.57	62.50	61.20	67.07	67.70	73.16	75.80	74.57	84.00	..
52.75	53.20	56.25	60.57	67.70	69.12	73.30	74.00	82.00	..	..
51.30	..	60.60	..	..	..	67.00	..	..	..	..

where these conditions do not prevail the effect is disastrous to healthy development during childhood.

These statistics of Dr. Arkle, however, only reveal the conditions produced by overcrowding at the commencement of life. Dr. Arkle unfortunately has not been able to take comparative statistics relating to the parents and adults in the classes from whom the children in the various types of schools spring. We can, however, obtain statistics from the Registrar-General's Return for the United Kingdom, which shows that the death-rate in England varies from about 9 per thousand in suburban areas to about 35 per thousand in congested slum areas, whilst the average death-rate in the United Kingdom is about 16 per thousand. The birth-rate also varies, the average for the United Kingdom being about 26 per thousand.

The statistics of death-rate and birth-rate for Port Sunlight are as follows (figures now brought up to 1917) :—

STATEMENT SHOWING THE RATIO OF BIRTHS AND DEATHS PER 1,000 OF POPULATION AT PORT SUNLIGHT.

Year.	Estimated Population.	Deaths per 1,000.	Births per 1,000.
1900	2,007	12·45	48·33
1901	2,331	12·87	51·48
1902	2,484	7·24	39·45
1903	2,580	8·14	52·71
1904	2,610	12·26	47·90
1905	2,700	5·55	42·70
1906	2,900	10·00	35·86
1907	2,981	8·05	31·36
1908	3,061	12·08	33·50
1909	3,137	10·08	28·17
1910	3,198	9·30	26·20
1911	3,604	8·14	26·68
1912	3,662	7·46	22·93
1913	3,864	8·28	24·80
1914	4,100	8·04	19·75
1915	4,146	7·90	19·05
1916	4,500	8·00	19·55
1917	4,600	9·13	16·73

In considering these figures of death-rate of Port Sunlight it is necessary to point out that the death-rate has repeatedly been swelled, both with regard to the deaths of children and of old people, by the fact that residents in Port Sunlight often invite their aged and infirm parents and the sick children of their relatives to come and live with them in Port Sunlight. This we know as a fact has often seriously swelled the death-rate. As far as we can ascertain, after making due allowance for the deaths in the village of non-residents, the death-rate of the inhabitants of Port Sunlight averages about 8 to 9 per thousand.

Another side of Garden City life is revealed by statistics with reference to marriage and the size of families. The following statistics relating to Port Sunlight have been drawn up by Mr. Duncan C. Fraser, the well-known actuary in Liverpool. Mr. Fraser took for his calculation those employees of Lever Brothers who, at the end of 1905, had seen ten years' service or over with the firm, their age and salary, married, widower, or single, and number of children under the age of seventeen years. Every employee of ten years' service and over, of the age of twenty-five or over, was included, from the highest official to the lowest labouring man. On this clear basis Mr. Fraser divided the employees into six grades :—

Lower grade workmen, earning on the average £67 a year.

Higher grade workmen, earning on the average £99 a year.

Lower grade clerks, with an average income of £128 a year.

Higher grade clerks, being the higher section of the clerical staff, heads of departments, and men in positions of responsibility, the average earnings being £191 a year.

Lower grade business men who were actually engaged in selling the products of the firm, the average income being £346.

Higher grade business men who were directors, managers, and controllers, with salaries of over £1,000 a year.

13

The above six grades therefore fall into three well-marked social divisions—working men, clerks, and business men—and each division is subdivided into lower and higher grades.

The following table gives the percentage of married men amongst these various grades :—

	Per cent.
Lower grade workmen	78
Higher grade workmen	96
Lower grade clerks	71
Higher grade clerks	66
Lower grade business men	96
Higher grade business men	92

The higher proportion of married men among the higher grade of working men is very striking, every man over the age of forty being married and having a wife living.

Mr. Fraser next compares the different grades with reference to the number of children (the children who were living and under the age of seventeen at the end of 1905 were classified according to the ages and grades of their fathers), and the *average* number of children *per married man* in each grade was found to be as follows :—

CHILDREN UNDER SEVENTEEN PER MARRIED MAN.

Ages of Fathers.	Workman, Lower Grade.	Workman, Higher Grade.	Clerk, Lower Grade.	Clerk, Higher Grade.	Business Man, Lower Grade.	Business Man, Higher Grade.
25–29	1·0	1·7	0·4	1·0	—	—
30–34	2·0	2·7	1·0	2·0	1·0	1·7
35–39	2·9	3·5	1·7	1·5	1·7	2·5
40–44	2·6	4·1	—	—	1·2	2·5
45–49	3·1	2·9	2·0	2·0	2·2	1·6
50–54	2·9	2·9	—	6·0	1·0	2·2
55–59	0·4	1·0	—	1·0	—	—
60–69	—	—	—	—	—	—

From this table it will be seen that the higher grade of working men take the lead in a most remarkable manner.

Mr. Fraser next calculated, taking the number of children per higher grade workman as the standard, the percentage there actually was in the other grades, and the result was shown to be as follows :—

PERCENTAGE OF CHILDREN UNDER SEVENTEEN PER MARRIED MAN COMPARED WITH THE STANDARD OF CHILDREN OF HIGHER GRADE WORKING MEN.

	Per cent.
Working men (higher grade)	100·0
,, (lower grade)	77·9
Clerks (higher grade)	61·1
,, (lower grade)..	42·6
Business men (higher grade)	62·4
,, (lower grade)	47·5

Mr. Fraser next considers the question of children from another point of view. The above table deals with the number of children per married man. Next Mr. Fraser calculates the number of children per male employee in each of the above grades, whether the employee be married or single. This table, it will be noted, introduces as a further factor in the calculation the percentage of men unmarried at each grade. The result obtained in calculating the number of children under seventeen per man to each grade, taking the higher grade working men as the standard, was as follows :—

	Per cent.
Working men (higher grade)	100·0
,, (lower grade)	65·2
Business men (higher grade)	58·3
,, (lower grade)	46·8
Clerks (higher grade)	45·5
,, (lower grade)	33·0

Practically it will be seen that the male employees of all the other grades, taken together, rise only half way to the standard set by the higher grade working men.

Mr. Fraser next prepared statistics in which the children are grouped in families, and the average number of children under seventeen per family arrived at was as follows :—

			Per cent.
Working men (higher grade)	..	..	3·1
,, (lower grade)	..	..	2·1
Business men (higher grade)	..	..	1·8
,, (lower grade)	..	..	1·4
Clerks (higher grade)	..	..	2·0
,, (lower grade)..	..	..	1·2

The preponderance of large families amongst the higher grade working men is very striking, and it was also found that more than half the children of the higher grade of working men were in families of more than four children. So far as Port Sunlight is concerned, it is clear that this is the grade which provides the increase of population. If Port Sunlight is representative of the general population of the United Kingdom, then we can assume that the increase of population, and in fact the great majority of the future population, will be provided by the higher grade of working men, the most intelligent and the fittest of their class, and we may take the most optimistic view of the future.

But if Port Sunlight is not representative of the general population of the United Kingdom, the figures are not the less interesting. They show that under favourable conditions, as regards employment and housing and general environment, such as exist at Port Sunlight, the most intelligent of the working classes will provide their full share and even more of the future population, and that Port Sunlight shows the way to the rest of England.

Another fact disclosed by Mr. Fraser's statistics is that it will be seen the marriage-rate varies in accordance with what may be called the surplus income of the man. By the word "surplus" income I wish to draw our thoughts away from actual income. A manager in receipt of a few hundreds a year, living in a certain style, may have little or no surplus income. A clerk on £2 a week dressing in cloth has less surplus income than a mechanic on 35s. per week. Bearing this fact in mind, the figures clearly show that the marriage-rate is higher among the better class artisans, which is the class that enjoys, of all workers, the largest amount of surplus income. A clerk stands at the lowest as far as surplus income is concerned. This you will see affects both the marriage-rate and birth-rate

I must apologize for occupying so much of your time with these statistics, but they are essentially necessary in considering Garden City life and its effect upon the development of the race. I am positive, from all the statistics available, that the most healthy conditions of the human race are obtained where the home unit exists in a self-contained house, with the living rooms on the ground floor and the bedrooms on the floor immediately over. All tenement dwellings, flats, and such devices for crowding a maximum amount of humanity in a minimum amount of ground space are destructive of healthy life, and whilst they may be endured possibly by adults, are seriously and permanently injurious to the growth and development of children. The building of ten to twelve houses to the acre is the maximum that ought to be allowed; any excess beyond this ought to be strictly prohibited by building by-laws, whilst the width of roadway ought to be increased to a minimum of 45 feet. The necessity for paving and macadamizing of the whole roadway and flagging the whole of the footpath, kerbing and channelling of the gutters, should be dispensed with in rural areas. A strip down the centre roadway of 15 to 18 feet wide, properly pitched and macadamized, for vehicular traffic, and strips 4 feet wide, flagged or gravelled, for footpaths down each side, the remainder of the roadway and footpaths being finished in grass, with, if possible, an avenue of trees on each side, will be found to be the cheapest and best form of road construction. Houses should be built a minimum of 15 feet from the roadway, and 25 feet or more where practicable; every house should have a space available in the rear for vegetable garden. Open spaces for recreation should be laid out at frequent and convenient centres. There is no difficulty in providing these conditions. Even taking the area of London, I find that these conditions could be enjoyed to-day if proper distribution of houses on the land within the area had been made. The metropolitan area of London is 74,839 acres, with a population of 4,536,541, which is at the rate of twelve houses to the acre, each house containing five persons. The fact is, we do our town planning after the mode of badly packed trunks. We all know that one's wardrobe badly packed in a trunk is spoiled, and the trunk appears all too small for what it has to hold. But on our wardrobe being carefully folded, the same trunk holds all that is required, without damage, and with greater convenience of access. Our by-laws already limit the number of lodgers allowed in a lodging-house, and there should be by-laws restricting the number of houses to the acre. If this is done and a relaxation of the building conditions as to the material to be used permits a greater range of selection of building material, thus reducing the heavy expense of building and of road-making to what is absolutely reasonable and necessary, then not only will building become cheaper and road-making cheaper, but infinitely superior in quality. Less elaboration in architectural effects would be needed to make a beautiful city, town, or village than under present conditions; a few sprays of ivy and a greensward in front of a house, a shrub here and there, and the plainest and most economical cottage, architecturally, becomes more beautiful than a more costly and elaborate one built right on the edge of the footpath without any intervening fringe of greensward. A home requires a greensward and garden in front of it, just as much as a cup requires a saucer or a hat the brim. Dust nuisance from passing traffic would be reduced in all such homes, and the conditions of living would become healthy and happy.

At Port Sunlight efforts have been made to carry out these conditions, with what success you will be better able to judge than ourselves.

IV

STANDARDIZING WELFARE

[The students of Sheffield University having expressed a desire to know something more of the practical side of Welfare Work than could ordinarily be learnt from speeches, Lord Leverhulme was invited to address them. He congratulated the University on possessing what he could well believe was the finest metallurgical laboratory in the world and on having provided the country with a Minister of Education. Under Mr. Fisher's guidance, he hoped, our past errors would be obliterated by our future victories. He proceeded :]

I THINK the first fact that we must recognize is that, in the coming days, the employer will not be considered to be the sole arbiter of the conditions of employment, nor will the employee. The time is coming—and coming very rapidly—when both employer and employee must be more subject than they are to-day to control by the State. It is not merely a question of the rights and duties of employer and employee, but we know now that the public, the consumer, and, in fact, the well-being of the State and of the Empire, have also to be considered. We have not yet developed to the point that we can be trusted, any of us, to be unselfish from the highest motives of enlightened self-interest. The education and health and training in efficiency of the whole nation depend upon the hours of labour and the conditions of employment.

I know that there is a preconceived false idea in many minds that welfare work in factories is largely a question of canteens, model villages, free libraries, and so on ; but, in my opinion, welfare work in factories is much more a question of wages and hours, of ventilation in the factory, of cubical air space, of heating and lighting and sanitation, than it is a question of any of the so-called welfare work of canteens and so on. Every fact, circumstance, and condition of employment affecting the workers engaged in a factory or office—mentally, physically, or materially—must come within its scope.

Our modern problem in considering industrial developments is merely one of size. The metallurgical laboratory you have shown to me this afternoon is probably many times larger than the largest engineering works in Sheffield a century and a half ago, and yet it is only an experimental and training college for students. A bigger development in industrialism than that made in the last fifty years will be made in the next fifty years ; and yet the progress and development made since, say 1860, to the present time are probably greater, in science and industrialism throughout the world, than achieved in all the centuries preceding that time. Up to now, the creation of our machinery with due suitability to the work it had to perform has been the only item in a factory that has received full consideration. The men and women operating the machines have been entirely forgotten and neglected. I need not enlarge on these points here; I am speaking to those who have become aware of this outstanding and appalling fact in the course of their study of welfare work. It is quite sufficient merely to mention this fact and to pass on, and I will, therefore, at once plunge into a consideration of some methods of standardizing welfare work in factories.

Before the employer approaches the consideration of welfare work for employees, the first care of all must be the factory building itself and its ventilation, lighting, and sanitation. Its position is much better in suburban or rural areas than in the town itself. The factory buildings must be well lighted and well ventilated. Canteens are a necessary part of the equipment, but appliances intended to produce the good health of the employees have not received in the past sufficient attention, and they are entitled to the fullest consideration.

Now that we have women workers doing the work of men away on war service, the factory clothing has been adapted to their new employment. Now, baths are an essential in factories. Rest-rooms are an essential as well as clothing and other items ; but of the greatest importance of all in these matters is the prevention of accidents—a movement called " Safety First," which, I believe, originated in the United States. But before I can explain a working system with regard to the prevention of accidents, I would like to explain to you a system of Works Committees, because it is through the Works Committees that the scheme for the prevention of accidents is carried on.

I am constantly being asked the question whether the rank-and-file workers cannot sit on Boards of Directors and engage in the highest policy of business management as Directors. Now, may I put the problem to you thus : As one who knew nothing at all about the business of soap-making thirty years ago, I had to begin in a small way. Each of our Directors has been a member of the staff, with one solitary exception, and it was only as I and my colleagues acquired knowledge and experience step by step that we were qualified for the larger business and ever-increasing business. That rule must apply throughout the whole of the staff, and therefore we must begin with a system of Works Committees.

Now, one system of Works Committees that I propose to describe may be briefly defined as follows : It commences with the formation of Divisional Works Committees ; these Divisional Works Committees are subsidiary to a General Works Council, which, in its turn, is subsidiary to the Works Control Board, so you see there are three lines of committees —Divisional Works Committees, General Works Council, and Works Control Board. The constitution and duties of the Divisional Committees are as follows : Each department of the works appoints its own Divisional Committee, consisting of ten members. That is, each department of the works, remember ; and in the example I refer to there are twenty of these Divisional Committees, which means a total of 200 members. Of the ten members of each Divisional Committee, five represent management and five represent the staff, and the chairman is elected from the five members of the management. The members of the staff, as well as of the management, must be co-partners, which means that they must have had at least four years' service with the firm. They are nominated and elected by the employees of the department they represent. Employee representatives sit for six months only and then retire, but are eligible for re-election after twelve months. This system is to obtain as wide an interest as possible. Where males and females are employed, separate committees of females may, if desired, be appointed.

The duties of Divisional Committees are : (a) Dealing with suggestions made by the staff. These suggestions cover a wide field : they relate to improvement in the conduct of the work, suggestions with regard to the safety and health of the employees, and any matter about which a member of the staff may desire to make a suggestion. (b) Suggestions can be made for the betterment of the division, or the works as a whole. (c) The third duty is to see to the observance of the rules and regulations and to suppress waste and irregularities. (d) To inquire into all accidents. (e) To hear appeals against dismissals—that is a very important matter ; and (f) to make general recommendations on any subject. Meetings may be held alternately in the Company's and in the employees' own time ; therefore, you see, half the meetings may be held in the Company's time, say morning or afternoon, and half in the employees' time, in the evening. No fees or payments attach to membership.

As I said before, there are twenty of these Divisional Committees. Of the duties mentioned, it is found that dealing with and investigating suggestions and making suggestions for betterment and prevention of accidents occupy the largest portion of the time and attention of the Divisional Committees. With regard to the first two, Suggestion Boxes are installed in conspicuous and convenient places throughout the works, containing necessary stationery forms and envelopes. An employee wishing to make a suggestion does so on the form provided for that purpose, signs his or her name or not, as either may wish, places it in an envelope, and puts it in the letter-box. The secretary of the Divisional Committee, on receipt of the suggestion, enters it on the register, gives a number to it, and sends a receipt for it to the suggestor. The Divisional Committee can, after discussion, recommend its adoption or rejection or modification, but has no other power, and then it passes on to the General Works Council.

With regard to accidents : When an employee meets with an accident, however trivial, he or she must immediately report to the foreman or forewoman, who in turn reports to the Divisional Manager, in order that a notice may be sent to the Safety Inspector. It is the duty of the Divisional Committee, after hearing evidence on the accident, to record the cause of the accident. Arising out of the inquiry, the Divisional Committee make recommendations for prevention of similar future accidents by the installation of suggested safety appliances. There is no branch of welfare work in factories that is so necessary and, in fact, so essential to efficiency as the installation of a Safety First Committee and a Safety First Inspector, and, in connection therewith, a surgery or first-aid room. Accident prevention pays. Prevention is not merely a question of guards. The education of the employee on lines of safety is most important. The axiom of all of us must be that it is always better to remove a source of danger than to set guards around it. Guards are of great value, but they are not the only means of protection. Careful and systematic education of the employees in the principles of Safety First are of, at least, equal importance. Now, there are Safety Museums in France and in the United States ; we have none in the United Kingdom. Our lack in this has been pointed out to the Home Office. The Home Office does nothing beyond expressing its blessing, but takes no action to grant the blessing of a Safety Museum. Now, safety and prevention of accident must not be merely a putting up of placards. I could give you an instance of a suggestion from the employees to show that mere notices in themselves are not as important as the education and arousing the personal interest of the staff. In the case of a machine operated by women serious accidents were continually occurring, and all attempts to adequately prevent them failed. A suggestion of a safety appliance to be fixed to the machine was made by one of the employees. It was so applied, and no accident has since occurred. The time taken up by these Divisional meetings is not large.

We have throughout the works a number of what are called " Safety Bulletin Boards." These are placed at the entrance to each factory building, and on these boards is exhibited a summary of the various safety notices, so that the principal ones are at all times on view to the employee. These occupy one-half of the board, and on the other half any special notices for the day or week are exhibited from time to time. When new notices are put up, a cut-out finger, printed, is pointed to the notices and placed above them. Mottoes are hung in various departments to get the various employees interested in reading the notices, and new mottoes are continually gathered and added to the list. The most frequent source of accidents is the neglect of employees to replace the guards on machinery after cleaning or oiling. To prevent this there has been originated a system of small tablets, printed in red, and so fixed as to come into view only when the guard is removed, so that if the guard is not replaced this tablet announces the fact to the operator. To superintend all this finds full employment for what is called a " Safety Inspector," who devotes the whole of his time to the duties of " Safety First." He makes a systematic inspection of guards and sees that they are maintained in an efficient manner. Now, I will give you the opinion of His Majesty's Chief Inspector of Factories for the North-Western Division. In reviewing the cases of accidents that came before him, he suggests " the adoption of a scheme in force in a very large works in his district which he thinks would do more to reduce accidents than any Act of Parliament or an army of inspectors." He then proceeds to describe the scheme I have just outlined to you—the Safety First scheme—but, of course, without naming the firm or giving any clue for identification.

I will now give you some figures. I have got here a Safety Inspector's Report for last August. It reads as follows :—

Since my appointment as Factory Safety Inspector of these works the number of accidents has been reduced to almost a minimum, and to achieve this end it was first of all necessary to educate our employees to the knowledge that " Safety " was for *them*. Safety Notices and Bulletins were freely exhibited on special Bulletin Boards throughout the factory, and at the commencement of this campaign the employees wondered what was meant by the steps taken. After accidents had occurred and safety devices had been installed to prevent their recurrence, they were quick to realize and appreciate the precautions taken to eliminate accidents, however trivial. Our employees are now almost as enthusiastic as myself, and from day to day I am in receipt of suggestions as to the treatment of what they themselves consider " danger zones."

It is evident to all that the number of accidents since the inauguration of our campaign has been materially reduced, as compared with the number reported during the corresponding period of the year 1916. This, in face of the fact that a very large proportion of our workpeople are new to our class of work, consequent upon the dilution of male labour entailed by the calling of our men to the Colours. Hundreds of women are now engaged on work previously executed by these men, and although working at abnormal pressure and under conditions which tend to an increased accident roll, I am happy to be able to report a reduction in the number of reportable accidents of 64 per cent. During the first six months of 1916, 113 accidents were reported to H.M. Inspector ; during the first six months of 1917 this number was reduced to 41, whilst the amount paid in compensation showed a reduction of nearly £100, and in loss of wages to employees of £160.

Notices for our bulletin cases are changed weekly, with the exception of those appearing in the left-hand portion of the case, which are of a permanent nature.

In addition to these bulletins and permanent notices we have also " Warning " Notices posted conspicuously throughout the factory, such as—

" Crossing."
" Railway Track."
" Look Out For Trains."
" Transporters."
" Speed Limit," etc.

A copy of our " Safety Rules " is also posted at frequent intervals throughout the works.

For a considerable time we had great difficulty in educating our employees in the use of goggles and respirators. Notices were therefore posted, and cases containing goggles and respirators fixed in the various departments in which the use of these safety devices was desirable, with the result that there is now no hesitation whatever on the part of the employee in using these, or in making application for the renewal of those worn out. With this enthusiasm on the part of our employees the efficiency of these safety devices has been proved by the fact that there has not been a single accident reported since their introduction.

The question of accident prevention is occupying much attention, and I am sure that, considering the short time the campaign has been in vogue, great and satisfactory results will be obtained, both as regards accidents through " machinery in motion " and accidents arising through other causes.

I would like to draw attention to some of our permanent notices on machines, particularly to one relating to " machine running." Many accidents have occurred owing to the machine-minder being called away from the machine and leaving it running, and to the interference of other employees who had no knowledge of its working. All machines worked by young people have a small card of instructions fitted into a tin frame, and the operator, after having been thoroughly instructed as to the machine's manipulation and the use of Safety devices in connection therewith, appends his or her signature to the card, which is then suspended from the machine in a prominent position. In the event of operators being moved from one machine to another, the same routine is again gone through. No operator who has occasion to leave a machine now allows it to run during his or her absence, and thus, through the notice under question, the risk of innumerable accidents is avoided. Another notice, referring to the question of men working on " shafting," is placed on the starting gear by the oiler whose duty it is to attend to the oiling of shaft bearings, and the person responsible for the starting up of the machine makes certain that all is clear before starting up. A warning notice is attached to every electric motor throughout the factory. In the past, many accidents have occurred in consequence of workmen removing guards and neglecting to replace them. The warning notices are now placed under each guard, and are not visible while the guards are in position. Immediately, however, a guard is removed, the notice is quite prominent, and reminds the worker of the necessity of carefully replacing the guard before starting the machine. We have not had a single accident from this cause since the inauguration of these notices.*

Another innovation is our Waste Campaign. Anti-Waste Bulletin Notices have been prepared and are placed in prominent positions throughout the factory. Permanent notice boards are fixed in all the main passages leading to the different departments, whilst portable notice boards are placed in the workrooms, and can be moved from one part of the room to the other, so that the bulletins are always kept fresh in the minds of the workers.

Now, from the Divisional Committee all reports and recommendations are passed on to the General Works Council. The General Works Council I wish to describe to you is com-

* For statistics see next page.

The following Port Sunlight Accident Statistics for 1916 and 1917 illustrate the results achieved by the "Safety First" Campaign which came into operation in the middle of 1916.

Nature of Accidents.	Number of Accidents.			
	1916.		1917.	
	M.	F.	M.	F.
Slipping, stumbling, falling on floors	30	11	18	6
„ „ „ gangways	1	—	1	—
Trapped in Hand Stamping Machines	1	6	1	7
„ Machinery in motion, Winch and Crane, Ropes and Slings, Belting, etc.	16	9	4	7
Trapped in Wagon Buffers, etc.	5	—	2	—
Tripping over Railway Metals	—	2	—	1
Self-inflicted through cutting, striking with hammers, etc.	10	3	2	3
Falling of tools, fittings, materials, etc.	23	5	15	1
Scalds and burns from acids, steam, caustic soda, etc.	13	—	8	1
Overcome by fumes	1	—	—	—
Slipping of tools, breaking of lifting gear, rope lashings, etc.	8	1	3	—
Strains and bruises from lifting, stacking, loading, trucking, etc.	16	6	9	5
(Many doubtful cases. See below.)				
Giving way of roofing, tilting of staging, etc. ...	2	—	1	—
Splinters	4	3	3	—
Protruding nails, etc.	6	3	1	—
Ironbound boxes, crushing, etc.	10	—	—	1
Chippings and filings in the eye	2	—	—	—
Other foreign bodies in the eye—as acids, soap, dust, etc.	4	—	—	1
	152	49	68	33

DEGREE OF INJURY.

1916.	Fatal.	Severe.	Moderately Severe.	Slight.	Total Accidents.	Per cent. to Total Employ.
Males	1	1	4	146	152	5·99
Females	—	1	—	48	49	1·66
	1	2	4	194	201	3·67
1917.						
Males	—	1	1	66	68	2·56
Females	—	1	—	32	33	0·89
	—	2	1	98	101	1·59

posed of the chairmen of the various Divisional Committees Its meetings are held monthly, and its chairman, in turn, is the General Works Manager. Its chief functions are : (a) To review recommendations from the Divisional Committees ; (b) to review accident recommendations from the Divisional Committees ; (c) to consider questions of repairs and renewals to the plant and buildings and to prepare estimates of the cost of same ; (d) to discuss generally any matter which members may bring forward ; and (e) other matters. Having expressed its views on suggestions and recommendations and added recommendations of its own thereto, the General Works Council passes on the various matters to the Works Control Board.

The Works Control Board consists of the Managing Director, who, as Director, has special charge of manufacture and of the works, with the General Manager and with such of the Divisional Managers as may be co-opted. The Control Board has full power of adoption or rejection, but if the adoption entails capital expenditure over a very small and limited amount, the approval of the full Board of Directors is required. The final decision having been obtained, instructions to management are given out on forms provided, and the work is proceeded with. Awards to the suggestors are made annually for suggestions made and adopted.

In addition to the above committees, there is a system of conferences composed of the Head Management, managers, heads of departments, foremen, and staff, for the purpose of encouraging suggestions and establishing closer co-operation between the various departments. The General Conference sits every four or six weeks, when matters of interest affecting the industrial position generally, or the firm in particular, are discussed. There has been also instituted a system of periodic visits of the foremen and managers of each department through the whole of the rest of the works. Nothing that has been introduced has given better results than that. Many of the foremen and managers only see their own department, and in going around other departments they make suggestions to the managers of those departments as to things they have found useful in their own experience, and what they have done in their own department in improvements, and they receive many suggestions from the departments they are visiting. These visits have been an unbounded success, just these little periodic visits to the other departments by the foremen and managers.

The managers, heads of departments, and foremen have formed a club called " The Progress Club." This club has a room and a special library of technical books and periodicals for the use of its members. It meets once a month for hearing papers read by the members, and discussion follows. The Progress Club is a thoroughly live institution, and has justified its existence and name.

Another institution which the employees have started for themselves is the " Co-Partnership in War-time Committee." The staff were anxious to do what they could during the war, and started this committee to consider on what lines they could best work under war conditions. It has been a thorough success, on lines similar to the Progress Club, but Co-Partners only are eligible for membership. I would like, if time had permitted, to say something on the great question of Co-Partnership. I am positive it is a binding and stimulating force throughout the whole organization of business, and represents a very long step in advance on the mere wages system alone.

Now, springing out of Co-Partnership, the firm I am taking as an example have had a body of men who have started themselves to work on their Co-Partnership motto, which is, " Waste not, want not." I have brought specimens of the notices of these, but I do not think it would serve any useful purpose to attempt to exhibit them, as they would not be seen, and, with your permission, I will not do so— but these mottoes are very helpful, and they are inspired by the Co-Partners themselves. Well, then, there are many other institutions, such as Long Service Awards. These are intended to encourage men to remain with the firm. The staff have got their own Sick, Funeral, and Medical Aid Society. There are an Employees' Benefit Fund, a Holiday Club, and a Savings Bank, and, with regard to Savings Banks, my own ideal, though I have never heard of any firm who have put it into practice, is that the wages of the rank-and-file worker ought to be paid to his credit in a bank in just the same way that the salaries of the managers are generally paid to their credit with their

14

bankers. I believe the system of his going to a pay-office and waiting his turn and drawing his wages in cash and slipping it into his pocket accounts for the excessive spending that takes place when wages are high. I believe that if the employee's wages were paid into his bank to the credit of his own private account, and he had to reverse the process and go to the bank when he wanted money for himself or for his wife, he would be inclined every week to leave a little in the bank. I have mentioned this suggested method of wage-paying to workers, and I find that more than half were most favourably disposed to it. The only objection I heard was from one man who said, " I like to see my wages in my hand."

Well, now I come to the question of education. The firm I am using as an example had for many years made it a condition of employment that all young persons of eighteen years of age and under, of both sexes, should attend the evening classes for certain nights each week. That was found to be a failure. Take the case of boys and girls of fourteen years of age leaving school and commencing work. They have been going to school at 9 a.m., they have had a quarter of an hour break for play, have gone home at twelve noon, going back again at 1.30 or 2 p.m., with another break during the afternoon, have gone home at four o'clock. To take them, at fourteen years of age, from such conditions and plunge them into work in a factory or office side by side with adults, and after working them during the whole day to expect these young boys and girls to attend evening classes, never was likely to prove a success. They have not the strength, and are tired out. They are not then in the mental or bodily condition to receive education, and you will not be surprised to hear the results were most unsatisfactory. So this method has been discarded, and the firm have got what they call a " Staff Training College." It was only started experimentally this year. Young people under eighteen in such departments as the firm are experimenting with—and the firm are experimenting with as many as the class-room accommodation will permit—take their education in the firm's time ; they do not take it in the evening. It is hoped in this way to give them a much better education. The firm have a great many volunteers from amongst their own staff who are undertaking the teaching, all expenses in connection therewith being paid by the firm.

Now I come, lastly, to what many people would place first, and that is the provision of a model village.   There is much to be said in favour of such welfare work ; but my own opinion is that the employer ought never to be in the position of landlord to the employee ; still, if the employer has to choose between being in the position of landlord and the people being badly housed, then the lesser evil is for him to build suitable houses and be landlord ; but it is not the right relationship.   There are various institutions spring up in such a village.   I would like to give you some statistics, which I can readily do, as to the number of births and deaths.   The death-rate in the village in 1916 was 8 per thousand, and the birth-rate 19·55 per thousand; the highest rate we had reached before the war for births was 52·71 per thousand in 1903.   So that if one has to choose between good homes built by the employer, with a high birth-rate and a low death-rate, and the objection to the employer being in the position of landlord, I think the lesser evil is that he should be in the position of landlord.

Of all welfare work in factories, a proper apportionment of the time is the one that will yield the best results.   .

A six-hour working day would give all that we require in production from our workers, so that we can pay to the workers the same rate of pay for the reduced hours that they receive for the longer hours : it would solve the education question for the boy and girl on first leaving school ; it would solve the question of physical training ; it would solve the question of military training, so that we could have a trained citizen army ; and it would solve the question of the outlook on life of our workers.

It was never the Creator's intention to send us into this world so many " hands "—He sent us with imagination, He sent us with the love of the country, He sent us with ideals and outlook, and these are simply stifled under our present industrial system.

EDUCATION AND BUSINESS

YOURSELF IS MASTER

Bolton, *December* 7, 1917.
[The address reproduced below was delivered by Lord Leverhulme at the Anniversary Meeting of the P.S.A. Brotherhood at Maudsley Congregational Church, Bolton.]

When we have won the war we shall have an opportunity that comes after most wars—a period of advancement in the social life of the people. Are we going on at the close of the war on the same lines, industrially, as we have been travelling along for the last century or more before the war ? True, we have progressed all the time—shorter hours, higher wages, and, coupled with these two, cheaper cost of production. Now, after the war we can make an enormous advance forward, and it will depend on how we approach this subject whether we are to be successful or not.

The lesson the Chairman read embodies the lines on which all progress is made. If Solomon had asked for money, honours, enjoyment, instead of asking for wisdom, he would have failed to attain them ; but because he asked for wisdom and knowledge, then in receiving wisdom and knowledge there followed, as a natural sequence, riches beyond anything the world had known before, and honour such as no king after him would receive.

If we approach the six-hour day from the point of view of more wages and shorter hours, and see only that in it, we shall assuredly fail. But if we approach it from the point of view of giving opportunity for acquiring greater knowledge, greater wisdom, doing our work in the world better and more faithfully for our fellow-men, then we shall achieve our end ; and not only shall we have a shorter working day, we shall have wages higher than we can dream of to-day, we shall have the cost of production of articles we buy cheaper than we can dream of to-day, and, after all, higher wages and higher cost of production must go together.

Increasing wages, as we see in these war-times, are a delusion and a snare if they mean corresponding advances in the cost of articles. Wages become merely nominal. Whether we have a shilling an hour or a sovereign an hour does not count; it is what the shilling or the sovereign will buy that rules the amount of comfort we shall have in our homes. Therefore, we have to consider this six-hour day problem from the point of view of increased production by machinery. Machinery is bound to be the great factor in cheapening products, increasing wages, reducing cost; and if we can so arrange and organize our industrial system that we can work our machinery more and obtain a larger output from it, then, certainly, we can reduce the hours of labour, and not only pay the same rate of wages for the shorter hours, but pay higher wages for the shorter hours than we were paying for the longer; but it all turns on the greater use of machinery.

I remember a conversation I had with the late Sir Hiram Maxim about ten years ago at a friend's house in London. He always took great interest in aviation, and he was struggling with the problem, as he had previously struggled with the problem of his machine gun, known as the Maxim gun, and he said to me in his characteristic way: " In trying to solve this problem, we can do nothing with a balloon sort of machine—one of the lighter-than-air type. That will not solve it. We shall require to fly, like the birds, with a machine that is heavier than air." (In this he has been proved to be right.) " We cannot do that until we can get one horse-power for the weight of a chicken." That meant 100 horse-power for 300 lb. weight. I read in the paper a fortnight ago that the King, when visiting a factory where these machines were made, was shown an engine with 500 horse-power for 600 lb. weight. That is $2\frac{1}{2}$ horse-power for the weight of a chicken, and so we have solved the problem. We had to come to the practical conditions on which everything depended, the generation of enormous mechanical power with light weight, and then the problem was solved.

We have to set our brains to solve the problem of the six-hour day on the same lines—enormous power in machinery, enormously productive power, enormously increased output at reduced cost.

Yes, but some one says : " If you manufacture in all your boot and shoe factories and your clothing factories and cotton mills as much as the machinery can turn out by working for two or three shifts of six hours a day, what will you do with all the product ? You will only fill the warehouses ; there will be no demand for these extra goods." Within this last week I have seen it suggested in a paper that the supposed difficulties of the absorption in industrial life of five million men who will return from the Army at the end of the war would be solved by reducing the output per man, or cutting down the number of hours he would work so that work might be found for other men. Let us see if that suggestion would do any good in solving unemployment.

Who are the consumers in the United Kingdom ? I will tell you who they are. Ninety per cent. of them are the workers. Remember that ! The workers are not producing goods to sell to some strange beings who live in the planets and have nothing to do with the conditions under which the goods are produced. Ninety per cent. of the consumers of goods in the United Kingdom are the workers themselves. The workers consume (to put this in the proper way) 90 per cent. of the goods produced—of boots and shoes, clothing, food, every commodity. Ninety per cent. is consumed by the producers—don't lose sight of that great fact. If you raise the price of the goods, the man who produces them has himself got to pay that higher price, and if you pay out with one hand the higher wages for the smaller production at a higher price, then the higher wages are of no value ; they buy no more goods than the lower wages purchased before. If, on the other hand, you think you will absorb these men by reduced output, cutting down production to find work for the five million men, the 90 per cent. of consumers will have to pay such fabulous prices for their goods that purchasing will be out of their reach.

Perhaps you will say all this can be done by a system of taxation of wealth—" Make the rich pay for this." Let us see who are the rich, and who are getting the advantage of the enormously increased demand for goods of all kinds at the present time.   The basis of this proposal is that if the wealth of the United Kingdom were confiscated, or conscripted, as some people prefer to call it, that course will solve the difficulty ; that taking that wealth and conscripting it and distributing it to everybody, or paying the cost of the war with it, will put the matter right.   You can scarcely take hold of some papers without finding that held as a basis for a possible solution of the financial difficulties at the end of the war.   Now, let us examine this proposal.   We have the income tax reports published ; and if we turn to those for 1913-14, which is the test year before the war and upon which excess profits tax is standardized, we find that all profits made above those of 1913–14 are subject to munitions levy and excess profits tax.   Take the profits in trade.   It is quite obvious we must eliminate entirely the amount of money that is paid in salaries to managers, foremen, and so on, because even if we conscripted all the mills and factories in Bolton and in the United Kingdom we should still require managers, still require overlookers, foremen, and so on, and we should have to pay them salaries, as we do pay salaries now in Corporation and Government offices. We must, therefore, eliminate all salaries from conscription.

Then, as far as the capitalist is concerned in mills and factories, it is perfectly true we might, if we were so stupid, conscript all the existing mills and factories, all the existing cottages and houses, every form of wealth that is to-day in existence.   Of course, that is the limit to our power of conscription.   We cannot conscript the houses we will build twenty years from now, because they are not in existence, nor the mills, because they are not in existence ; but, if it were considered wise, and Parliament passed such a law, we could conscript anything that is in existence.   But the minute that we have conscripted all the mills in Bolton they will begin to wear out, and not only would they wear out by use, but they would wear out by better spinning and weaving and manufacturing methods being discovered.   We are not going to stand still in the next twenty years.   We shall see as big advances and improvements in the next twenty years as we have seen in the last twenty.   Machinery that was in existence in Bolton twenty years ago, as we know, is getting not only worn out but old-fashioned, and that will be true in twenty years from now. Therefore, from the minute capital is conscripted, we shall have to provide some fund out of which we can rebuild, repair, renew, and reconstruct, for there is no scheme suggested under which we can go to mechanics, engineers, carpenters, joiners, and bricklayers and say they must build new mills and fill them with machinery without receiving wages in the meantime. And whether these payments for wages are in money, or merely in paper which can be printed by a printing machine, and is merely the token of the amount of work a man has done, which he can change into the commodities he requires, or whatever the system might be, you would immediately have to begin and pay out to the men who are building and constructing ; and from that moment when you had con-scripted all the wealth in existence, you would have to begin to pay out, and these payments would have to be charged to some fund or other. The money must be raised as a loan. To raise this wages fund by direct taxation in the year in which the rebuilding and refitting has been made would lay an enormous burden upon all the existing workers of the country, 90 per cent. of whom, remember, are consumers —a burden they ought not to be called upon to bear. By calling these loans capital and merely charging interest, as we do in a waterworks or any scheme of construction, we can defer the payment of that capital until we have the income ; and out of that income we can pay interest and sinking fund and so gradually wipe out this expenditure. So, twenty years from now we shall be back in the same posi-tion that we are in to-day, but we ought to be on this different footing, that we should have Government ownership of mills, factories, workshops, houses, land, etc., and officials instead of employers. Instead of what we call the master we should have the Government official. If that would be better for us, and give better results, by all means let us have it.

There is no earthly reason why the people of any country, and less reason why the hard-headed, sensible people of Great Britain, should work under any system other than the one that will give them the best results, the greatest comfort and happiness and enjoyment of life, and the capacity to acquire all that is needed to make a full, complete and happy life for the greatest number. Let us see what is meant by some texts you find in the Bible on the subject of masters.

St. Luke says, in chapter xvi. verse 13: "No servant can serve two masters."

St. Matthew, in chapter xxiii. verse 10, says: "Neither be ye called masters: for one is your Master, even Christ."

St. Paul, in Ephesians, chapter vi. verse 5, says: "Servants, be obedient to them that are your masters according to the flesh, with fear and trembling, in singleness of your heart, as unto Christ."

I make no claim to be able to expound Bible truths, but I am convinced of this, that there is not a verse in the Bible that has been written carelessly, thoughtlessly, or at haphazard, and that if we cannot see thoroughly the meaning, that is our short-sightedness, not the error of the Bible. When we come to read that no one can serve two masters, and that we have to serve our masters in fear and trembling, I think we must link them to the true master and employer, ourselves as consumer. I am confident St. Paul was not a man who would ever go in fear and trembling of any other man; and I am certain he never intended a servant should be in fear and trembling of any other man, whatever position he was in. St. Paul fought wild beasts, and faced every danger and difficulty, and he never intended that any one should work in fear and trembling of another man—never! Therefore, St. Paul was merely cautioning all servants as to the inevitable results of their own acts on themselves. Well, he said that. The other verse says, "One is your Master, even Christ, and ye are brethren." Have we not just agreed that 90 per cent. of consumers are working men? Therefore, there are not two masters—the employer and the consumer—but only one master, who is the consumer; one servant, who is also the consumer, and over and above all there is Christ.

You will, perhaps, think I am a master and, perhaps, that men who are working for the Company of which I am Chairman come under the description of servants. Think a little more deeply for a moment. There is not a man in this room, not one in this church, who has so hard a taskmaster over him as the so-called masters have. So far as this world is concerned, the master of every employer of labour in Bolton and in the United Kingdom is the consumer. You can see this every day. Articles go up in demand, and the enterprise that produces such articles is flourishing. Then the consumer ceases to demand that article, takes to something else—and the man who, as employer, was prosperous and successful is reduced to the Bankruptcy Court, and is as much discharged as the so-called servant. Take any employer's case, and imagine an article that is being made at his works, and that the consumer ceases to demand ; it is as much a dismissal of the employer as it is the dismissal of the workman or servant.

There is not a master in the United Kingdom to-day who has not a supreme master over him in the form of the consumer. The so-called masters have to consider the consumer and consult the wishes of the consumer or their business falls away and they have no opportunity of employing any one. Therefore, you cannot serve two masters. You are your own masters as consumers and must fear and tremble for the result if you do not serve yourselves faithfully as consumers. If you are to serve " ca' canny " as master, reduce output as the way to make for prosperity—you can't so attain success for yourselves as consumers. It is impossible. The servants, as consumers, are the masters, and it is for the consumers to say on what basis they will have an article supplied. If the consumer can truthfully say, " It will give me better and cheaper goods to have Government officials going round looking after all factories," then let the workers as consumers and the consumers as workers equitably arrange for all the factories in the country to be put on that system. I say, " By all means." The consumer is the master, and if he thinks that will give more and better commodities at less money, give greater enjoyment to life, not only will it not be possible to prevent such a course being taken on fair, honest lines, but it would be wrong to oppose it. But if we are to get all enjoyments and wealth that life can yield, we must first, just as did King Solomon, ask for wisdom, because only as wisdom is granted us shall we realize our aims.

Take the position of two men who are held up to public odium before this country, especially the first of them, and in the great country across the herring-pond, the United

States.   Take Rockefeller and the Standard Oil Company, and Carnegie.   If any man has been held up to odium for a long time it is Rockefeller, and, in a lesser degree, Carnegie and other men.   They were not born capitalists ;   they began life with nothing but ideas.   Rockefeller's ideas were these : He saw single oil wells, single pumping stations, single refineries for single oil wells, and the oil had to be filled into barrels and high freightage had to be paid on the railway to the point of distribution.   And this young fellow had the idea that he could refine oil better and cheaper than that, and organize pumping stations much better than that.   If he had a group of oil wells and a central refinery to refine for many wells, and if he could do away with casks and lay pipes from the oil refineries to carry his mineral oil, as we bring water to Bolton from Belmont, and save freightage, and so on, he would have made a tremendous advance.   Then he had an idea that he could build tank steamers and convey his mineral oil across the Atlantic to Liverpool without the cost of barrels.

By putting all this into execution he made his fortune, on the only basis that fortunes can be made, except gambling fortunes—and it is rare that a man who makes a gambling fortune dies a rich man, because gamblers are dealing with something that is not adding to the value of the goods they are handling, and are depending upon their brains being a little smarter than the brains of other people ; and when one man sets his brains for smartness against the brains of his fellow-men he always goes under.   But when a man sets his brain to see how he can serve his fellow-men better, he becomes a rich man in proportion as he serves his fellow-men.   Rockefeller made a fortune on the only lines fortunes can be made, by cheapening his product, and in time the oil came to be reduced in price from one shilling per gallon, when he commenced, to fourpence per gallon, as it was before the war.   In the process he made his fortune, and if he had lowered his price still more it would have been no advantage to the world, because he was already making the pace very hot for other producers, and, indeed, it has been said against him that he ruined many people in the process of lowering prices.   If he did ruin any one, he did so on the same lines as we have all seen many men ruined in life, by their own neglect and love of ease. When I was a wholesale grocer in Bolton, I knew, when I saw a customer coming into his shop in carpet slippers at eleven o'clock in the morning, what to expect. It is always the same. Such men grumble at some one who, they say, is ruining them. They never think that their carpet slippers are the cause of their ruin. If we carry ourselves back to the days of the first cab, the men who carried the sedan chairs no doubt said they were being ruined by the cab, and we have seen cabs ruined by taxicabs. There has always been an absorption by other industries, and the consumer has always greatly and enormously benefited, far in excess of either temporary inconvenience or real hardship that may have been suffered by a section.

Then take the case of Mr. Ford. As you know, he was a farmer, but with some bent for mechanics. His mechanical ambitions got so strong with him that he told his wife he would give up farming, go into Detroit, and see if he could put an idea into effect for a motor that would deal with the work on a farm. He gave up the farm and went to Detroit, and engaged himself at a quarter or less of what he had been making on the farm, and worked long hours to get to know all about motors and electricity. After a while he was running a motor-car of his own amateur make about the streets. His wife grumbled when she knew he was working in a shed until three o'clock in the morning and had to be at his work at six o'clock. But he won through. To-day we hear criticisms that when he is making five millions sterling a year he is making too much. It is said that twenty-five million dollars for any man is too much. True, the people who say that agree that he pays double the wages paid by his competitors. He starts a boy from school at £1 a day, because he will not have any one at less than £1 a day. He sells his motors cheaper than they can be made by other makers of motor-cars, and for their price Ford's cars are wonderfully good cars.

You have seen that the master of all so-called masters is ourselves as consumers. It is a fact that we are the employers of our masters. It is the consumers' benefit that must be considered, and only that ; and if there is any better system than the present one we ought to have it. The world ought to have it. The present system is this : The man has his Union, a necessary and important and successful organization ; the Union arranges the rate of pay for which its members shall work, and the general tendency is, and always must be, for increasing rates of pay. Therefore the workers, the consumers, say to the employers : " We will only make those goods which we consume on the basis that you pay the highest rate of wages we can get anywhere." The workers are engaged on those terms, but when the workers go to buy the goods they have been producing, every good, careful, and thrifty housewife in Bolton says to the person who is distributing the goods, " We will only buy the goods that are made and sold the cheapest. We are not going to buy goods from the manufacturer who charges the highest prices, even if he pays the highest wages. We demand the highest wages and we equally demand as our right to spend those wages where we can buy the cheapest goods."

This is the present economic position. On these lines we ought to strive for a six-hour working day, because by working our machinery for two or three shifts, and therefore a greater number of hours, we can undoubtedly produce cheaper goods. And we ought to organize for a six-hour working day, because the reports on the health of munition workers show that after a certain length of time spent at work the output decreases as soon as fatigue is present, and that the output increases by the reduction of hours so long as work can then be carried on without fatigue. We want only 33⅓ per cent. increase to make it possible for each of us to produce as much in six hours as in eight, and that is less than the average scale which has been shown to be possible.

With shorter hours we can have better education. From better education springs the wisdom which was asked for by Solomon, and our children and children's children can receive, under a properly organized system of a six-hour working day, as good an education as can be given to the children of the master.

So you will see that in a few generations a great, healthy, strong, and ambitious race of men would be produced who could help to control the industries in which they worked, but all this can only be realized by wisdom brought about by education. On these lines, working with wisdom, after a generation or two, there could be a complete revolution in our industries.   We know that the consumers are the masters, that wages must advance along with cheaper production and increased purchasing power.   All this can be done with a six-hour working day, which will give the worker leisure for two hours a day to devote to education ; and by working on these lines we can achieve a condition of prosperity in this country by increased wages, reduced cost of production, and more leisure for enjoyment of all things likely to add happiness to the workman as to the master. On these lines, keeping reduced cost of production steadily in mind, we can have an England and an empire spreading throughout the world, founded on lines that are so wise and practical that poverty becomes unknown, unemployment is never heard of, goods are produced in increasing volume at lowest price, and happiness reigns supreme.

II

FAST ASLEEP ON A GOLD MINE

BOLTON, *December* 5, 1915.

[On revisiting Bolton and addressing, as on other occasions, the
Mawdsley Street Congregational Church P.S.A. Brotherhood,
Lord Leverhulme recalled that he was born in the town,
and that his father, who settled there as a young man, was
a worshipper at the Mawdsley Street Church. He said :]

YOU are, perhaps, wondering why I chose the subject
for this address—" Fast asleep on a gold mine." You are
quite right if you say, "What does he know about gold
mines ? " Well, I don't know much about gold mines,
I must confess it. And yet I feel that there are men who
unconsciously are sitting on gold mines and are unaware
of the fact.

Some say all the great men died years ago. Don't believe
it. There's not a word of truth in it. There are finer young
men in England to-day than ever there were in the past.
We are not like potatoes, with the best of us underground
and only wurzels on the top. I believe each age produces
its right quantity of the very best. It is only that we should
take the right view and bring the best that is in us out.
Everything is possible to the young man. It is only for
himself to decide what course he will take. No, the danger
in good old England is that we are inclined to belittle the
young men, and the young women also. And the danger
to all young men and young women is that they think too
much of this belittling. Throw it aside, disregard it. You
know that lack of encouragement is the greatest stimulus
that a young man can have applied to him. You remember
the story of Lord Beaconsfield. When he first spoke in
the House of Commons they would not listen to him. But

he was not discouraged because he was belittled.   He told them the day would come when they would have to listen to him ; and it did come.   After all, it is only a matter of how we take these rebuffs.

Let me give you an illustration of what power we have over ourselves.   If we had a furnace in this building, and two rods of iron and some brimstone, I could show you this experiment.   I could take one of the rods of iron and make it white hot in the furnace, and if I then plunged it into the brimstone, it would turn to slag and be useless.   If I took the other rod of iron and made it equally white hot, and then put it on an anvil and struck it with a hammer, I could beat it out, and then, if I made it hot again and plunged it in cold water, I could harden and temper it and make it a piece of iron that would do good service for any use iron can be put to.   Let us learn to despise those who would belittle us, and learn to hate pity and sympathy and coddling.   If we want people to be praising us, saying kind things of us, it only enervates us.   We are not a parcel of blind puppies, wanting warm blankets to keep us from perishing, but men and women every one of us.

You will remember the story of the Irishman who, every now and then, used to take too much whisky ; and when he had had too much whisky he thought he was going to die.   About three o'clock in the morning he would wake up certain he was going to die, and would send for the Catholic priest.   The priest got a little tired of this trapesing out at three o'clock in the morning to a man who was only imagining he was going to die, and decided he would not go again.   But when the call came again he said, " I had better go, it may be something serious the matter."   So he put his Bible under his arm and off he went through the rain at three o'clock in the morning, and when he got there Pat said : " Oh, Father, I am going to die this time !   Look at the rats crawling all over the bed, up the curtains, and all over the walls ; I shall never live till morning."   " Why did you send for me ? " said the priest.   " It's not a priest you want ; it's a fox-terrier."   Believe me, any one who wants sympathy and pity and to be coddled up is weakening himself or herself.   When we are determined to go our own way, and believe that way to be right, it is not sympathy and pity we want, it is a fox-terrier to shake us up. Opportunity will come to each one of us ; and don't let Fortune, when she knocks at our door, find us asleep. We are every one of us—myself, perhaps, the greatest sinner in this respect of all—fast asleep on some gold mine or other and don't know of it.

I remember my first visit to Australia in 1892, two years before this P.S.A. was inaugurated. Whilst there I heard of a wonderful gold mine—Mount Morgan. A farmer owned the site for a farm at first. It was not very good land and never had done much as a farm. One day a man came along and thought he detected on the farm traces of gold, so he went to the farmer and said, " This is not much of a farm ; I will give you £600 for it." Well, £600 does not seem much for a farm of over 100 acres, but in Australia you can get land given to you free, and if you have enough money to move your things you are all right. So the farmer said, " All right, I sell." The farmer was farming to make money. That was why he was in the business. That was his object in farming ; and when he sold the farm he sold it because he didn't think he could make money on it. He had not found it easy to make money on it. The man who bought it thought he saw gold, and it would be easy to make money on it. With pick and shovel, the land being his own, he digged down and found his ambitions confirmed, for the rocks contained some gold. Another man came along and said " Look here, I will give you £6,000 for it." Well, a profit of £5,400 and only a week's work put in, he thought he would have it ; so he said, " All right." The man who paid £6,000 delved deeper still and found more gold ; and a syndicate came along and said, " We will give you £60,000 for your mine." Well, £60,000 is a lot of money, and he took it. When I was there the mine had been floated for £600,000, and the £1 shares were £10 each, so it was worth six millions. That farmer wanted money when he had it at his feet.

I will give you another instance. There is an island in the Pacific that was the property of a firm in Sydney. It was not much good to them ; only a few coco-nut trees that would not yield much profit. They sold it ; but before they did, one of the captains of one of their small schooners visiting the island had picked up a rock, and he brought it home for some reason or other.   When he got to Sydney it was carried to the office, and the people at the office used it to keep the office door open on warm days. One day a man coming in from Sydney University nearly fell over the stone, and picked it up and looked at it, and said, "Where did you get this from ? "   They replied, "It came from Ocean Island, in the Pacific, one of the islands we used to have."   "Do you know what it is ? " he asked.   "No ; it is rock."   "I think it is phosphate.   If you will allow me to take it, I will analyse it."   It proved to be the richest phosphate the world had ever known, and the man who had sold the island for a trifling few hundreds of pounds had in his possession an island that contained some thirty or forty million tons of phosphates, each ton worth £2.   But he didn't know it ; he was asleep on it.

There was a young fellow in America, brought up on a farm with his father, but he didn't think much of farming, so he went to a University.   He was a clever, bright young fellow, and he passed his examinations and was appointed to one of the junior professorships at £3 a week.   He thought he had passed his old dad tremendously.   He decided to take up the study of mineral oil, the oil from which paraffin and petrol are made, and he took it up.   He became expert in it, and because he had specialized on this subject the University gave him a chair, specially dealing with mineral oil, and he got £10 a week—50 dollars a week.   His father died, and without going to look at the farm, he sold it.   The new man who came in looked up the stream.   The old man, to water his cattle, had had to put a plank across the stream at the point where it came gushing out, to take off what the old man called the "scum," because under the scum the water was clear and good.   He put a plank to clear the scum off.   The new-comer found the scum was mineral oil, the very thing that the young man who was born on the farm knew all about ; but he did not know there was mineral oil gushing out of the earth on his father's farm.   He had been fast asleep when he was at the farm.   He had never gone up the stream to see where the cattle were watered ; he had never seen the plank which took the scum off.   That farm and the oil became worth over twenty million pounds sterling.

You will find that money is required for every good work that is done in the world. I hear some one ask, ". Can any one, as a Christian, devote his mind to making money ? " I say " Yes ! " " But surely not a religious, Christian young man ? " I say again, " Yes ! "

Here comes in the confusion of thought. Money-making and a good life are said not to be in accord ; the suggestion is that you can take your choice of one or the other, but you can't have both. That is a wrong impression about life, responsible for the idea that the strong, virile young man is not so religious as the weakling. The fact is that the opposite is the truth. Religion is not a sickly sentimentality or the practice of a maudlin mutual admiration society. Religion is not solemnity, but solemnity is stupidity.

A strong belief in God and the Bible, and the everlasting struggle to live a better life, are the mark and sign of true manhood. Without this belief and this eternal struggle after the good, a man will be hindered and crippled in all he undertakes. The weakling is the man who gives up the struggle for good. All have sinned, but the unpardonable sin of all is to give up the struggle for good. Do you think any one believes the worse of Paul because in his youth he was Saul ? Not a bit of it. He stands higher because of the fact that he was once Saul, than if he had always been Paul and never had the experience of Saul. Ridicule turns the weakling, but cannot turn the strong. Ridicule has been directed against those who attend P.S.A.'s, Sunday schools, churches and chapels, and it is hard to stand against it. In my opinion, it is easier to fight in the trenches against the enemy than to stand the ridicule of friends at home. Ridicule has been truly described as " The icy cold north wind, endurance of which makes men into Vikings. "

The fact is that the foundation of business success and of Christianity are the same, and that foundation is service for others. In rendering service to others, money is the most effective means of removing our limitations. You are, no doubt, saying and thinking you would have been glad to have helped to make some life happier, but you had not the money to do it. But let me say right here, you must not think money is the only essential to doing good. I have said nothing of the sort. I say money will relieve your limitations, but you can do good without money : you can do good in anything you set your heart to do, if you are not limiting yourself by saying, " It is impossible for me to do it—I have not the money."

I hear some say, " What chance has a man in Bolton of finding a gold mine, or a phosphate mine, or an oil field ? " None at all. But because of that it does not follow you have not better chances and better opportunities than all of these three added together. It is our duty—every one of us—to make money, as much as it is our duty to worship God and love our fellow-men. " What ! " you say ; " is it the duty of a Christian to make money ? " And I say " Yes." You reply that the Bible says money is the root of all evil. I read the Bible somewhat, and I have never found that in the Bible yet. If I challenged you, you would, I have no doubt, be able to turn up the page in your Bible, chapter and verse, where you think you have read that money is the root of all evil. But you will find what the Bible does say is, " The love of money is the root of all evil." But there is a great difference between the two. It means that making money—holding on to it—hugging it to our hearts, as we would our God, is wrong, and is the root of all evil. Yes ; but if making money is right, and you want to make money, you will have to pay the price. That is necessary in order to get money.

We know that everything in this world is said to have its price, and, believe me, the price that you have to pay for money-making is within the reach of every boy or man in this room. It is not outside the reach of any one of us. It would be grossly monstrous and unfair, and I would not myself believe in a Deity who could treat His children so unjustly and unfairly as to make money-making possible to some and impossible to others. It is within the reach of every one of us, it is a gold mine on which we are every one asleep—but we have to pay the price, which is hard work and self-sacrifice. I know this sounds an anti-climax ; but, believe me, in whatever form you look at money-making you will have to make a great deal of self-denial—give up a great deal and sacrifice indulgences. But there is nothing in life worth having to be got at any cheaper price, and we can all pay it. Think of that. There is money to be got at a price that is well within the reach of every one of us. Some of us in this chapel may never have a chance to fight for our country. We are past the fighting age, maybe, or medically unfit ; others may be unable to go for other reasons. Some women who attend, this church may never have the chance to be a Florence Nightingale or a Miss Cavell, but all of us can make money, much or little, and do some good with that money.

I heard recently of a noble act, only this last summer, in connection with the Red Cross Society. Two young ladies in London, daughters of wealthy parents, decided that for their summer holiday they would go into Wales. They were amateur artists. They had no need to paint, but they decided they would paint pictures of Welsh scenery, and then they would put their work up for sale for the benefit of the Red Cross Society. In a letter I received last week I heard they had jointly made over £500 for the funds of the Red Cross Society by the sale of their pictures. They sacrificed their pleasures; they sacrificed their indulgences in many ways and worked hard; and, as a result, they got this money, which will help towards the care of some wounded soldiers, and do such an amount of good that it could not possibly be the root of evil.

But I think some of you say, " We never get the chance." I have heard that said by so many—by school teachers. " What chance has a school teacher of making money ? " Do you know, one of the richest dry-goods store men in America, who died a multimillionaire, even in English terms, let alone dollars, was a school teacher when he began life ; and his first venture in trade was to buy 1 dollar 50 cents worth of goods, and he lost 87½ cents in selling it. He determined to make another effort, but he did not buy on his own judgment. He went from door to door and inquired what people wanted. Then he set to work to buy articles so as to sell at a profit. He considered public wants in order to make money ; in other words, service for others; for that was what it amounted to. I have heard shopkeepers say they cannot make money. I would like to ask any such, " Have you ever studied what your customers want, or taken a kindly, fatherly interest in them—inquired after them if they are ill, or tried to help them in any way ? Have you made yourself indispensable to them ? " If you have not, you cannot make money out of them. You only make money out of people when you have made yourself indispensable to them.

I hear a shop assistant ask what chance he has of making money. There are scores of the wealthy men in America and in Europe to-day who started life as shop assistants, and who would answer the same as I, that the basis of their life was service to others. They made themselves indispensable to their employers. That was the stepping-stone to their wealth. Mechanics—what chance has a mechanic ? Ford was a mechanic only a few years ago, but he has rendered a service to mankind in producing a cheap and, at the price, a good car. He rendered a distinct service to the whole civilized world, and the world poured its money on to him. It is said he makes five millions sterling a year. He has earned it by rendering service to the people. Office-boys —every rich man in America was an office-boy, from Carnegie downwards. No, let me say right here, at once, our jobs are all right ; there is no fault with the job. We ought to remember that man himself has always been the best part of the opportunity. The secret of success is no secret at all. Will a man pay the price of success ? That is the point. That is all there is in it. There is only one certainty—hard work and self-sacrifice and service for others. It must be hard and unflagging, persistent work ; the self-sacrifice and surrender of indulgences.

Hard work and self-sacrifice must be so practised as to become habits. Some think hard work may kill a man. It never did so in this world. It is a good habit, is hard work, and it is bad habits that kill. The basis of all business success is hard work combined with service. It is not sufficient to say, when we are serving a customer, or whatever we are doing, " That will do." That is not the question. The question is, " Is that right ? " And only when we aspire to that, determined that whatever we are supplying shall be the right article supplied in the right way, shall we succeed.

How many young men there are who believe that if they are punctual in attendance at the shop, the factory, or the office ; if they do their work fairly well, so as to escape censure, keep honest and respectable, they have paid the cost price of success. There are millions who are willing to pay this

price, and bidding this price every day.   But the hammer
never comes down to one of these bids.   Success is never
knocked down to that sort of bidder.   They say they do
everything they are told to do, and ask what more they can
do.   To occupy the position we are in counts for nothing.
Success alone can be found in the way in which we fill the
position.

Yes, but some say, " There is no advancement for me;
my employer does not appreciate me."   What a false idea !
What does it matter about your employer at all ?   Never
mind your employer.   Do more than you are obliged to do,
and better, and be independent of your employer.   If he
will not appreciate you—and there are employers who can
be as fast asleep on the gold mine of a good assistant as on
any other kind of gold mine—some other employer will.
Make yourself indispensable to your employer, and be independent of him, and then you will be wanted, either by him
or by a better man.   But only then will you be wanted,
and only when you are wanted can you make money.   Whatever your job may be makes not the slightest difference.
It is our business, each of us, to make ourselves indispensable.
That is the gold mine.

Yes, and some say, " I am short of capital.   I could do
all sorts of things if I had capital."   Don't believe a word
of it.   Who are the men in the big world beyond who have
capital ?   They are the poor, penniless boys of forty or
fifty years ago.   Now, having made yourself indispensable,
try to find out the wants that are not yet filled, and don't
be afraid of competition.   Believe me, it is only by finding
out these wants that we can succeed.

Don't be afraid of competition, for there is one great rule
in this universe—the law of resistance.   We are apt to think
we would do very much better if there were no resistance.
It is not true.   Remember that none of us could walk if
the ground did not resist the tread of our feet ; we could
not bicycle if there were no resistance to the muscles of the
leg in pedalling the bicycle ; we could not fly in a flying machine
if the air did not resist the spread of the wings of the
machine ; the ship that sails on the water only sails to the
extent of the force of the wind it is able to resist ; the steamer
only progresses through the ocean because the water resists

the propeller or paddle; we can only row in a boat because the water resists the stroke of the oar. If the leaves of the trees and of the plants did not resist the rays of the sun, there would be no flowers; if the drum of the ear did not resist the sound-waves there would be no hearing; if the eye did not resist the rays of light there would be no seeing. I could go on repeating the value of resistance *ad infinitum.* Do not think competition, then, is hurtful; without competition we cannot succeed. There is no growth, no life, no progress, without resistance—merely stagnation. It is the struggle with resistance that makes a man strong, virile, and successful. A life without resistance is a life of ease—ignoble and leading to poverty and rags. If we take the right view, fighting with resistance can only help us. Resistance is good and brings opportunity; resistance is life. But if the forces of resistance overcome our strength, they can only do it momentarily. The struggle against them increases our strength, and by that struggle we so increase until, finally, we can overcome resistance and succeed. The worst about our failure is not the failure itself, but the oft-time effect of failure on ourselves; the important thing is never to give up, but to keep on with our ideal aim persistently and perseveringly.

Is success worth the price? That is for each man to decide for himself; and what, after all, is the final achievement?—happiness. We are all in this world for happiness; our life was intended by our Creator to be one long span of happiness. All this effort, if it brings us happiness, has put us severally on a gold mine that will give us riches that we never dreamt of. John Bright said, "Happiness is a congenial occupation, with a sense of progress." There is a world of truth in that. I have always thought, also, this, the description of the happiest day in his life, given by a distinguished man, is the finest picture of happiness you could conjure up. He said, "When I took my bride home to the house I had furnished, and taking her by the hand, said to her, 'Darling, every piece of furniture in this house I have worked hard to buy, and it has been bought with my savings, the result of my work, darling; it is here, and in future it is ours, it is yours and mine, and we join and share together in it'"—that, he said, was the happiest

day. of his life. · Why ?   Because that was the nucleus·
of the home he had worked and struggled for..   The man
who has made and saved money and can say this, and has
won the love of a woman worthy of such a home and of such
a man, has found a gold mine which will yield. money and
happiness beyond the dreams of the wildest imagination.
Such a home is the living temple of the soul, in which nothing
vile or unworthy can endure ; and out of such a home come
opportunities for good and service to others, which is the
purest metal of the richest gold mine the world has
ever seen.

III

VICTIMS OF EDUCATION

LIVERPOOL, *October* 29, 1917.

[Whilst regarding education as the root and basis of all national progress, Lord Leverhulme is a severe critic of the past and present errors and misdirections of the public education system of this country. It was with these that his address to the Liverpool Literary and Philosophical Society was mainly concerned.]

WE are spending forty millions to-day sterling in this country on education, out of the public purse, depleted already, and with so many demands now coming upon it ; and I am not sure that we are quite satisfied that we are getting what we are entitled to get from this expenditure. We have no clear aim and objective in our educational system ; we are not preparing our boys and girls for their after-vocations in life ; and firms in Liverpool, I am sure, would bear me out in saying that boys and girls who come fresh from the Board School are, practically, almost raw material, and have to be made fit for their situations almost as much as was the case forty years ago or more, before we had the present elaborate educational system. Now, what do we mean by an uneducated boy or girl, or man or woman ? I believe that really what we mean when we make use of this phrase is simply a person without book knowledge. The boys and girls before 1870 were educated for their business, but they had no book education. Now, the so-called uneducated person may be superior in knowledge of the rules of life, superior in knowledge of the moral laws, superior in common sense, but if that person is not book-learned, he will be called uneducated. Are the boys and girls, after nine years in Council and Board Schools, going to be worthy of the descrip-

tion " educated " ?   What smattering of knowledge they
will have gathered will be of little or no help to them, except
to enable them to read a daily paper and a " penny dreadful."
You know what Herbert Spencer said of our Education
Act after it was passed. He said it was " a measure for
increasing stupidity," and one of our great statesmen of
the nineteenth century, Lord Melbourne, said that " circumstances were the best education," and that all great
men had been educated by circumstances. And a cynic
has said that the key to all our difficulties in the United
Kingdom (and this best explains our difficulties in education)
is " imbecility."

Now, our special imbecility in education affairs has been that
we have left ourselves too much in the hands of scholastics.
The scholastic builds his edifice on book learning. With
these men the belief is established that mankind knows
nothing except what it has learned out of books. In any
case, they act as if they believed that ; whilst most of our
best education—the best education of every one of us in
this room—we never get out of books at all, but in the daily
affairs of life. An unread ploughboy or mechanic can put
many scholars to the blush with his knowledge of life and
of many matters that are of vital interest to the well-being
of the individual. We know that many bookworms are
veritable ignoramuses, and many so-called uneducated persons
—uneducated, that is, in book learning—may be veritable
encyclopædias in all the affairs of life. We worship book
learning to the summit of adulation. Yet what can it help
us ? Except in painting and sculpture, everything practical
in the way of handicrafts is despised. We despise a boy
who, at fourteen, is earning his own pocket money ; we
admire a boy who, at fourteen, is writing Greek plays. And
as to our daughters—the daughter who is earning her own
living is, to-day, almost considered scarcely an eligible future
wife ; and whilst our sons who have taken a University
degree and have adopted, say, the medical profession or
the legal profession would be welcomed in every house as
eligible and desirable future husbands, the girl who has
adopted a profession, however high the University degree
may be that she has taken, does not receive invitations to
house parties, and does not receive invitations to receptions,

"At Homes," and garden parties, because she is not quite in the "Class." Yet every man or woman who has attained to any eminence has supported himself, or herself, more or less, according to his or her necessity, from very early in life.

Our whole system of education is carried on, as I said at the beginning, without aim or objective. In fact, the Education Act was passed without any scheme of a national course of training to fit the scholars for their after business-life being prepared, and, as far as I know, no proper and complete system of national education on those lines is even in existence to-day.

The cry has been for a ladder to reach from the Board School to the University; but there has been no asking of questions as to what vocations in life are in want of men or women who have had a University education. Why, to-day, there is a greater demand for craftsmen than for University men; there is more demand for girls as cooks and housemaids than as graduates from Newnham. A chauffeur or a skilled mechanic will often command a higher salary, with more constant employment, than an M.A. or B.A., or a Senior Wrangler who is merely a book-educated man. We owe more to the craftsman than to the mere scholar or bookworm, yet we still act as if books alone were the only training for the intellect. We educate our students to depend on books, and as practical units in after-life they are in less demand than the chauffeur or the artisan. Do not think for a moment that I am ridiculing book learning. I would regret sincerely if you interpreted that as what I have said; but I am pointing out, and desire strongly to call attention to, our failures through having no definite system of training for vocation in life, so that we may, as far as possible, get better results in the future from our educational system.

The cure is not less book learning but some practical application of book learning. It is not book learning that we must scrap—it is our vague wool-gathering aims and objectives that we must scrap. A boy or girl Board School scholar, and man or woman University student, who have been well taught from books will make, if taught to apply the knowledge so gained, superior craftsmen, or business men, or housewives. May I give you an illustration from elec-

tricity of what the idea exactly is that I wish to convey?
Suppose we consider education as, say, equivalent to an
electric current. For transmission you must have a copper
wire : for the transmission of education you must have book
learning. If with electricity we worship only the transmitter, what use would electricity be to us? But take
that copper wire that acts as transmitter, with the electric
current running through it, then cut that copper wire, connect
the two ends by a fine wire, and you will find that that fine
wire will glow with heat. You have produced heat. Now,
cut again the wire in another place and attach to it a carbon
filament lamp, and you will find you have produced light ;
cut again in a third place, and suitably connect the two ends
with what is called a motor, and you will find you have produced power ; but there was neither heat, light, nor power
until you made the break from the transmission. So in
education, you must make a break from book learning to
actual practice. The current of book learning must be
applied to definite ends and aims within the powers of utility.
We should get nothing out of the electric current if we had
vague ideas as to its application for heating, lighting, and
power ; and so it is with book learning.

Now, the United States and Canada—if I may give you
a definite illustration of applied education taken from these
two countries—show the greatest interest in agricultural
education. In England the total number of students studying agriculture is under two thousand ; and yet agriculture is
our greatest industry of all, and employs more persons than
any other single industry. We have our Universities full
of book students ; how many have been studying Forestry ?
Yet we have millions of acres of waste land awaiting re-afforest-
ation. We are giving the same Board School education
to the sons of dwellers in towns to fit them as mechanics,
carpenters, or labourers for work in factories as we give to
the sons of dwellers in villages to fit them for the farm. Now,
if education is to pay the nation for the forty millions a year
it costs, then it must have a practical bearing on the after-
school vocation in life, otherwise education can only make
victims of scholars. We are sometimes inclined to ask
ourselves the question on this point—we do not really in
our hearts and minds believe it possible—but still we ask :

Are people less efficient by book education ? Often it seems to a business man that the University-trained man makes less use of what brain he has than does a so-called uneducated man. Edison, the great inventor, filled his laboratories with University-trained men ; and yet no one was more fond than he of showing that this University knowledge had to be applied practically, and that University men were lacking in the practical application of their knowledge. On one occasion he took an electric candle, such as we have here, and he handed it to a man who had taken the very highest degrees in mathematics at one of the Universities. " Now," he said, " just calculate for me the cubical contents of this bulb." There you see a bulb overhead, and how it tapers, and it is not an easy thing to calculate. Well, this man took several hours, and covered several sheets of paper with calculations, and finally brought the result to Mr. Edison. " No," said Mr. Edison, " you are at least 10 per cent. wrong." Well, the man went back and calculated all over again, but could arrive at no different result ; so he came again and rather insisted that he was right. " No," Mr. Edison said, " I know you are at least 10 per cent. wrong ; let me have the bulb." Edison took the bulb ; he took a common plumber's diamond, cut round the projecting glass point at the end, gave the end a tap and it fell out, leaving the bulb as a cup or bottle. Edison then took it to the tap, filled it with water, poured the water into a beaker, read off the cubical contents, and did all this in a minute, and the record proved that the man was, as Edison had said, 10 per cent. wrong. Now, that University man, with the book learning, had his whole brain on calculations. The practical man would know nothing about calculations. Edison had not had a University education, and in trying to think of the cubical contents, he made the bulb into what you might call a cup or bottle, and then measured what water it contained.

|So, after a certain point, what we want is not mere book learning, but more practical training and education. It is well known that nothing is so fatal to thought as continuous reading. In handicraft, the mind can follow its own train of thought, and notorious in English history has been the deep thinking of the village cobbler, and his great influence

on village politics, all springing from the practical use of his hands, his eyes, and his brains. Working these together he could think better and clearer. It is said that the late Sir Hiram Maxim discovered the principle of using the recoil of a gun to place the next cartridge in position, in what is known as the Maxim gun, when out shooting one day with an old gun that kicked badly. The principle of the safety-valve was discovered by a fourteen-year-old boy, whose duty, for which he received his wages, was to watch the gauge of a boiler, and, when the gauge recorded a certain pressure of steam, to pull a string which opened the safety-valve and reduced the pressure, and let the record on the gauge go down. He wanted to go away and play, and he arranged a series of weights to take the place of his hands on the cord, and he found that when the steam got to a certain pressure it would lift the weights, and allow the steam to blow off, and so he was able to go and play marbles. I only mention this to show that the brains of each of us— I am convinced of this more and more every day I live— are like, say, this room ; you have to have some light in this room before you can see anything, and our brains require some stimulus outside to set them to work, and they respond immediately to the stimulus. The stimulus to Sir Hiram Maxim was the kick of the gun ; the stimulus to the boy was the desire to go and play marbles with his companions ; that stimulus would not have come by reading about guns, would not have come by reading about pressure of steam ; it came by the actual experience of life.

The educated who are nurtured on books alone are the victims of education, and not the efficients of the nation. And how do we arrive at our final gauge of the book-educated man ? The final acid test of book education is an examination, and if the student passes this examination he receives the hall-mark of College or University, with an assortment of letters added to his name. But what about the great world outside ? The late Sir Alfred Jones told me himself that he would not have a University man in his office. I argued and debated with him because, at the time, I intended to send my own son to the University, which I did, and have never regretted it, and I thought that the only point was the question of application. I argued that a University-trained brain, if it applied itself to business, must be a superior brain to the untrained brain of a man who has not had a University training; but there is no sequence from the passing of these examinations to the progress in after-life. Senior Wranglers have often proved the biggest failures of all amongst those who have gone through Universities. Do you think that passing examinations gives us what the nation wants in our Civil Service? Could you pick out, by any system of examination in their youth, future Sir Alfred Joneses, or Thomas Ismays, Andrew Carnegies, or Cecil Rhodeses, H. M. Stanleys, or Nelsons, or Wellingtons? An examination would not help us in any of these, yet we worship the results of examinations. But private firms, as far as my knowledge goes, have never adopted the examination system of entry into their business, or for a seat on their Board of Directors. No, the injustice of our education is that it does not look beyond the cramming with book learning; that it victimizes the student and condemns him, or her, to an after-life of hard and toilsome drudgery, merely because the learning has not been applied to a definite object, such as I mention in the illustration of the electric current, of either heat, or light, or power.

Now, when the Franchise Bill was passed in 1869, we were told by a statesman it would now be necessary for us to " educate our masters "; but, instead of training and educating, we are producing an untrained, uneducated boy or girl, who leaves school at the age of fourteen, and we, naturally, are not satisfied with our product.

We are beginning to find the wisdom of the poet Pope, who wrote :—

> A little learning is a dangerous thing;
> Drink deep, or taste not the Pierian spring :
> There shallow draughts intoxicate the brain.

And an ancient saw runs :—

> Who are a little wise the best fools be.

Now, how can we find a remedy? It is perfectly useless in any affair of life to call attention to what one believes to be an evil without at any rate making some attempt to

apply a remedy There is no remedy in evening classes
In a business I know it was made a condition of employment
that all young persons between fourteen and eighteen years
of age must attend evening classes. The parents consented
and it was tried for many years, but it was not a success,
and the reason is obvious. You take a boy and girl of
fourteen from school, and what has their previous life been ?
They have gone to school at nine o'clock, they have had
a quarter of an hour's break in the forenoon and gone home
at twelve o'clock ; they have come again at one-thirty or
two o'clock, had another break in the afternoon and gone
home at four o'clock, and immediately on leaving school
you take the boy or girl and you put him or her in a works
or office. They are working alongside adults and working
the adult hours. You do not say to the adult, after a hard
day's work, " Go and attend an evening class " ; but you
say to these immature, growing boys and girls that you want
them to give three evenings a week to evening classes for
the improvement and development of their brain. Neither
their brain nor body is capable of receiving education under
such conditions.

So we must seek for some other remedy, and the remedy
is not easy to find. There is such a great variety of industries in the United Kingdom that what might suit one
industry would not suit another ; but I do not think that
that should be any reason why we should not apply a system
to such industries as it might suit, and which would include
the great bulk of the people such as are employed to-day
in factories and workshops. Whilst it is true that agriculture is the greatest single industry, it is not true that
agriculture employs the most people, for in all the variety
of factory work the aggregate runs into many millions more
than in agriculture alone. Now, in factories you have
two elements of production : you have the mechanical
utility, the engine and the machine, and you have the human
being, commonly called " hand," as if a human being could
be without a soul and have no horizon or outlook in life other
than the machines they are tending—a brutal description
which must be made impossible. Now, at any rate in factories where we have mechanical utilities, we know that
we could work these mechanical utilities, with a little extra

oil, a little quicker wearing out perhaps, a little extra attention, continuously for twenty-four hours each day. But
the strength of the human being is limited, and it is limited
not only because of its physical capacities, but it is also
limited because a human being must have something 'more
in life than merely working for a living. It must not be a
question of a whole life passed in work to produce and buy
food, washing, and lodging, then sleeping to prepare for the
next day's work, with no view of green fields, no time to
read books and elevate the mind—that is a feature in modern
industries that cannot be tolerated. Now, in the employment
of mechanical utilities our great burden of expense is interest,
depreciation, repairs, and renewals ; and before I come to
consider the human element, suppose I just deal with these
four items of expense in connection with mechanical production, because we must be aware of this great fact—whatever
hours are worked in British factories, we are in competition
with the whole world, and we cannot maintain our enormous
export trade, nor, indeed, can we produce for the people
in the United Kingdom a sufficient supply of boots, shoes,
clothing, and houses unless each individual can produce
to the total of his capacity.

We exchange and barter, in one form or another, the
labour of one individual with others, and if the people in
the United Kingdom who are working in factories were to
produce less, then, obviously, there would not be enough
for themselves, to say nothing about others. We must
consider the output, and, I believe, it is equally an axiom
in economics that we have got to consider the price of the
output. If we do not, then, however much wages advance, they
will purchase no more boots, shoes, clothing, and houses than
the lower rate did when these were all cheaper. We must
continually aim to cheapen the product, for cheapening of
product increases the demand for the product ; it increases
the wages of the producer two ways—first, in actual cash
and, secondly, in purchasing power. Any reversal of that
process, whatever increase there may be in wages, reduces
the purchasing power of the wages and leaves a wage-earner
worse off. Now, I want us to accept that because it is vital
to the points we have got to consider ; but I want us to accept
it with a knowledge of what benefit we can get from mechanical

utilities.   First of all, wages are the highest in the countries
that have the most mechanical utilities in proportion to the
people ; that is to say, wages are the highest in the countries
that have the most capital invested in the mechanical utilities in proportion to the population, and lowest where these
conditions are reversed.

IV

GIRLS AND BOYS

BOLTON, *October 7*, 1916.

[Lord Leverhulme, addressing the Girls' Side of the Bolton School
at their Prize Distribution, subjected the traditional views
on the relation of the sexes in education to the fresh thoughts
of a practical man.]

THIS School has been founded without any idea that it was
a work of philanthropy, or any nonsense or humbug of that
kind. I have never found that dukes ever objected to
send their sons to Eton, Cambridge, or Oxford because they
would be receiving an education that was not entirely paid
for by the school fees. All they ask for is good education,
and for the rest—whether the endowment goes back to the
time of Edward VI or not—this does not raise any difficulties
for the Duke who is sending his son to school or college. I
want to make it quite clear that the education of the Bolton
School can be accepted without any sense of humiliation
on the part of very wealthy parents, and without any sense
of patronage by less wealthy parents.

Why do not boys and girls always attend together in the
same school building? The opinion is that the mentality
of girls and boys is not identical; the same ideals are not
applicable to the teaching of boys and girls, except in certain
classes. It is a mistake to separate scholars and to put
the students in separate buildings for girls or boys. In my
boyhood's days girls and boys were taken at the same school
up to a certain age, and I attended a girls' school myself
until I was eight or nine years of age. But I want boys
and girls to be educated at the same school together up to
a much higher age than that. I have always argued to
myself that if it was ever intended that the sexes should not

be mixed there would be families consisting entirely of girls and other families consisting entirely of boys. Mrs. Smith's babies would be always girls and Mrs. Brown's babies always boys, but not both boys and girls in the same family. Those families are better, and the children grow up better, where there is a mixture of boys and girls. You can always tell if a boy has had a sister or if a girl has had a brother, because the influence of one on the other has been for good. I have felt that if the Bolton Grammar School and Bolton High School pupils could be brought together it would be of advantage. I think there are many classes, such as drawing classes and science classes, and certainly the classes for music, where, with advantage, the two sexes might be educated together in the same class. You may depend upon it, it is perfectly healthy, natural, and sane for the two sexes to meet together in this perfectly natural way. Girls and boys played games together in my younger days. There was one game called " tig." I don't know whether you have that to-day ; and there was another called " rounders " which we used to play. One of the girls, who afterwards became the wife of my oldest friend, was the best runner of any of us. I met my own wife in that way. Boys and girls were brought up together and played together. That is the most natural way—through games and schooling, in a perfectly healthy way—for the sexes to meet together. You may depend upon it that in bicycling, motoring, in sketching parties, and in many other ways, this perfectly natural affinity is seeking expression.

Now, what is the object of the School ? We have here, in the United Kingdom, and the British Empire generally, the finest material in the world, and Lancashire is second to none in its possession of the best of that material. There is not any town in Lancashire superior to Bolton. Here, then, we have the best material with which to commence. The idea is to give to the boys and girls an equipment, an education, which will prepare them for the battle of life and to take their places in discharging all the responsibilities and duties that will await them in after-life. In doing this we feel we shall be giving them a broader and more enlightened outlook on all affairs and on matters connected with their native town of Bolton, so that the future generation of Bolton will be the better able to take advantage of all that science and discoveries are daily placing within our reach, if they have only got what we commonly call the " nous " to seize it. What we are to-day we owe to yesterday, and those who lived then entrusted to us this great work. What we are to be to-morrow depends upon what we do to-day. With this retrospect and with this way of looking forward we can set our hands to work on this task which we have undertaken.

The war will make great changes. The war will not leave England as it found it. England will be a different England for the boys and girls in this room from what it has been for us who have lived most of our lives before the war. This war has discovered Woman. Women are in evidence everywhere, engaged in hundreds of useful and honourable occupations, and discharging their duties excellently. It was never imagined prior to the war what women could accomplish in other work than was then open to them. We are proud of the work undertaken by all classes of women in England to-day in this great war. I often wonder what those grand dames, who danced in Brussels on the eve of the Battle of Waterloo, would have said could they have seen their great-grand-daughters and great-great-grand-daughters doing the work the women of England are engaged in to-day. They would have been shocked at the idea of women working side by side with men without affectation —easily and naturally—in munition factories, and making shot and shell to kill the enemies of their country. It is a grand work, and it is also grand to be engaged in taking care of the sick and wounded, a work which is being well discharged by delicate girls, and by matrons, and by those who are no longer young. The whole nation is working together in a way that could not have been possible in either the Crimean War or the great Napoleonic wars, because the ground had not then been prepared by education. We owe all this response and patriotism to the passing of the Education Act of 1870, but even education to-day is not as good as we would have it, although superior to any there was in this country at the time of any of the preceding wars. We are reaping, in the advancement of this war and the victory which is surely, if tardily, coming, the results of a better educated England than ever before. We want to extend that and to see in the years to come that we shall not fall behind.

This war has taught us that, however valuable material Education may be, its function of most value is to teach us to think aright, and to realize that success in life depends most of all on character, and that unless a high character and high ideals are aimed for in Education, it may even be a curse rather than a blessing.

The old idea of women has got to go ; woman has to be the companion and helpmeet of man, as was originally intended, and it can only be done if she receives an equal education in every way and an equal equipment with man. Our ideas are very much mixed on this subject.

It is admitted by every one that they have an equal right to earn their own living, and so long as they earn an honourable living and follow an honourable career they have a right to choose for themselves. A brother and sister decide, say, to enter some profession, say that of a doctor ; both are equally well educated and take equally high degrees at their respective Universities. Similarly if they had each chosen commercial careers. Well, somehow we feel that when the young man has launched himself on a professional or commercial career which may lead to great distinction, he is a very fine fellow indeed. Our ideas about his sister are not quite the same.

The young man is received everywhere. Fathers with marriageable daughters are glad to receive him at their houses, and the mothers give him equally flattering welcomes, whilst the sister will be coldly received everywhere. Society admits her brilliant ability, her cleverness and efficiency, and that she has a perfect right to enter a profession and earn her own livelihood, but does not want her to do so. The modern young man nowadays without definite aim and calling in life is looked on with contempt ; whilst the woman who has a definite aim and calling, and is earning her own living, is despised and neglected socially, and finds that few invitations ever reach her. We are not so backward, perhaps, as the Japanese, who, when a girl baby is born, hang over their door a doll ; or as the Chinese, who do not consider women quite human beings, but who believe that if a woman is a good woman, she will after death be allowed to return to this world as a boy baby, and so, as a man, become a human being.

It is perfectly true that the destination and goal of the majority of girls must be the home, marriage, and the household cares that come upon them in their position as mothers of the household ; but it is equally true that a girl has a perfect right to choose whether she will adopt that career or another, and she ought not to be under the slightest reproach if she has chosen contrary to the majority of girls. If it is a career which gives distinction, then she should be able to win for herself distinction. In all these careers there will be a dozen openings and a dozen outstretched hands to welcome a brother, whilst there will scarcely be one opening or one outstretched hand to welcome a sister. Women are, for instance, absolutely prohibited in law from practising at the Bar. This will all have to disappear after the war. We cannot, as we have done, accept it as vital to the existence of this country that a woman can go into a munition factory and yet not be fitted to become the head of a business. It is no wonder if woman does sometimes fail to make a success in business. Method, regularity, and system in doing the daily task are also rare in men as well as rare in women ; but it is to the advantage of the State that they should occupy whatever position they are best fitted for. The bringing together of the two sexes will make in this direction. The war will clear out all preconceived ideas on this question. And the Bolton School will, without doubt, take a prominent lead in the good work of education, and of nationalizing a clearer, more definite, and wiser recognition of Woman's true position and equal right with men to full opportunities for useful, intelligent, efficient, and honourable service for the Empire and Humanity.

V

OUTPUT AND INTAKE

BOLTON, *August* 1, 1917.

[The text of old sermons on thrift was : " Take care of the pence, and the pounds will take care of themselves." Lord Lever-hulme, in an address on the Annual Speech Day at Bolton School (Boys' Division), announced a more vital principle, which may be summed up in the motto : " Make the best of your output, and your intake will grow of itself."]

I WILL tell you a story of a benevolent old gentleman who, coming home one day, saw right in front of his house an overturned load of hay blocking up the road. A boy about the size of one of you was trying to get the hay back into the cart. The gentleman said to the boy, " Have you to put all that hay back into the cart ? " " Yes, sir," said the boy. " Have you had your dinner ? " asked the gentleman. " No, sir." " Well, then, come inside and have your dinner. You will work better for it." " I don't think my father would like it," replied the boy. " Oh ! your father would not mind. Why should he mind you having a good dinner ? " Then he took him into the house and gave him a good dinner. After dinner he said to the boy, " Now, just you have a walk round my garden, and then you will be ready for your work." " Please, sir, I don't think my father would like it," said the boy. " Oh ! your father won't mind. He will be glad for you to do it. You have a walk round." And the boy did. On his returning to the house the gentleman said, " Now, I have a nice book here. Just look at a few pictures, and then you will be ready for your work." " But, please sir, I don't think my father would like it." " Oh ! it's all right, I am sure your father will not mind. But what makes you keep saying you do not think your father would like.it ? "   " Please, sir, he's under the hay." Well, boys, every father is under the hay, and must be until his son eases his burden.

The future of the nation depends on the boys and girls, and I am quite certain it is still more true that the future of the boys and girls depends on the nation. Don't you think so ? I do. You can accomplish much more than the grown-ups can. I have travelled a good many thousands of miles in the Congo I am very fond of the Congo. I like the elephants and other animals there, and I am delighted with the stories the natives have there. The most excellent folklore stories I have heard have been in the Congo. I will tell you one. It is a Congo tale, and you must remember that the people there are in the same state of civilization as the people of Bolton were a hundred thousand years ago. They are in the Stone Age. They know little or nothing about metals, but they know a good deal about fighting. Nations learn that very early.

The story is about a hen which was sitting on a nest of eggs. One day she left them for a walk round, and when she came back a serpent was coiled round them. The poor hen did not know what to do. She could not get the serpent off, because every time she went near the serpent hissed. So she went to the elephant and asked him to drive the serpent away. The elephant came with his big feet, but when the hen saw him she said, " Oh ! you go away, you will break my eggs ; go away ! " She then went for a buffalo. The buffalo came along with his big feet, and she saw that he, too, would break the eggs and sent him away ; and she went for the giraffe and all the other big animals in turn. But it was just the same in every case : she was afraid of their big feet breaking the eggs, and they all went away in disgust. Then a tiny ant came out of the ground and said, " Let me try." " You try to drive the serpent away ! Not a bit of it." " Well, let me try," said the ant, " it will do no harm." " No, it is only a waste of time if the elephant and the buffalo and the giraffe cannot do it." " Well, let me try," persisted the ant. " Very well, try," said the hen. So the ant went back to the hole out of which it had come and gave a signal. Ants came out of the hole in swarms and went all over the serpent and stung it and nipped it and pinched it. And the serpent, in order to get rid of them, went away.

You can do many things we grown-ups cannot do. I want you to remember how you can do them. You can accomplish anything you want only in one way, and that is by doing your best. A boy who has done his best has done everything, and a boy who has not done his best has done nothing. I do not care if he has taken prizes here this afternoon : if he has not done his best he has done nothing. If the boy who has not won a prize has done his best, he has done everything. It is only by doing the task we have to do to-day that we fit ourselves for a bigger task to-morrow. Some people say there is so much chance in life. I dare say there may be something they call chance. I do not know ; but a great English poet of about four centuries ago, Gascoyne, said a boy had better never be born than be untaught. Think of that. I think it was true. And it is truer to-day than ever.

Do you know what the teaching you get here is like ? I will tell you. If you take a trained boy and an untrained boy, they are, if I might compare them, like a workman with tools and a workman without tools. The trained boy is the workman with tools. He has got them. He may use them or he may not, but he has got them. It is like the Cadet troop we have been seeing this afternoon. I am sure the School is proud of the Cadets and of the Boy Scouts, and I congratulate their officers. You know perfectly well that all this training is for a definite purpose. The boy without education would be like a soldier without a weapon. It is no good going into war if you have not the right weapons. A boy without training would be merely like a soldier going to war without weapons. Of course, having got them, it depends upon us how we use them. Why take these books we have given out to-day ? If you have not been trained how to read a book and how to assimilate a book, they will be no good to you.

Have you ever been to a circus ? I used to love a circus. I dare say they don't come to Bolton now ; but when I was a boy, at Christmas and New Year and other times, there used to be Wombwell's and Bostock's and Mander's Menageries and a circus or two, and I used to love to go to them.

I used to watch the acrobats swinging on parallel bars and doing all sorts of wonderful things. It is all only a question of training. I believe any of us could do it if we had the training, though I should not like to start training for them now ; but any one can do those things if they start training at the right time. There is nothing marvellous about it. The curious thing is that when we see a conjurer or an acrobat we think he is doing something marvellous. It is all training, and you can be trained by Mr. Lipscomb and the masters to do far more wonderful things than that.

There are many people who think a college education, or a University education, is not comparable to practical experience in the cotton factory, at business, or in the office. Well, I hold the opposite view. The better the training he gets, the better the man will be for all positions in life ; but, of course, we need to have the practical knowledge added to the theoretical.

I will tell you an amusing story of Edison. He never had a University education, and every now and then he delights in showing a University man that the practical man is superior. On one occasion he took an electric light bulb, and said to his most highly trained University man, " Tell me the cubical contents of the bulb." Well, it looked about as impossible as squaring the circle—pear-shaped tapering— and he had to tell the cubical contents of it. Well, this man, who had taken high degrees in mathematics, got sheets of foolscap and covered them with calculations and figures and, eventually, took the result to Edison. " No, you are at least 10 per cent. wrong," said he, and the young man went back and worked it out again and again, getting the same result, so he was inclined to argue. Edison said, " I know you are about 10 per cent. wrong. Give me the bulb." He took a plumber's diamond for cutting glass and cut round the sharp point at the end of the bulb and then knocked it off. Then he filled the bulb with water, poured the water out and measured it, and in something less than two minutes, he knew the exact contents of the bulb, and proved his assistant wrong. Of course, the man was thinking merely of calculations ; he had not got his brain settled on the practical side. There were many other ways of ascertaining the contents besides calculations. He might have submerged it in water and seen what it displaced, allowing for the thickness of the glass. The point is that you should always try to think beyond the book you have learned. Don't assume the book method is the only method, but try to think of another.

We talk about the circumstances of life. There are two great elements in life—one is power and the other is circumstance. Now, there is in a boy or girl the greatest power the world knows—that is life, a power greater than the steam engine, or electricity, or hydraulic power. But this power has a great tyrant, and that is circumstance. Even from the tiny seed you can learn a lesson. Botanists will tell you that when a seed lies on the ground, especially certain seeds, they can be carried by the wind; they will not attach themselves to the soil until they get to soil that suits them. That is a well-known fact. They roll along with the wind, but as soon as they get on soil that suits them they settle down and make the most of it. That is the control over circumstance; so circumstance is not such a great tyrant after all. We have a say in what we are going to be. Each of you boys is thinking of a career in life, and preparing for it, and learning such lessons as will help you in your future career, and having settled it, you are going to anchor yourselves down. I know you are.

Do you know that one of the most tremendous cumulative forces in this world is the power of persistence? Settle on a plan and persist in it, and every year it gains in power and weight until finally it becomes irresistible. All this training will have a definite effect upon you, and it will lead you to something greater. I suppose if we dig down 20 feet under where we stand we should come to a stratum of clay, or something that is exactly the same as it was twenty thousand or a hundred thousand years ago. That has not changed, but on the surface here there have been all sorts of changes. Look how many changes have taken place even in your lifetime. Why? Because there have been men here in the good old town of Bolton who have been developing it all the time.

Many people think success in life—the greatest success in life—is a question of intake and no output. Get all you can and stick to it—that is the way to succeed in life, they think. You might as well try to run a cotton-mill on the principle of all intake and no output; it would soon come to an end. This good old town of Bolton, whilst the clay 20 feet below the surface has not changed, has gone through all the changes of thousands of years of history. Why is Bolton so .much a better town to-day than ever before? I will tell you. It is because Bolton has been supplying the wants of people in India, China, and all over the world, and in supplying the wants of others Bolton has acquired the means of making a better Bolton, leading a happier life, a fuller and more complete life. I was in Japan four years ago, and I went into a cotton-mill there, and there was machinery made in Bolton. Sending out machinery from Bolton, and doing something for other people, is what has made Bolton what it is. The invention of the spinning mule by Crompton, making machinery by Hick, Hargreaves, and Dobson & Barlow's, and cotton goods by Barlow & Jones, and other firms. That will apply to every one of you. It will be by making yourselves wanted, badly wanted, that you will succeed.

I know many people believe that it is capital a man wants to start him. Believe me, there is not a single large firm in the United Kingdom that is short of capital. They can get all the capital they want. But there is not a single large firm in the United Kingdom that has got all the best men it wants, the men they want to pay big salaries to. There is plenty of capital; no trouble about that, but the greatest trouble and difficulty is filling up their staff with the men who can draw the biggest salaries. I do not mean that there are not men who would like to draw them, plenty of such men. But drawing a big salary means earning more than you draw. That is the output. The intake is the salary, but the output must be greater. It is the same all over the world. A friend of mine in America says he has on his list three positions vacant, for each of which he can afford to pay 100,000 dollars a year salary, and he cannot fill them. If he wanted 100 million dollars for his business he could get it without trouble, but he cannot get three men capable of earning 100,000 dollars a year each. Bear that in mind. Never mind about the salary—that will be seeking you all the time if you are worth it. Never mind about capital—you will never be short of that if you are worth a big salary. It is the difference between output

17

and intake which has made the good old town of Bolton prosperous beyond the wildest dreams of our ancestors of a century ago, and it is as applicable to every boy and girl here as ever it was in Bolton. It applies to every one of us.

I want to say a word now to the teachers. I want you to remember that boys need so much encouragement, and it is in your power to fix in the minds of these boys the highest ideals. In business we take stock periodically, and in taking stock we have a debit side and a credit side, and so show whether we have made a profit or loss. That is an excellent plan, both in business and in every other walk of life, including your boy pupils in this School. In taking stock of your boys in school, why not put all the drawbacks and disadvantages on one side? There is not a single boy in the world of whom you can say everything is in his favour. On the other side put all the good points that help, and when that is done by teachers they will find that the predominant characteristic in human nature is goodness. The predominant element in boys' nature is goodness, and it is for the teacher, by pulling out the right stop—not the same stop for every boy—to appeal to his ambition and ideals and to elevate the boy to the highest pinnacle.

Might I say a word to parents? I don't think parents quite realize, and I don't think boys and girls do when they are children—I know I didn't—the enormous influence that passes from parents to children. It is in the power of parents to encourage the boys and girls when they come home, and make their task easier. A boy came home one day from school, and it was obvious that he had been badly caned. His father looked very severely at him and said, " You have been caned." " Yes, father." " Well," said his father, " you must have been doing something wrong and deserved it." " No, father, I didn't," said the boy. " You must have," the father insisted. " No, father, I didn't." " Well, what was it for? " " Well, father, you remember me asking you, last night, how much a million pennies was? " " Yes," said his father. " And you said it was a devil of a lot? " " Yes." " Well, the schoolmaster says that is not the right answer, and he caned me for it." When the children come and ask these questions I dare say it is a nuisance, but a little encouragement at the time will reap the biggest harvest that can be reaped.

I am very proud to have been here. It has been a very great pleasure to me. It always is, and I feel that under Mr. Lipscomb, and the masters and the Governors, the future of this School is being laid on solid foundations, that it will, every year, add to the future prosperity of the good old town of Bolton, by producing the type of citizen who will be proud of Bolton, proud to help Bolton and of whom Bolton will be proud, and who will look with pleasure on the days they passed at the Bolton School.

Now, boys, I want you to remember some poetry. Can you learn it ? See if you can remember this :—

Some ships go East, and some go West,
    Whilst the self-same wind doth blow ;
For it's rudder and sail, and not the gale,
    Decide where the ship shall go.

Nor wind, nor gale control our fate,
    As we journey along through life ;
It's the set of the soul decides the goal,
    And not the calm and the strife.

SOME INDUSTRIAL QUESTIONS

INDUSTRIAL ADMINISTRATION

LIVERPOOL, *November* 8, 1916.

[Having spoken so often, and out of such long and successful experience, on the subject of Co-Partnership, Lord Leverhulme devoted the speech here presented to those basic principles of industrial administration which cannot be ignored, even under the most harmonious scheme, without entailing serious limitations to the expansion of industries and actual curtailment of both wages and profits. Incidentally, he grappled with the great Trade Union question of " restriction of output." His audience was the Liverpool Social Problem Circle.]

THE answer to the question, " What is the employer's position at the present time ? " depends, like the answer to so many other questions, upon the point of view that this position is regarded from. You will remember the story of the painter who was explaining to his sitter for a portrait that he could only paint his portrait as he saw the sitter, to which the sitter promptly replied, " But, unfortunately, I can only see my portrait as you paint it." However, I may, perhaps, better answer the question by adopting the answer given to the question, " Is life worth living ? "—the answer to which was, you will remember, that " It all depends upon the liver." If the employer's liver is out of order he is apt to take the view that " the times are out of joint " ; and it is not impossible, under similar circumstances, that the workman, even when working in good conditions of employment, might, if he was told, as was the Irishman, that he could not do too much for a good master, give the answer, " No more will I." However, we shall all agree that to-day it were wise if both employer and employee examined their relationships in the past and looked well ahead into the future.

And the first point in the near future that will present itself to both will be the consideration of after-war conditions. The experience gained by both employer and employee during this war makes it impossible for either to resume work after the war with conditions quite the same as they were when the war broke out. For one thing alone, the war has added nearly one and a half millions of income-tax payers to the previous number who came within the net of the Chancellor of the Exchequer, which of itself is a revolution. This increase in numbers is not only the natural effect of lowering the limit of exemption, but mainly, as far as is ascertainable at present, from actual increases in wages and salary. This is a grand fact and, if the employer can take a far-sighted view, is an immense gain to the strength of industrial production.

Statistics of incomes and income-tax payers, when carefully examined, reveal this great truth, that to bring a larger body of wage-earners within the scope of the income-tax collector has the undoubted tendency to increase the efforts of each to earn a larger income out of which to pay the tax. Equally, every raising of the rate at which income tax is levied has been followed by increased efforts, successfully made, to increase incomes out of which to pay the increased tax. Therefore the effect of placing one and a half million additional income-tax payers on this higher platform has been to place an increased number of employers and employees side by side as income-tax payers, and give them one common object to strive for, viz. to maintain and to increase incomes. We are all inclined to say, with the Irishman, " Be jabers to the tax, if you will give me the income," and having got the income, we are all inclined to make increased efforts to make the income sufficiently large to stand the contribution demanded by the Chancellor of the Exchequer, in the form of income tax, without diminishing the balance remaining for the income earner.

To ensure the highest degree of efficiency in plant, machinery, and all the mechanical utilities required for production and distribution, the employer requires good profits ; and, equally, to ensure the highest degree of efficiency for employees, high wages and reasonable hours of employment are necessary. Good profits for the employer enable the prompt scrapping of old plant and machinery, and the installation of better equipment, to be successfully accomplished. Equally, high wages and reasonable hours for the employee react in increasing the physical and mental tone and efficiency of the worker. Therefore, the tendency of modern conditions is to bring the interests of employers and employees nearer and nearer together, if these interests are rightly understood, but not otherwise.

And what are the problems to be faced ? The biggest problem the employer has to face, and one that is always present with him, is to surround himself with a permanent efficient staff, happy and contented in their employment, who will not only work *for* him, but, what is much more valuable, will work *with* him. I knew a manufacturer in America, a very successful man, who was once asked which he would prefer—a fire that burnt out his factory, his buildings, machinery, and plant to total extinction, or some plague or epidemic that killed off all his staff. There was no hesitation in the answer, which was prompt and quick, that he would prefer the fire ; because he could sooner replace the factory, buildings, machinery, and plant than he could get together another staff ; besides, with his staff remaining to him, he declared, he could worry through all right without the factory, the plant, and machinery, until he got the same replaced. And the reason for this preference is obvious. An efficient staff is a staff trained to their duties, and this training depends upon constant repetition in performance of the same duties, and in solving the same problems of the business. Repetition is the basis of efficiency, which can only be achieved as the result of long service. Therefore, one of the principal objects of the employer must be to attach to himself an efficient staff ; but, to ensure this, it is absolutely essential to convince the employee working for salary or wages that the welfare of the employer and employee are identical. We are all agreed that, to ensure ideal conditions and an ideal relationship between employers and employees, employment must be so organized that profits earned shall not only be sufficient to provide good living conditions for the employees, and a reasonable return on the capital invested for the employer, but shall be such as to ensure the advancement of the industry and the contentment and satisfaction of both employers and employees. Mere desire to attach a staff to a particular industry, and to ensure long service, is not sufficient. The solution of this problem can only be found in the actual working conditions themselves, and until these working conditions are acceptable to both employers and employees, neither are yet prepared to surrender their weapons of attack and defence, or to " beat their swords into ploughshares and their spears into pruning-hooks " in order the better to cultivate a larger and richer harvest.

The gulf at present separating employers and employees is very largely a misunderstanding of the conditions affecting each. The employee has an exaggerated idea of the volume of the profits produced under ordinary normal conditions of the industry in which he is engaged. The employer, faced with demands for higher wages and knowing the competition he has to face, is nervous in granting advances for fear his small margin of profit shall be turned into an actual loss. As you know, a minority of employers, myself included, hold very strongly the view that only under a system of actual Co-Partnership can the spirit of greed and fear be eliminated and a just division of profits as between employer and employee be obtained.

But I propose that we devote ourselves to the consideration, not of Profit-Sharing or Co-Partnership, which subject I have dealt with elsewhere as fully as my limited capacity has permitted me, but rather of what, for want of a better name, I propose to call " Industrial Administration," and of those principles that must be recognized if there are to be any profits available for division. But I would here again repeat that under no scheme of Co-Partnership can the basic principles of industrial administration be ignored without entailing serious injury to employers and employees, and serious limitations to the expansion of industries and actual curtailment of both wages and profits.

Now, what are a few of the principles that, combined, must form and under all circumstances include both the employers' point of view, viz. good profits, with the employees' point of view, high wages and reasonable hours ? The chief of these basic principles are increased production with consequent reduction of overhead charges and reduced operating costs, combined with shorter hours for workers, resulting in better working conditions, leading to greater efficiency and producing higher wages and better profits. To ensure the attainment of these aims and objects and of these sound economic conditions, and as part of the control of labour, the words " Scientific Management " have been applied. Unfortunately, much that is preached and sometimes practised by this school of employers is neither scientific nor worthy of the name of management. But underlying all the error of this school of thought are some good, sound, wholesome practices. But perhaps a less stilted and less irritating title would be " Industrial Administration." The supreme spirit of scientific management worthy of that description must be that of administration. " Management " rarely considers the workman other than from the point of view of control, and to thrust the antagonizing spirit of control to the front place, as so-called " Scientific Management " would appear to be doing, is not to make the relations between employers and employees less irritating, but rather the contrary. The whole idea associated with " Management " is that of control, which idea has embalmed itself, and its meaning, in the name " boss." But workmen have grown and developed much during the last quarter century, and are no longer blindly consenting to be " bossed " or controlled as if they were children. Workmen have become responsible human beings, and claim some just and sane share in the management of their own lives and conditions. The workman to-day claims rights, and does not deny that the exercise of rights will bring with it the responsibility for the performance of duties, and these duties he is willing to undertake. But to show how inapplicable the word " Management " is, it is obvious that you cannot have management of rights nor management of duties. To show the better applicability of the word " Administration," you can have administration of rights and administration of duties. Therefore, if employers and employees are to be brought to work together, and if all suspicion and distrust, not to say actual and active opposition, are to be abolished, then the idea of " Management " as " bossism " must be surrendered by the employer.

At this point, I think I can read the thoughts of many

in the room, who will be wondering whether I am, advocating the surrender of all discipline in Industrialism. Nothing of the sort. There must now, and for all time, be authority and law in Industrialism as in the Army, and as in all places where communities have to live and act and work together. Both employer and employee must agree fully and without reserve in this, otherwise Industrialism and the working together of an organized system for production would be impossible, and mankind would degenerate into a mob.

We must have authority and law and due observance of discipline in the factory and workshop as on the steamship, and as for the nation and State. But do not let us confuse ourselves over this essential. The question is, Has the authority to be autocratic? If so, have your management as " boss," and endeavour to make it as scientific as possible. Or shall the authority be democratic? In that case, let us adopt the description for the authority we must provide that best fits our aims and intentions, viz. administration. You will find that whilst the dictionary gives " control " as one of the meanings of management, that word does not appear as one of the meanings of administration, but the words " to direct," " to dispense" ; and the word " guardian " is given as the meaning of the word " administrator." These latter all form a good democratic basis, and the necessity for authority, law, discipline, and obedience, under these conditions, is at once admitted, and can be accepted without humiliation or loss of self-respect, when " bossism," even if called " Scientific Management," would raise a spirit of opposition founded on the resentment we all feel to that very idea when applied to ourselves.

Scientific Administration we would all welcome as applying to established principles supporting the laws for the working together of hundreds, or thousands, or millions of men and women in productive enterprises for the combined benefit of employers, employees, and of the whole community. Scientific Management is apt to be viewed as entirely designed to increase the profits and advantages of the employer at the expense of the employee, whereas Scientific Administration would be welcomed as merely the science of production in the simplest, easiest way which would secure the highest wages and the greatest prosperity for employers and employees.

Scientific Administration can be honestly based on the assumption that the interests of employers and employees are identical, and opposition thereto can only be possible on the assumption of the obvious error that these interests never can be honestly identical.

Scientific administration will make clear that restriction of output is not only immoral for the man who might have made two articles but who only made one, but that he has thus robbed his fellow-man even more wickedly than the thief who had stolen one out of any two articles one of his fellowmen might have made; for whilst, in the case of the robber, there would still be the two articles, and both would be of service, there would be only one article in the case of restriction of output, and the lapse in production could never be made good.

Parliament has intervened to prevent the thraldom of labour by passing Industrial Acts, limiting hours and conditions of labour, fixing rates of wages, providing for employers' liability for the safety and health of employees, and the employers' responsibility for accident, ill-health, or death the direct result of employment.   And just as Parliament has made these laws for preventing the thraldom of labour, Parliament may also be forced to pass laws to prevent restriction of output as an act of robbery against the common weal, and, as an act of adulteration of service, just as wrong as the adulteration of milk or any article of food or commerce.

Just as attempts by combinations of employers to cheat the public in quality and price have been met, when and where attempted, by laws to prevent the same, so similar attempts by combinations of Labour to cheat their fellow-men by restriction of output must, and can be, prevented by laws directed to that end.

Such a state of affairs, however, need never to arise, and ought never to arise, if the whole position of industrial administration is properly understood.

The employers' contribution to the world's progress and betterment is organization of mechanical utilities and machine efficiency, in order to give enormously increased output. Industrial administration, by providing the means for intensive mechanical production by increased steam-power and more efficient plant and machinery, demanding less and less exhaustive strain on the employees, has unlimited opportunity for increased output at reduced cost after paying wages on the highest world's scale; and this can all be accomplished provided the fallacy of restriction of output is not permitted to spoil the working of these economic principles. Mechanical utilities, mechanical horse-power, and standardization of products are the keystone of the arch of better conditions for employer and, still more so, of better conditions for employee.

High wages cannot be paid without correspondingly increased output by employees. Surely the employees' point of view must be the amount of wages received, the length of hours worked, and the strain of mind and muscle involved. If opportunity of earning high wages can be assured in a reasonable eight-hour day without strain or exhaustion, then the amount of product need not worry the employee. The employee cannot in his own interest wisely assume an attitude of approval of restriction of output.

Under these conditions, industrial administration scientifically applied will provide that the profits resulting from the enormously increased output are not all to go as dividends on the capital employed, but shall be shared in fair and equitable proportion between both Capital and Labour.

Let us see if practical examples of the effect of a high scale of output with high mechanical horse-power per wage-earner can be given as showing the direct bearing and connection on high wages and shorter hours for the workman. The lowest output and the longest working hours per wage-earner in the world are to be found in China and India; and in these countries there is also the lowest mechanical horse-power per wage-earner and the lowest wages earned per wage earner. The example of the highest of all these will be found in the United States. Let us compare these with the same in the United Kingdom. Mechanical horse-power per wage-earner in China or India is so low as to be negligible. The mechanical horse-power per wage-earner in the United States, as given in Government records of industrial production, is two to three times that of the United Kingdom. The value of the product per wage-earner per year in the United

States is also found to be two to three times that of the wage-earner, in the United Kingdom. And how do the wages paid per wage-earner compare under these conditions? In India and China the average wages do not exceed, for unskilled labour, 4s. per week, and for skilled labour 6s. per week. The weekly wages in the United Kingdom and the United States for the year 1912, being the latest year available for comparison, are stated to be :—

	U.K.	U.S.A.
Carpenters.. .. .. £2 0 0	£9 0 0
Foundrymen £2 1 0	£9 0 0
Builders' labourers .. £1 6 0	£6 0 0
Other skilled labour .. £2 0 0	£6 4 0
Other unskilled labour .. £1 2 0	£2 11 0

Of course, the rates of wages vary in different parts of the United States, as in various parts of the United Kingdom, and these figures are merely quoted as illustrations, and subject to such variations. Hence, whilst in the United States the mechanical horse-power is two to three times per wage-earner of that per wage-earner in the United Kingdom, and the output is also two to three times of that per wage-earner in the United Kingdom, the wages in the highly skilled trades in the United States are over four times per wage-earner of those paid in the United Kingdom, and in the less skilled trades over three times, and the unskilled labour two to four times that of the same grade of wage-earner in the United Kingdom.

Now let us see if we can find a direct example of reduced output per wage-earner in the United Kingdom as compared with the same industry and increased output in the United States. We can find this example most readily in the statistics relating to coal, and whether this reduction of output in the United Kingdom has been brought about by the " ca' canny " policy in the restriction of output or not is quite immaterial to the point it illustrates. I do not know, not being connected with the coal industry, how the reduced production in the United Kingdom is to be accounted for, and I make no attempt at guessing ; but whatever the cause may have been does not affect the resulting injury to the

consumer and the industries of this country in competition
with the rest of the world.

TONS OF COAL PRODUCED PER WAGE-EARNER PER ANNUM.

	U.K.	U.S.A.
1886–90	312	400
1911	260	613

VALUE AT THE PIT MOUTH.

1886–90	4s. 10d.	6s. 4d.
1911	8s. 1d.	5s. 10d.

So that we see in the United States by increased mechanical
horse-power, combined with increased output, the cost of
coal to the consumer has been reduced, and the employers
have been enabled to pay more than two to three times the
rate of wages per wage-earner in mines, as in all other industries in the United States, than can be paid in the United
Kingdom.　Let me point out that these rates and statistics
are all pre-war rates and subject to pre-war conditions.　This
increased cost of coal does not benefit either employer or
employee, and certainly injures the consumer.　In fact,
under these conditions, the employer (or capitalist) in the
United States also makes better returns on his capital than
his fellow-employer in the United Kingdom.　But the tragedy
of it is that it makes the cost of cooking, heating, and lighting oppressive for the wage-earner, and creates a handicap
to every British industry that uses coal, making the cost
of production of all articles higher.　It threatens our iron
and steel industries and, with them, our world supremacy
in shipbuilding and our mercantile marine, upon which we
absolutely depend for our very existence as a nation.

And now let me give you figures of our greatest national
industry of all—a national industry which is even greater
than the iron, steel, and coal industries added together, viz.
agriculture.　In this industry restriction of output is unknown.
The farmer has a free hand in the cultivation of his crops
and the rearing of his live stock.　If we examine the pedigree
of the live stock that is most highly prized all over the world,

whether of horses, cattle, pigs, sheep, or whatever it may
be, we find the pedigree of this stock British ; and if we turn
to crops per acre we shall again see that British farmers,
untrammelled by restriction of output, hold the highest
place in their productive enterprise of any nation in the
world. We will compare the four leading agricultural
products in the three leading nations.

QUINTALS PER ACRE, 1913–14.

	Wheat.	Barley.	Oats.	Potatoes.
United Kingdom ..	10·0	8·4	7·6	64
United States	4·4	5·5	4·4	29·4
Germany	8·0	8·0	8·4	54

And we must not overlook the fact that, in obtaining this
high production, our agricultural industry has had to submit
to the handicap of underpaid, underfed labour, backward
position in mechanical appliances, and lack of knowledge
of the science of chemistry as applied to soils and fertilizers.

Just as we have seen that the highest proportion of
mechanical horse-power per wage-earner, aided by science
in administration, has raised the rate of wages in all industries, so when we get these modern aids applied to British
agriculture, so surely will the cost of production be reduced
by still further increased output, with greatly increased
wages to labour and better returns to the farmer. The
low wages of labour in agriculture have been a handicap
in every way to the farmer by greatly reducing the
efficiency of his labour and the attractiveness of farm work
to the wage-earner. He has had to stand impotently by
and see his best labour leave the country and seek the higher
rate of pay obtainable in the town and city.

We see clearly what an awful blunder for the Empire the
policy of restriction of output proves itself to be. Where
high mechanical horse-power per wage-earner is found, there
the greatest output per wage-earner exists side by side with
the highest scale of wages. Restriction of output is not
only an economic fallacy but is the robbery, by the worker,
of his mates of their rightful due in wages, food, clothing,
houses, and welfare conditions. It is the duty of every

18

Trade Union official to fight this false doctrine with all his strength and might; and I say this because I know, and I am convinced by a lifelong friendship and acquaintance with Trade Unions, that they have one sincere aim and object which they pursue with devotion—the welfare of the wage-earner.

There is nothing in mechanical horse-power, new and improved machinery, producing enormously increased output, to incur the opposition and enmity of Trade Unions. If it pays, as it does, scientific administration to scrap obsolete plant, buildings, and machinery (and we know that there is no scrapping and destruction of obsolete property which will not, in the long run, prove immensely profitable when it represents the price to be paid for superior and more efficient methods), then similarly it may be said with equal truth that it will pay the wage-earner to scrap obsolete, false economic methods and worn-out policies. And first of all of these policies to be scrapped ought to be that of restriction of output.

There is a much broader sphere for the operations of Trade Unions, providing ample work for many years to come, in bettering the industrial conditions of this country. The scrapping of the policy of " ca' canny," or restriction of output, will give all the more liberty and power for the advancement of these higher aims and activities; and, in addition, this broader, better outlook and higher activities for Trade Unionism will prove to the world that Trade Unions are fighting not only for the betterment of the workers, but are considering the interests of the consumer and of the British Empire in competition with all other nations in the world.

When the British public are convinced that the good of the community as a whole, and the progress and strength of the British Empire in competition with all nations of the world, are also receiving the attention and special care of Trade Unions, then woe to the capitalist or employer who attempts to oppose any just demands made for the furtherance of these aims and objects.

The times are changed, thank God! from when, in 1858, Ruskin addressed these sentences to a British audience as being the then thoughts of Capital and of the general public towards Labour :—

" Be assured, my good man," you say to him, " that if you work steadily for ten hours a day all your life, and if you drink nothing but water, or the very mildest beer, and live on very plain food, and never lose your temper, and go to church every Sunday, and always remain content in the position in which Providence has placed you, and never grumble, nor swear ; and always keep your clothes decent, and rise early, and use every opportunity of improving yourself, you will get on very well, and never come to the parish."

Ruskin's biting sarcasm passed without effecting any material change ; but what biting sarcasm has failed to bring home to the intelligence of employers and the public may, perhaps, be learned by both from our common necessities in the evolution of industrialism.

When peace comes, bringing us victory over our enemies and giving us rest from the clash of arms, we shall still have to enter the field of struggle for commercial position amongst the nations of the world.   It is unthinkable that we and our Allies, proving victorious in this cruel war, fighting for right and liberty, justice and freedom, should be defeated in the struggle for industrial position by our present enemies and Neutral nations.   And yet defeat is certain if our industrial organization is founded on attempted oppression of Labour on the one hand or restriction of output by Labour on the other hand.

Our victorious Army has been drawn from all classes, from the highest to the most humble in the land, who have been loyal and true comrades in the trenches, and it is unthinkable that when the war is over industrial antagonism should prevent the Empire maintaining her former proud commercial position.   Let both employer and employee scrap their old, antiquated, false ideas as to their mutual relationships, and work with a better understanding of each other's rights and duties, recognizing that this good old world is far too small to hold any more than two classes in the classification of people, viz. those who do their duty and those who fail to do their duty.   It is certain that in the next world there will be only these two classes, whatever artificial divisions between employer and employee may have existed in this world.

II

COMBINES

PORT SUNLIGHT, *January* 11' 1903.

[The following address has the special interest attaching to a friendly talk by a great employer to an audience consisting very largely of his own workmen on topics of intimate concern to both parties. They met on the common ground afforded by the annual gathering of the Port Sunlight Men's Meeting. Lord Leverhulme said :]

THE subject I have chosen for my address is best described by the word "Combines." I do not care whether it is a combination of masters, in which case we probably call it a Trust, or a combination of men, in which case we should probably call it a Trade Union—there is nothing new in Combines. And I am afraid that there is nothing new which can be brought forward as to the principles that will govern them. In my opinion, the principles that govern Combines are just as old as the law of gravitation and just as immutable. The difficulty is sometimes to find out what these principles are, but the principles are there, we may depend upon it, and we may also depend upon it that they apply equally certainly to the masters as to the men. I can best illustrate that by imagining for the moment that a master and a man (his workman) were walking down, we'll say, one of the corridors of a cotton-mill, and we will imagine that the master, by some mishap, became entangled in the machinery on the left, and the workman became entangled in the machinery on the right. The machines, we know, would be no respecters of either master or man ; they would not stop on the master's side nor on the man's side. If either got entangled in the machinery, the mishap would be just the same whether master or man. And so in my opinion it is if by any mishap we forget economic conditions in dealing with Combines. I believe that if we make a mistake destruction will just as surely come on the master if he makes a mistake as upon the employee if he makes a mistake.

Well, I believe there is a general impression sometimes in the minds of employees that the master is a sort of tyrant, who could pay very handsome wages if he would, and who does not do it just merely out of cussedness and an ill-will towards his men. And there is an opinion among some masters that they are very unfortunate, they don't make as much money as they ought; but that it is certainly not their fault, and that it is probably anybody's fault but their own. Well, now, I would like just, if we can, to inquire what are the conditions that would prevail to make a successful combination of masters, and what would be the conditions that would prevail to make a successful combination of men. It does not matter which we take first—there is no order of priority in the matter. The century that has just closed has seen an equally large advance in combinations of men as we have seen in combinations of masters. The number of Trade Unions in England to-day is larger than it ever was in the whole of the preceding centuries of the world's history, and combines of masters are larger to-day and represent a larger amount of capital than was ever known in the preceding history of the world.

Well, now, suppose we take the question of the combines on the masters' side first—we shall find upon a close examination into the combines of employers that those combines have succeeded when one of the results of combination has been an opportunity for producing a cheaper product, an opportunity for producing a more abundant product, and an opportunity for producing a better product; and we invariably find that combinations of masters have failed when the object has been, without having the advantages I have just mentioned, to increase the profits of the masters—in other words, their wages—or to bolster up decaying industries. I will just give you one illustration of a successful combination in our own country, that is Coats' thread. They combined a number of thread-makers, and they were enabled to save enormously in salesmen's salaries and expenses. An enormous amount of money is saved in advertising, and enormous sums of money are saved in various other ways, with the result that the undertaking is successful. Now, I might mention many, but it would be invidious to do so, that have been gross failures—you know of them; I hope none of you have put your money into them—which have never had for their object the cheapening of the product. They had no opportunity springing out of the effect of the combination for cheapening their product. Their object, prominently held forth in prospectus and dangled before the eyes of possible investors, has been to increase the profits by doing away with competition, and this object they have always failed to realize. I have never heard yet of a single instance where, for even a small number of years, a combination, brought about with that object, and without the other advantages I have mentioned, has succeeded. Now, the position from the employer's point of view is this : the market that he caters for is no longer the local one. There was a time when the manufacturer did not even make for all England, but he made for the town, village, or district in which he lived. The products were small and unimportant ; they were what were called cottage industries, and many people lament their disappearance ; but they have had to go in the march of progress, and the manufacturer has had to face all the consequences brought about by the invention of steam, by the extension of railways and steamboats, and the enormously increased capital required in consequence of these things. In the old days a manufactory would be an individual concern. Next, we can imagine, after that would come the time when two or three individuals would join their capital together and form a partnership, and that was a state of affairs which continued until quite recently. Then it grew beyond the capital available by two or three joining together as a partnership, and limited companies became necessary, with appeals to be made to thousands of investors, in order that still larger capital might be got together. Now we have reached a further stage again, when a number of limited companies require to be grouped together into what we call a Combine, the object being the concentration of capital and the concentration of effort. If these Combines result in cheaper production and a more abundant supply, such undertakings will be successful; if not, they will be failures.

The very idea of large combinations is always alarming to us at first. It is only when we become accustomed to the altered conditions that we cease to fear it; but we may, I think, feel certain that as inventions progress the amount of capital required in business will be larger and larger, and so Combines on a larger scale even than we know them to-day will become necessary, practicable, and successful. We may regret the disappearance of the small manufacturers, but, after all, it is certain that the destruction of the small manufacturer is simply his smallness. It is not himself, it is merely a matter of size. The law is undoubtedly " For whosoever hath, to him shall be given, and he shall have more abundance : but whosoever hath not, from him shall be taken away even that he hath." If the small manufacturer could produce more cheaply than the large manufacturer, it is as clear as the sun at noonday that before many years were over the positions would be reversed, and the former small manufacturer would have become the large manufacturer, and the former large manufacturer would have disappeared altogether. Therefore, it is clear that large manufacturers are going to be the rule. They receive many advantages— advantages of large capital enabling them to make large purchases, to buy improved machinery, to engage a large and experienced and talented staff; and they have facilities for the utilization of waste products which small manufacturers do not enjoy, and never can enjoy. And then they can live on a smaller percentage of profits. What would be a ruinous profit to the small manufacturer becomes an ample fortune to the large manufacturer doing an enormous turnover. The public cry all over the world is always for cheapness, and I do not mean, when I say cheapness, for nasty cheapness, but cheap good quality. The public are continually supporting and rushing after the man who can give them the best goods at the lowest possible price. The third of a farthing a pound on the sugar consumed in the United Kingdom would amount to somewhere about one million sterling. I venture to say that the small sugar refiner would find so small a profit as that probably spell ruin, but a large manufacturer, you can readily understand, could make an ample profit out of such a margin.

Now, I have ventured to impress upon you the conditions that prevail with regard to employers. If every one of you in this room were a manufacturer, that is the state of affairs you would have to face at the beginning of the twentieth century. It is an iron law, and any manufacturer who feels competition keen to-day and seeks relief in combination with other manufacturers in the same line of business, thinking thereby to avoid what he calls cut-throat competition, unless he can prove to himself that such combination will enable him to produce cheaper and to save expenses, will be simply putting off the evil day, and the firms he has combined with will simply drag each other down, down, down, until they disappear. Their place will be taken by men who are producing more cheaply, with probably improved machinery and other better conditions. If, as a result of the combination, he can produce cheaper, he may also depend upon it as an absolute certainty that he will make better profits, otherwise called wages, because the fund available for so-called profits or wages will have been increased.

Now, what is the position with regard to the employees? We know that the employees are feeble if single ; we know that if you take a number of employees and put them, say, on a desert island in the Pacific, with merely their hands, they would be not in any one bit superior, and probably very much inferior, to the savages living on the island. An employee's capital is not cash like the employer's ; an employee's capital is his intellectual and bodily attainments, and the knowledge he has acquired and his natural aptitudes. But all the same, man is a machine just as much as the engine he is driving, and is subject to just the same unchangeable law. We all of us know that the machine which can produce, in proportion to its consumption of fuel, the largest amount of goods is the best, and the one that will be secured at the highest price—and the same it is with man. An employee has the responsibility resting upon him to elevate and improve his condition—an employee has just the same ambitions in that direction as his employer —and if an employer can consider the question of combinations as to whether they are going to benefit him, the employee has not only an equal right to do it—which I venture to say no one would be so foolish as to dispute—but he has the responsibility resting upon him to seek out how he may do it for the benefit of himself, his wife, and family ; and it is his duty to seek out whether he can improve his condition by combination, and if he finds he can on solid, sound business lines, then it is his duty to do it.

Now, in what way can an employee (to go back to the illustration of the engine) improve his power of production, and, consequently, his own value ; and what are the laws that govern him ? I venture to support the views that have most strongly appealed to me under this head, and they are these : firstly, the value of a man is in proportion to his power and ability, mental and physical, and the power of the implements he works with ; secondly, it is in proportion to the abundance of circulating capital ; and thirdly, the value of a man is affected by the cost of rent, food, and clothing. Now, suppose we take the first of these three—firstly, that the value of a man is in proportion to his power and ability, mental and physical, and the power of the implements he works with. We have often seen through lack of knowledge on this point that workmen have declared over and over again that machinery was throwing them out of employment, destroying their labour, and lowering their wages. We find that the hand-loom cotton-spinners in Lancashire declared, when Crompton and Arkwright made their discoveries which have resulted in the present basis of cotton-spinning, that they were being ruined ; and some of these men took extreme measures and smashed the models of these inventors. In Samuel Crompton's house you can be shown the hole in which Crompton had to bury his model of his machine from his own class, his own fellow-workmen living in cottages, his neighbours, who, if they could have got at it, would have smashed it to pieces. What was the fact at that time ? Before the inventions of Crompton and Arkwright there were only 8,000 cotton operatives in all England, and no associated trades to speak of, going with them. Of course, I am not including in that the wife, who did a little bit of spinning for her family at home, as most farmers' wives did. Twenty-seven years after these machines had come into operation—these machines that these men

wanted to break up—there were 300,000 workmen engaged,
and wages had advanced. Eighty years later wages had
still further advanced, and there were 800,000 men engaged
in England in the cotton industry, and to-day wages are
higher than ever, and including the associated trades that
go with cotton-spinning—such as calico-printing and the
making of the machinery—it is estimated that not less
than two and a half millions of people are engaged in
the cotton industry in this kingdom.

We see now that it was machinery that enabled us to do this.
It has enabled the Lancashire spinner to buy cotton in India,
to pay the carriage from India to Lancashire, to make it into
cotton goods, to ship it back to India, and whilst paying
weavers and spinners from 24s. to 36s. a week, to sell that
product cheaper on the Indian market than Hindoos getting
6d. a day. It is enabling Lancashire cotton-spinners to do
all that and yet beat the native Hindoo labourer working
at the rate of 6d. a day. What is the reason? The reason
is that whatever increases the product increases the fund
out of which wages are paid. There is no other way of
paying wages. You cannot pay wages except from the fund
from which wages are produced—the product of the man,
or the man and the machine he works—and therefore every
invention, every discovery, every machine, every improved
organization, every increase in product, increases the fund
available for wages. Now what could decrease the fund
available for wages? Many things, but one thing most
certainly, and that is the employees rendering the task of
the employer more difficult, either by slovenliness or laziness,
or by compelling him to go to expensive and costly supervision; all this would decrease the fund available for wages,
and tend therefore to lessen the sum paid in wages.

Now we come to the second point. The value of a
man, as of all producing machinery, is in proportion to
the abundance of circulating capital. The circulating
capital is the money that will bring produce to the
machine and be responsible for all the floating capital
required in the business. It is found that as capital in any
country increases, the wages invariably increase. It is a fact
that in all countries where wealth increases wages increase.
The reason for that is clear : that in countries that are wealthy

there is so much more capital available to purchase machinery, for the payment of inventors, for the building of railways and steamboats, for floating capital, for the purchase of stocks, for opening up fresh markets, for providing for stability of credit. All these things require money, and every one of these tends to increase the fund out of which wages are paid, and consequently tends to increase the amount of wages. The shrewd employer with ample capital, and who apparently is making the very largest profits, and who very often is considered to be making them out of his workpeople, is really producing a fund available for wages and salaries, and every such employer that there is through the country must have the effect of increasing the fund available for payment of wages and salaries ; and every employer making small profits or no profits, short of shrewdness, short of capital, unable to meet modern improvements, to get rid of his old machinery and put in new, is tending to decrease the fund available for wages.

The next position is that the value of labour is in proportion to the cost of rent, food, and clothing. We all know that money value is only relative. If you go to a country and you find that rent is high, clothes dear, food dear, why, you naturally require a larger sum of money to live in that country than in one in which rent and clothing and food are cheap. It does not matter, when I pull a penny out of my pocket, whether I call it a penny or a shilling ; if the purchasing power of the penny in a certain place is equal to the purchasing power of a shilling in another place, I shall find it is immaterial to me as long as I can buy as much for the penny in one place as for the shilling in another. You might just as well, for all practical purposes, call the penny a shilling or the shilling a penny. In Egypt a workman can keep his wife and family, and live well, on 6d. a day. In the United States a man can scarcely live—he cannot live in comfort—on 6s. a day. It is, therefore, perfectly clear that it is not the amount of money received but what money will buy that is the standard.

Professor Thorold Rogers, who investigated this subject very closely, was one of the first to draw attention to what was the golden age for labour in this country, and what I believe was the golden age for labour in the world, and that was here

in England in the fifteenth century. Guilds, which preceded
our present Trade Unions, were prevalent in all trades ; they
were extremely wealthy, and we have many of them existing
right down to the present time, as the City Guilds of London.
The wages paid then—if I tell you the amount you will say
they were very badly paid, shockingly paid—the standard
wages for stone-masons, bricklayers, joiners, and most other
trades was 6d. a day, but they were paid for all days—
15s. a month. Let us see what the sixpence would do.
Supposing you formed a club here for buying each other
clothing, food, and paying your rents here in Port Sunlight,
and you took a thousand of your number, and said, " We'll
put all our wages into a common pool." Well, imagine you
have such a club in Port Sunlight, and one man is buying
as cheaply as he can all your mutton, beef, pork, eggs, geese,
pigeons, etc., calico, clothing, and paying your rent. Well,
imagine there was another club like that in the fifteenth
century, let us see what your wages would have to be to do
what the men could do in the fifteenth century. Each man's
wages would need to be £10 a week to pay your rent as
you pay it in Port Sunlight ; for buying beef, mutton, and
pork, £3 10s. a week ; geese, £5 5s. a week ; chickens, £4 a
week ; pigeons, £6 a week ; cheese and butter, £4 a week ;
bread only £1 a week—that is entirely caused by the cheapness of transport by rail and steam ; eggs, £3 15s. a week ;
calico, 3s. 6d. a week—that is caused, again, by the machinery
I have mentioned, the inventions of Crompton and Arkwright ; for the clothes you wear your wages would have
to be 15s. a week.

These men in the fifteenth century, therefore, were
extremely well paid ; in fact, food was so cheap in those
days that when these men went to work on the monas-
teries and the cathedrals which we see now in the country,
some in ruins and some still in existence, as York Minster,
it was perfectly immaterial to the master whether he
gave the man food in addition or not. The man got his
wages, and if he liked to have his food he could have it.
They worked eight hours a day in the fifteenth century ;
therefore, the workmen of to-day are only striving for what
their forefathers enjoyed five hundred years ago. Another
feature of that age is the quality of the work. It has survived

to the present time ; it is unquestionable that each mason took a pride in his work, and put a mark on each stone he worked, and those masons' marks on the old stones are known well throughout the country, very much hke signed pictures by a Royal Academician of to-day.   I won't say we cannot, but we do not produce such quality in stone-masons' work and brickwork to-day.   Won't you agree with me that such a high quality of work would have been impossible if the men had been paid starvation wages and worked long hours ? I am perfectly certain of it, and when I know, as above illustrated, that men were paid in purchasing power at double the rate of wages that men are receiving to-day, and working an eight-hour day, then when I see the quality of the work that went with it, I see not, necessarily, cause and effect, but I see an effect which might have been utterly impossible of attainment under other conditions ; and I also see that when the work is excellent its value is increased, and when you increase the value you again increase the fund out of which wages are to be paid.

Now, these Labour Associations in the fifteenth century were extremely strong, but one of the special features of them—and we see it in some of the lodges that come down to us to-day—was that they inculcated temperance, religion, good, honest work.   The vices of the age had not then reached the workmen.   Whatever they were, they had certainly not reached the working man of those days.   That was the high-water mark for workmen ; and the low-water mark was just about one hundred years ago.   The Civil Wars, the Wars of the Roses, brought about a great change, for as soon as you have war, you are reducing the fund out of which wages are paid.   There might be honour and glory, but you are destroying product, and as surely as you destroy product you destroy the fund out of which wages are paid.   Then, when the wars in France ceased— for in those days we used to have periodical wars with France —the soldiers who returned began to maraud the country ; they never settled down to work again : they became bands of robbers, preying on industries and making the country unsettled.   Then bad government followed, resulting in the great Civil War of Cromwell's time.   All these things, I want to impress upon you, are the factors that govern the case ;

these things reduce the fund out of which wages are paid—
they reduce it so much that, in 1651, only two hundred years
after the golden age for labour—the magistrates attempted
to fix by law a minimum wage for a man equal to 5s. a week
in its purchasing power to-day, and during the first twenty
years of the last century the wages paid were only equal,
in present purchasing power, to 6s. a week for a man. We
wonder how they could live on it—they did not live, they
starved. I have read reports concerning the workpeople
in some of the towns of Lancashire, at the period of one
hundred years ago, and there find there was often not a bed
in many families, in some towns only a bed for five
families, and they had to sleep on straw and anything
they could get.

The three conditions I have mentioned are the only
conditions that can affect labour and increase wages, and
as in the fifteenth century, so in the twentieth century,
Trade Unions are absolutely necessary; but don't let us
mistake their vocation! In the fifteenth century the unions
insisted upon absolutely a high standard of excellence in a
workman before he was admitted. Trade Unions are
powerless to raise wages other than by widening, broaden-
ing, and increasing the only three sources out of which
the fund available for wages can spring. If Trade Unions
could raise wages they could maintain them. The Trade
Unions of the fifteenth century, rich and powerful beyond
anything we have to-day, would have done so, but they were
a broken reed, feeble as water, against the neglect and viola-
tion of the three sources above mentioned, powerless against
the destructive effects of war, bad government, and a waste
of capital. The present improved conditions of labour have
not been brought about by Trade Unions, else how can you
explain the fact that domestic service, which is absolutely
without any union at all, and which numbers more people
than any other single industry, has been able to obtain
larger increases of wages than any of the organized industries?
The reason is this: that in domestic servants you have got
these three conditions fulfilled. Domestic servants, as a
class, have immensely improved in the last fifty years; they
have improved in the quality of the service they have rendered,
and, consequently, there has been an increased demand

for their services ; but, further than that, there has been a large and enormous increase of capital and of wealth in this country : consequently, there has been a larger number of people who have wanted domestic servants. Lastly, there has been a reduced cost for food and other things, and as the cost of keeping and paying for the mere food of a domestic servant has gone down, the fund available for payment of wages to a domestic has increased, and the domestic has had the advantage of it.

If Trade Unions were to force wages up in any industry higher than that industry could pay out of its funds available for wages, that industry would soon cease to exist—there can be no doubt about that. And is not this a better footing to have the question upon than that of mere bargaining between master and man, in which the workman asks for a rise of wages somewhat as if it were a favour, and believes that if he fought hard enough, and struggled long enough, he would get it ? I think that idea is degrading to every one of us ; and look at the false position such a system places the master in. There is no master who is a master literally : he is just as much the servant of the public, and just as much dependent upon the quality of the service he renders to the public, as the men he employs are his servants. The sooner we recognize the economic conditions that govern these matters, the sooner we shall find that we are all on one common platform, that we can work together to increase the fund out of which wages are paid, but no amount of bargaining, no matter of asking as a favour for higher wages, no question of refusing as an act of tyranny, has any effect upon the question whatever. I prefer it so, and I believe every one of you, as I know you do, prefers it to be on that footing. Trade Unions, I think, have recognized these last twenty years this fact, and do recognize it more and more ; they see that their greatest sphere of usefulness is in increasing the power of the three main influences that tend to enlarge the fund available for the payment of wages.

The Trade Unions Parliamentary Committees have striven for good government to protect their members from injustice ; they have agitated in Parliament for improved conditions of labour ; they have agitated for employers' liability; they have agitated for reforms of administration of justice; for the appointment of factory inspectors; for the improvement of patent laws—a most important matter; they have agitated for certificates of competency for engine-drivers, and for various improvements of the Friendly Societies Acts.   These are the lines along which, I venture to say, Trade Unions can best gain their object. Trade Unions are absolutely necessary; there must be combinations of men, but don't let us mistake either what a combination of employers can do for employers or what a combination of employees can do for employees.   If we take the right view of this, we shall see that any attempt at restriction of output is only another way of reducing the fund out of which wages are paid, and can only have one effect, and that is to reduce wages.   I venture to say that Trade Unions might take just one little lesson from their predecessors, the Guilds of the fifteenth century, and whilst determined as these Guilds were in protecting their members in the maintenance of the standard wage, that they should accompany that by an equally strong insistence upon a maximum of efficiency in their members.   By doing so the fund available for wages would be again increased.

Perhaps it might be argued that self-interest is quite strong enough to deal with these matters; that the man who wants his wages increased will take such measures as he thinks right to get them increased, and his own self-interest will keep him right. I have never known the man who did right merely because it was his self-interest to do so.   It is to no one's self-interest to get drunk, or to get locked in prison or to commit any crime.   We don't find self-interest strong enough to keep men out of prison or to make them lead good lives, and the reason is that self-interest must be an enlightened self-interest. If you will add the word " enlightened," and say " enlightened self-interest is a strong factor," I will agree with you; and, therefore, it is extremely necessary, when we are discussing the points of self-interest, to see that we have enlightened self-interest.   And if we do that, we shall find as years roll on that we are improving our conditions.   Not suddenly, perhaps—sudden changes are not very desirable—but gradually improving our conditions; and we may rest assured of this: that anything that tends to violate the three conditions that

I have ventured to call your attention to will, sooner or later, and in my opinion sooner than later, reduce the fund available for wages. We are suffering a little from that now. We have just come through a war,[1] and war, altogether apart from whether necessary or unnecessary, is destructive; and as surely as we go to war, righteous war just as much as un-righteous war, war of self-defence just as much as war of attack, we shall have to pay the penalty. Whenever we go to war, let us know and realize the step we are taking. Don't let us think we can go to war any more than go to law, and not have the bill to pay afterwards. The three conditions I have mentioned are the three conditions we must keep steadily in mind.

[1] The Boer War.

III

X PROBLEMS

LIVERPOOL, *November* 23, 1917.

[In the plain terms of a worker speaking to workers, Lord
Leverhulme addressed the representatives of the Liverpool
Trades and Labour Council on topics to which the Great
War has given a new urgency.]

WE have all of us ideals, and the following of our ideals
brings us into contact with many aspects of life, but we are
conscious that the only part worth living of our lives is following those ideals ; and I know every one of us in this room
realizes that fact, and that we are all anxious to do everything we can to realize our ideals. We recognize, fully and
completely, that present conditions are not right. When
we talk of Labour Unrest, then I say, if Labour were quiet
under present conditions it would be a bad look-out for this
country fifty years from now. The healthiest signs we have
got to-day are Labour Unrest and all the aspirations of Labour
—and I may be allowed to use the word "labour," because I
think I have worked as hard as any one in this room, and
have done so all my life.

As an ideal, we see urged on some hands that the confiscation of all the wealth to-day, the cancellation of all the
war loans and so on, would be a short-cut to a more equal
enjoyment by Labour of all that wealth can place within the
reach of each of us. Believe me, that is a delusion. If all
the money possessed by each of us here in this room to-night
were placed on this table and pooled and divided out equally
to us as we left the room, the only result that such division
could have would be this, that those who had been thrifty
and worked hard, and had saved a little money, would be
asking themselves to-morrow, knowing that the same process

would require to be repeated over and over again, Why should they live laborious days and deny themselves enjoyments and luxuries when this was the only result ? And, equally, those who had received money that they had not worked for would feel that this and future divisions would abolish the necessity of their working to-morrow and their practice of thrift to-morrow, so that both sections of us in this room would go away discouraged from the exercise of our full ability for work and thrift.

There can be no other way in which we can get greater comfort and happiness for each of us than by producing more goods. That is the keynote of all, and there is no reason why in the production of more goods we should not do so on such lines as will ensure a more equal distribution of the result of our labour, because that is what we do want. Well, we are apt to think that unless there is going to be a more equal distribution of wealth, there is something in the distribution at fault, and we are quite right in considering in what way we can deal with the problem and rectify abuses. Now, the only way in which we can increase wages—because that is the first step to advancement—is by increasing production. The only way in which we can soundly increase production is by employing more machinery. The only way in which we can make a demand, a consuming demand, for this increased production is by cheapening the product, otherwise, no matter what the wages are, the price of the product is so high that, as we are feeling now in war-time, the extra wages are of very little increased value. And, finally— and here is where I want to lay great emphasis—you cannot increase demand greatly, notwithstanding that you have raised wages, notwithstanding that you have cheapened the product, unless you have elevated and increased the wants of the people. You have to increase wants. You can only raise their wants by giving them more leisure. I believe that reduced hours of labour and more leisure for a proper outlook on life are as essential to an increased consumption of articles that can be produced as is a cheaper cost.

Now, we will imagine, for instance, that away in the Congo we talked of greatly increasing the production of, say calico. I have been through the Congo ; the native there has few or no wants. A piece of calico the size of a towel makes a full dress suit for the husband ; another piece the same size makes the full dress suit for the wife, and the children need no dress at all. Now, if we were to produce any quantity of calico, as soon as these simple wants were satisfied there would be no demand for the remainder. We would have to start in the Congo by first of all inspiring in men and women a love for more clothing—blouses, skirts, trousers, coats, and so on; and for houses that required table-cloths, sheets, curtains to the windows and all the rest that makes for comfort, and then we would find that with these new wants came such a demand that however much calico we could produce in reason, it would be all required and all be sold. Now, I believe as firmly that the workmen of this country—I have endeavoured to practise it in my own limited way—have as much right to an artistic home, a comfortable home in a garden, with all the amenities of life, as their employer. Now, I say that that is the first essential to the enjoyment of this leisure. What use is it talking to a workman about a nice artistic home with pictures or engravings on the wall, taste shown in everything, when he only comes home to sleep and to rest for the next day, leaves early, and his only time at home is an occasional Sunday ? You won't raise a taste for an artistic home under these conditions. Art flourishes only where there is leisure and all that art means, in increased demand for books and everything that makes for comfort, and, believe me, reduced hours of labour are essential for increased demand.

Now, if we have such a production that wages can be raised, a greater volume of articles produced, costing less money, and increased demand to sell them off as fast as they are produced, that is an ideal and it is worth striving for. We can only achieve this with machinery. There must be no antipathy to enlarged output by machinery, and, believe me, wages increases then would become quite a matter of secondary importance. You know that there is automatic machinery in which the wages of the operator, however high, are a very small part of the cost of production. The great part of cost of production is interest, depreciation, repairs and renewals, and the cost of the central power station for running the machinery. Now, we have these machines, and if we are wanting a greater increased output we are simultaneously wanting more ships and we are wanting more machinery for the ships; and how can we greatly in the next few years duplicate our machinery for factories? All our men will be wanted on shipbuilding, house-building, and repairing of the devastation of war; but we can run our existing machinery double time, and it does not cost us anything more for interest, for depreciation; only a little more for raising steam in the boiler, a little more for oil, a little more for repairs, and we get all that increased production, with just those trifling expenses. Labour working six hours a day, as has been proved over and over again, can produce in six hours the maximum it is capable of in monotonous occupations. We shall, therefore, be able to pay for six hours' work at least the same rate of pay as we pay for eight, because labour will be capable of as much work in six as in eight hours. The machinery will produce more, and out of this combined effort, the human element working two shifts of six hours each, the mechanical element working twelve hours, or more, we shall have two funds created, one for reducing the price of the article and another for increasing the wages on the top of the reduction of hours.

These results are certain, provided we have the demand for the goods when they are produced. Apart from export trade, which we shall be bound to cultivate, and which is an enormous trade and one which we can make still greater, we must have the increased demand from the home trade, and that I believe the six-hour day, by giving us more leisure, will ensure to us. Now, why do I talk so positively about this? Do you know that we find all over the world that wages are the highest where, *per capita* of the people, the greatest amount of machinery is in existence and in employment—the wages are the highest there—and as a result the wealth invested in machinery in these countries has always an ever-increasing force compelling it to still further similar investment in that direction because it pays. In the United States the capital per head in machinery is the highest of anywhere in the world, and wages there, as we know, before the war and maybe even to-day, were the highest also. In China and India the amount invested in machinery is the lowest of any countries in the world, and the wages are the lowest. And, curiously enough, it was India, where the

cotton is grown, where the men in the cotton-mill get pence
a day—eightpence and ninepence a day—and where native
engineers when I was last in that part of the world were only
getting ninepence a day—it was India, that grows the cotton,
and where labour works long hours for these low wages, that
within this very year, only a few months ago, appealed to
the British Parliament to be protected—from whom ? From
people working longer hours and being paid less money ?
No ; but from Lancashire, where the workers receive more
shillings per day than the Hindoo receives pence, and where
they work less hours, and where they have to pay freight
on the cotton from India to Lancashire, make it into goods,
and again pay freight to send it back to India. So that
higher wages go with machinery and lower cost of production,
and lower wages and less machinery go with higher cost of
production and strangle any attempt to raise and uplift labour,
as we see in India.

Now, I think we can claim at this point that all employers
must abandon their idea that low wages mean cheap production and high profits, and I think the workman must equally
abandon his idea that limited production means more labour
employed and at higher wages. They are both wrong, and
two wrongs do not make one right.

Now then, can we arrive at a prospect of some direction
in which we can work to lift the workers ? We want more
capital invested in labour-saving machinery to give us
increased output, higher wages, shorter hours, reduced cost
of production, and we want to eliminate the element of fatigue
by the reduced hours of labour as well.

Now, there is a theory, and you know the theory as well
as I, that labour produces all wealth. It was started by
Adam Smith, and is worshipped by many to-day. If that
were true, don't you think that the Manchester Ship Canal,
and other undertakings that I could mention, would be veritable gold mines ? In the making of a canal the cost is practically all labour—digging—it is practically all labour, and yet
we know that the original shareholders in the Manchester Ship
Canal, instead of making wealth, have never seen a penny
return on their capital in the last thirty years. If the theory
were true, not only would the Manchester Ship Canal be a
veritable gold mine, but the mere act of loading a ship,

which is the greatest labour, I imagine, in connection with shipping, and the mere act of shovelling the coal on the boiler fires, which is, perhaps, in many parts of the world a still more laborious piece of work, ought to ensure a profit on the voyage, but we know they do not. We know that profits are not made because of the labour of loading the ship or merely putting coal upon the fire. The men who can make money are few. They are less than one per thousand who can make money at all other than by the receipt of wages for employment. They are less than one in a hundred thousand in the very high undertakings, and in the highest undertakings of all they are fewer than one in a million who can organize large undertakings to make money. This good old world has only produced one Ford, one Rockefeller, one Carnegie. I know these men are held up to odium because it is the fashion Let us see if they deserve it. Don't you think it was just as sensible of the old man who blew the organ to say that he produced the music as to say that it is labour that is the source of all wealth ? I like this illustration, because it is quite obvious that if the man ceases blowing the organ there will be no music ; but it is equally true that he may blow the organ as much and as laboriously as he likes, and that unless there is some one there to play and touch the notes with discrimination and skill there would be no music. And when we search how these fortunes have been made by the three men I mention and by all others, what do we find ? We find that fortunes have only been made by producing goods cheaper and selling them cheaper, and by increasing the rate of wages paid to the worker and reducing the hours of labour.

Take Ford's cars, for example. Ford started as a young man, and I think his first occupation was on a farm—his father's farm. Then he got an idea that he could make a motor that would do a lot of the farm work ; just the idea that he is putting into practice now, thirty years later. He had thought on the farm, and he wondered if he could not make a motor to do a lot of the work on the farm, and he told his wife he would go to Detroit and see some of the machines ; so he went. He was a fairly successful farmer and he was making a fair sum of money. He closed down his farm, and he and his wife moved to Detroit, and he. engaged him-

self as engineer on the night shift to look after the Edison
plant for lighting the city of Detroit, at something like a
quarter of what he had been making as a farmer.   He was
quite content ; he had made up his mind he would get to
the bottom, as far as he could, of the electrical problem ;
he found he would have to acquire a knowledge of electricity
to make his motor, and he worked on and on, and you know
the result.   Now, does any man begrudge Ford his five
millions sterling a year that he is making ?   Fancy, that is
£100,000 every week.   Does any one begrudge it ?   If any
do I could imagine them saying to themselves—they would
say it truthfully, I know—something like this : " It is true
Ford serves the public with a cheap car and, for the price,
a good car.   It is true Ford serves his workers in his
factories well, because he pays them double wages ; in fact,
he starts a boy fresh from school at a pound a day.   But,
but, but, Mr. Ford, you make too much money ; you give
the public cheap cars, you pay double wages in your factories, but you make too much money for yourself ; that
is our objection."   Well, what would happen ?   Would
other men be encouraged to emulate Ford's example if, after
all this toil of leaving the farm, working for a quarter of the
wage while he mastered the subject, all this laborious work,
he and his wife (a loyal and true wife, as every successful
man has always had) working together—if the result of all
that was to be told that he was making too much money ?
You might as well tell some of his men who were drawing
double pay that they were making too much money.   The result
would be the race of Fords would die out, cars would cost
the public more money, the wages to workmen would fall to
the lowest Trade Union rate—that is, to half the rate Ford
is paying—and the future Fords would have hard work to
make bare interest on their capital.   It would operate
against all three.

Now, let us imagine a scene at Ford's works.   We will
imagine that his 20,000 or so operatives—I am not sure how
many he has, but we will say 20,000, it may be 40,000—
read in the paper, the local paper, that Ford has made
five million pounds sterling, twenty-five million dollars,
the year before, and they have discussed that fact the night
before, and they have come to the conclusion that Mr. Ford

is making far too much and have decided that they will go and interview him, because "labour creates all wealth," say they, "Adam Smith told us so, and, therefore, this money is not Ford's; we make that money, we ought to have it." They go and wait on Ford and they lay their case before him fairly, perfectly fairly. Now we will imagine his reply. Now, Ford I imagine would say this: " Now, my men, I don't want you to make a penny of this money for me. Go right away and make it for some other motor man, one of my competitors, who cannot make money for himself, who is perhaps losing money. Leave me right away and go and engage with that man; he will give you nearly all the profit; he is losing money now or making none. You can make your own terms with him. He will give you at least nine-tenths of the profit, because if he got a tenth he would be content. You go and make him five millions and he will give you nine-tenths, or he will give you even more—perhaps he will give you nineteen-twentieths, perhaps even ninety-nine one-hundredths of it; but you can make your own terms with him. You will get splendid terms from him; in fact, you can dictate your own terms. As to myself, those men who will be sacked from this motor man who is not making money, why, I will engage them; it will be merely a change over. You men who are making my money will go and make it for these other people; their workmen will come and work for me and I will pay them double wages as I am paying you, and I will see if I cannot make as much money without you as with you. I will put them in my factory and they can work for me. I do not want discontented men. I will engage these men, who will be perfectly contented as soon as they come to me, because they will be drawing the double amount of what they are drawing to-day; I will pay them double wages. But I want you to be sure," he would say to them with a twinkle in his eye, " when you engage with your new masters you stipulate to receive the double wages whether he makes the profit or not—the same as I am paying you now; do not trust yourselves or him to make profits for you; insist on having the double wages I am paying you, and then, of course, make your claim for the profits in addition, because you say labour creates all wealth. Now, if you draw double wages from my competitors, it will make it easier for me; for, paying only half my rate of wages, their cars are already dearer in price than my cars, and I shall have the trade more and more in my hands. This, of course, you will be able to do easily because you create the wealth ; out of that wealth you will draw the double wages, and you will draw the ninety-nine hundredths of the five millions you will be making for your new master, because you say you create it ; you make it ; it is yours, and take it and do not delay for a moment ; start right away, and I will swop employees with these men."

Now, let us see, dismissing that picture—I will just leave it at that to you—what is the wealth that the masters make in the United Kingdom per head of the population and per head of the workers, because it is estimated that only three out of every five are workers. In the three I am including the wife—you will understand I am including all workers. Now, it is only pre-war income tax figures I can take, but on the top of pre-war figures we can add excess profits. If you will take the returns for 1913–14 you will find the income from land and houses, which I am quite willing to throw in because we are going to divide every-thing else ; let us divide all there is. We cannot divide salaries, because we shall always want some one to do the work, and they will always want salaries paid in proportion to their appointments ; and the salaries paid to Govern-ment officials and Corporation officials also will have to be paid. I am merely speaking of the profits in business which we are proposing to confiscate ; and see how they work out. Now, the income from business, worked out per head of the population, is 4½d. per head per day of the people, and the income from land and rents of houses is 2¼d.; total, 6¾d. The excess profits tax divides out at 3d. per head per day of the people—that is what the Government take.[1] The Govern-ment began by taking 50 per cent., then 60 per cent., and now it is 80 per cent. There is another 2¼d. per head per day of the people that the maker of the excess profits is per-mitted to retain—total, 1s. per head per day ; now, dividing this over three out of every five, it is 1s. 8d. per head per day of the workers. Now, that would not eliminate poverty if we took it all, if we did not pay a penny to employers in England ; if we could get employers for nothing, that would

[1] In 1917.

not remove poverty. In fact, since this war began, covered by the period when these excess profits have been made, wages, as you know, have risen from 2s. 6d. in some industries for unskilled labour to 5s. in others for skilled, and in a few, 10s. per day per head ; so that in dealing with this money in the sense of confiscation, or any name we like to give it, all the wealth of the country would not relieve poverty or lift the workman much. No scheme of confiscation or redistribution can do that. The only way is the one we mentioned —increased production. This will enable wages to be advanced as I mentioned, hours of labour to be reduced, cost of production to be reduced.

A policy of "ca' canny" defeats its own end. We can see in the building trade the policy of "ca' canny" can only increase the cost of building ; and whether the houses are built by the municipality or the State, or by private enterprise, wages will have to be paid in the building, material will have to be bought—and material is largely labour cost right up to the point of being on the job where the material is going to be used—and the amount of rent, either directly as rent or in rates and taxes, will be in proportion to the cost. If "ca' canny" is in the coal mine, then coals will be dearer. If "ca' canny" is in the factory, then boots, shoes, and clothes will be dearer. No "ca' canny" policy can produce wealth ; it is a robber of wealth and of fellow-workmen and reduces and lowers the level of every workman. It is not an uplifting force, it is a suffocating poison ; but it has its devoted disciples in many industries throughout the land, mistaken—don't think I am judging these men hardly ; I believe they are as honest in their efforts by "ca' canny" to help the working man as I am honest in my conviction that "ca' canny" is a blunder. All I want to endeavour to show is that the policy is wrong, not that the men's motives are wrong. If it was mere laziness, I would say it was a wrong motive ; if it was to save their own backs, I would say it was the wrong motive ; but when it is a belief that "ca' canny" will employ more labour, will make wages go up, and so on, then I say it is a mistaken policy.

Now, it may be thought that we could get relief from Acts of Parliament. A noted man said—I think it was Herbert Spencer—that he had inquired into thirty-two Acts

of Parliament that had been passed to benefit the worker
and to relieve poverty, and twenty-nine out of the thirty-two
Acts had produced exactly the opposite effect. Why, the
so-called People's Budget, for which I voted with great
pride and pleasure in 1909—and I am not ashamed of
having voted for it, because that Budget was sound so far
as its taxation of wealth, its graduated income tax, its
graduated death duties, and so on, went, all of which
taxation ought to make us look gently on such clauses of the
Bill as have failed to achieve the objects intended—now,
that Budget has discouraged undoubtedly the building of
houses for workmen throughout the land; it has discouraged
the landowner in developing his land; it has not made
prospective builders eager to buy building land; in fact, for
the scarcity of houses the workman is suffering from to-day
the Budget of 1909 is partly responsible—not entirely responsible, but it has tended in that direction.

When the war first broke out, we thought employment
was going to be very bad for the workman, and the Prince
of Wales's Fund was started and five million pounds subscribed
at once to assist the unemployed. People were urged not
to discontinue any work that employed labour, but to start
fresh work that employed labour—anything that employed
labour. We all expected that the war was going to make
employment very bad. The war has proved us all to be
very bad prophets. Wages have risen, employment is to-
day in the position that there are two jobs for one man. Now,
why is this? Why should a Bill called the People's Budget
have failed to achieve the building of more houses, that part
of the Bill which was intended to so achieve, and war has
produced employment when it was expected that it would
reduce employment? Why is that? Well, in the first
place, the one has discouraged and, in the second place, not
only in munition factories but in all other occupations, the
war has been a stimulus and an invigorator to both men and
women. From patriotism, from every motive, we have all
worked harder in munition factories and in our ordinary
occupations since the war. This has increased the wages
fund, this harder work, greater employment, men, women,
and girls employed who were formerly not employed. This
has produced more wealth, not Acts of Parliament. It is

our determination to win this war, the high, patriotic effort we have put forth, that has increased wages. Of course, there has always been the destruction of property in the form of shells, cartridges, guns, battleships, and ordinary ships, and so on—that is going on all the time—but the big factor has been the stimulus to us to work harder, the opportunity to work harder. With equal stimulus to work and without war, the demand for munitions would have been a demand for more boots and shoes, more houses; but it has been the stimulus behind us to do our bit, and without that stimulus we would have been in chaos in this country, as many nations are. No; we cannot increase our wealth by Acts of Parliament, because we cannot see far enough what are the cross-currents and under-currents that we have to face; but we can organize our time and our work so that all shall have equal opportunities and none be overworked, and on that line, with increased machinery and a six-hour working day, higher wages, reduced cost and improved leisure, increased consumption can be attained.

Now, who are the employers to-day? You think I am one—great delusion. You think Ford is one—another delusion. We are not employers; the people who employ myself, and every one who works in the business I am connected with, are the consumers. Let consumers buy other products made by other firms, and where are we all at our works? Let the consumer of motor-cars buy other cars than Ford's, where are Ford and his workmen? The employer of Ford is the consumer. The employer of every master in the country to-day is the consumer, and 90 per cent. of the consuming power of products made by machinery in this country are the workmen themselves. Therefore, 90 per cent. of those that employ me are working men and their families. I want you to bear that fact in mind. My employer is the consumer, and 90 per cent. of the consumers of my article are working men, and so with all the articles made in cotton-mills, boot and shoe factories, and so on. Well, now, don't you see that the real employer is the consumer, and not the capitalist—the so-called employer? Don't you see that the consumer's own best interests must be to see that whoever is the nominal employer he shall be stimulated to bring out the best that is in him? If you choose a chairman for any of your committees, you choose one who has your confidence, and who you consider is likely to give the best results. If the capitalist is a Rockefeller, the consumer practically employs Rockefeller on the understanding, and only on that condition, that he shall bore oil wells, build oil refineries, lay pipe-lines, and build tank steamers to transport the oil, and that he does this work cheaper than any other capitalist can do it. That is the only basis on which Rockefeller was ever employed. If the capitalist is a Ford, the consumer says to him that he can make motor-cars on condition that he build them better in quality for the price, and lower in price than any other capitalist can build motor-cars for. But that is the consumer's bargain with the capitalist. There is not one of your wives going into a shop to-day who must not be satisfied as to the quality and the price before she purchases an article, and she will buy where—I know you have all got good wives—she gets you the best value for your money always. But the workman, how does he approach the capitalist ? Labour says to Rockefeller or to Ford that they will only work for him on condition that he pays them the maximum wages ; Labour in effect says, "We are going to reverse this process on which we buy our goods, and we are going to apply our rights as consumers in buying goods on that principle ; but when we come to sell our labour we are going to sell it to the capitalist who gives us the most wages for our work, and we claim our right to both these privileges." And Labour can honestly claim the right when spending wages to get the best value obtainable, and when seeking employment to get the highest wages for producing articles bought at lowest prices. It is as if Labour said to Capital : "You are only our agent or broker. If you can give us the highest price for what we have to sell and sell to us the products of our own labour at the lowest price we can obtain the same for anywhere, then we will pay you a commission for so doing ; but if you lose money over the transaction you go down and out and into the bankruptcy court and you must not look to us for help."

And what is this brokerage or commission ? I have shown you that the profits on trade would be 4½d. per head per day of the population : the excess profits retained by the capitalist 2¼d. per head per day ; total, 6¾d. (for the purpose of this illustration we are now dealing only with profits in trade, therefore I am leaving out, at the moment, land and houses) or about 11d. per head per day of the workers. But from this we ought to deduct certain items that do not appear in the income tax returns. The bankrupt employers—employers who reach the bankrupcy court—their losses are not deducted from the income tax of the successful; there is no deduction for interest on capital. Income tax returns include interest on capital. Whether our factories and machinery are State-owned, or whether they are owned by private enterprise, we shall always have to employ capital to pay out wages to the workman whilst building our new factories and new machinery. If we had obtained all our existing factories and machinery by confiscation, in twenty years we should have just as much capital raised to pay workmen to build new machines and build new factories. We could not get away from capital and interest. Now, if you deduct interest on capital and losses of bankrupt capitalists, you will find that the net profits do not work out at more than 3d. per head per day of the workers ; in other words, a most modest commission on the basis of the bargain, which is the highest wages for the workman and the cheapest selling price for the product of his labour. Abolish private enterprise, and you would not save the 11d., you would not save the 3d. For competitive capital you would get State Civil Service; every Government department, it is essential, must be run on what we call the lines of red tape. Wages would become nominal, not real, and whatever wages were nominally, they would always represent reduced purchasing power to the consumer.

Now, all I want us to ask ourselves is this ; whether working on lines such as we have hitherto worked consistently has not increased wages solidly and substantially ? Every opportunity for advancing wages—and, believe me, the prosperity of a country depends as much upon high wages as upon any other element that can make a country prosperous—must be taken advantage of. But this means more machinery, and it has to mean, also, cheaper production. Wage increases must not be sham increases; they must be real increases, with increased purchasing power, as well as increases in amount. I want us to realize that, and then on sound lines we can, I believe, realize all our ideals.

But behind all this is the ambition that I rejoice at of the workers to control their own industries. I think that is one of the healthy signs of the day, and I can see it and feel it in the very fibre of my being, because, as I mentioned at the beginning, I began in a modest way and I have worked up, and I can realize your desire, the desire of every healthy man in the kingdom to raise himself and become pilot of his destiny. How can this be done ? The greatest attraction to me of the six-hour working day is the education of the young. I ask myself, Why should not the sons of the workman have the same education as the sons of the master ? They must have, if they are going to control industries in the next generation. Do not think for a moment that control can be achieved on any other lines ; but, with better education and with the same ambition to control industries, who can say nay to Labour ? But merely a desire to sit on a Board of Directors, without a knowledge of all that that position means, can help neither the workman, nor the industry, nor the country ; there must be a period of training.

But if we get this training we shall be a better nation physically, we shall be better in brain power ; and note well this, and I say it without any hesitation : sons and daughters who are trained with hand and eye as well as brain will make better educated men and women than the mere University bookworm—infinitely better ; and, you may depend upon it, the control of industries in the future will go to those who can work them to the greatest advantage. The circumstance that gave Ford his to-day's position was that he was thirty years ahead of anybody else when he was working on a farm, and he set himself to realize his ideals, and gave up the farm to obtain a bigger field for his energies. The circumstance that made Rockefeller was that he had the conviction that single oil wells and single oil refineries, putting oil into casks and sending it on the train at high freights, was stupid, and he bought a number of oil wells ; he combined big oil refineries, he laid pipe-lines from the refineries to the coast, he put tankers on the ocean to bring the oil to England, and he brought the price of oil down from 1s. to 4d. a gallon, and in that process he made a fortune. Now, that is the way it will be for your sons, for my son, if they have to make money, if they have to raise themselves, have more comforts for themselves and their children than we have had. We can only achieve these ideals by increased production.

Education, the consideration of which I have left to the finish as the crown of all, is the keynote of the situation, and I would rejoice, as every one of you would, that the sons of the workman should be the equal in education of the sons of the master. But behind the master, behind the hollow title of employer, is the consumer, and the fact that 90 per cent. of the consumers are the working men and women, that the whole mass of the consumers of the country will be elevated and raised, the whole of our industries in which they are employed will be elevated and raised, and we shall march forward a proud nation to further achievements undreamt of even to-day ; and Great Britain, at home and overseas, the largest Empire the world has ever seen, will contain a people whose joyous lives are spent in such happy surroundings as are unknown to us in this room to-night, where life will lengthen and joy will deepen, and where happiness will be assured for all.

IV

ZERO YIELDS OF CAPITAL AND LABOUR

LONDON, *February* 13, 1918.

[The Royal Society of Arts devoted a considerable proportion of
its proceedings during the winter of 1917–18 to problems of
Reconstruction, and in pursuance of this design Lord Leverhulme was invited to read a paper at one of its meetings.
He gave cogent reasons against what is called " Conscription
of Wealth," and set up instead an ideal of comradeship in
the mutual relations of Capital and Labour. Mr. Robert
Tootill, M.P. for Bolton, who presided on this occasion, and
spoke with the authority of a Labour leader of many years'
experience, echoed Lord Leverhulme's call for a real comradeship of Capital and Labour, and the late Sir Swire Smith,
M.P., said the paper opened up a vision of what the country
could do even in the present difficult circumstances. Here
follows the paper :]

WE are living in strenuous times, and are making sacrifices
of life and treasure on a scale that we are apt to believe is
greater than our forefathers, even in their most difficult wars,
were ever called upon to endure. But this is obviously only
true of dimensions. It is not true of proportions to scale
with the resources or wealth of the present British Empire,
as compared with her former war periods ; nor is it true in
relation to the resources Science has placed at our disposal
for our more rapid recuperation from the effects of this war,
by the exploitation and development of the nascent wealth
that Nature, with lavish hand, has stored up for us within
our boundaries. To realize the natural strength of the
British Empire, let us think of it in the words of the poet :—

As some tall cliff that lifts its awful form,
Swells from the vale, and midway leaves the storm,
Though round its breast the rolling clouds are spread,
Eternal sunshine settles on its head.

Our most cruel and deplorable loss in this war is the awfu
sacrifice of human life. The irreparable, disastrous consequences to civilization and the progress of the world that
must result from so many of the flower of our manhood having
been taken from us it would be impossible to overstate. This
welter of blood has made the world one huge sob and stifled
moan. There is not one single family group in the whole
of the peoples of the belligerent nations that has not to mourn
some loved dear ones lost or returned mutilated and torn,
blinded or crippled—the wreck and shadow of their former
selves. No loving care nor patient toil can restore these or
make good to us their loss.

But for the rest the loss can, on certain well-known and
proved established lines, be fully recovered, and most speedily
of all the money wastage. Many worthy good souls are worrying themselves and the nation as to the undoubted load and
enormous burden of national war indebtedness we shall
have to carry when this war is over, and are worrying still
more as to our ability as a nation to repay these debts. In
their alarm, and suffering from an attack of nerves and cold
feet, some openly advocate unblushing repudiation of our
war debts, and call the same by some such specious name as
Conscription of Wealth. And in their haste to propound
this " cure all " for our ills they cannot even wait until we have
won a decisive victory on the battlefield and obtained the
unconditional surrender of our enemies, but must needs weaken
the national credit by advocating this impossible policy
even whilst the necessity for further borrowing still continues.

There are seven pillars of national and individual prosperity
and happiness. These are :—

Justice.	Science.
Truth.	Art.
Labour.	Leisure.
Capital.	

The unit of the Empire, as of all democracies, is the home
and fireside, and along the lines defined by the seven pillars
of prosperity, individual nations and the home units have
progressed from slavery to fullest liberty. What were the
conditions of life in Great Britain in, say, Oliver Cromwell's
time, when we experienced our greatest advance towards

our present ideal form of Government—a Constitutional Monarchy? London, even then, was the largest, the richest, and most populous city in the then-known world. Yet it was indescribably dirty, overcrowded, insanitary, badly lighted and worse drained, and neither health nor life was safe from attacks from disease, pestilence, or robbers and footpads. The then death-rate was over 49 per thousand in ordinary years, and much higher in years of special visitations of plague. In Oliver Cromwell's time, close to the then London, were 25 square miles of swamps, which to-day are absorbed within the boundaries of the Metropolitan area, drained dry and made healthy and built over. In wet weather the streets and roads were impassable, a quagmire of mud, in which chariots, wagons, and carts sank to their axles. Robbers, footpads, and high-waymen made it dangerous to travel in daylight, and impossible at night to do so without being under convoy of a guard. In the United Kingdom at that time there were 34 counties without any, even the most primitive, form of printing press. The master flogged his apprentice, and the husband flogged his wife. The stocks, the ducking-stool, and the whipping-post were national institutions in the most public centres of every town and village. Even a century later we were very little improved in our social life.

What has changed all this to conditions such as exist in the United Kingdom to-day? It has been the discoveries of science and the inventions of mechanics. About the close of the eighteenth century, Watt, Arkwright, Hargreaves, Crompton, Cartwright, and others invented various of our most important " key " mechanical utilities, such as the steam-engine, the spinning-jenny, the mule, the power-loom, the carding-machine, and scores of others. It is said that as a result of these inventions, twenty-five men and fifty women and boys can produce to-day as much cotton goods as could have been produced by the hand labour of all the men, women and boys that were engaged in the cotton industry in Lanca-shire in Oliver Cromwell's time.

And what is the condition of London to-day? The popula-tion is more than a scorefold what it was then, and it has be-come the cleanest, most healthy and sanitary, the best lighted and the best drained city, as it is also the largest city in the world. And all traces of special visitations of plague or pestilence have ceased, and the death-rate is the lowest of any of the largest cities of the world, being no more than 15 per thousand.

And corresponding progress has been made in every city, town, and village in the country, and in the social betterment of the lives of the people, and the British Empire has become the greatest Empire in the world, not by repudiation of the Napoleonic War debts, not by Acts of Parliament, but by the steady maintenance of the beneficent support of the seven pillars of prosperity, and by the labour of employer-capitalist and employee-workman. These, as inventors, manufacturers, merchants, explorers, and shipowners, have often been handicapped in the march of progress in competition with other nations by stupid Acts of Parliament and ignorant statesmen ; but in rectifying this handicap of progress let us be careful that we do not commit still greater errors of government in the future. Our best hope for the future is that the whole of the difficulties to be overcome, and of our social betterment to be achieved, shall be fully considered in all their bearings, shall be fully discussed and understood, before we enter upon the putting into effect of immature and ill-considered new and experimental policies. We must approach the consideration of the problem with minds free from thoughts founded on prejudice, hatred, or temper—free from taint of selfishness or injustice. Above all we must dismiss from our minds and souls any idea of what, for want of a better name, we call " class against class " antagonism. In all countries, throughout all ages, there have been numerous divisions of peoples into so-called " classes," but this good old world, large as it is, has never been big enough to contain more than a division into two great classes—the class that is doing its duty and the class that fails to do its duty. These two great divisions are wide enough and deep enough to include the whole human race, and all other distinctions are purely artificial. But we have got into a slipshod way of thinking of mankind as existing in " classes," and nothing, in the present temper of the world, is more unjust or dangerous. Peer and peasant, employer-capitalist and employee-workman, have fought side by side in the trenches, and laid down their lives side by side on the battlefield in this great war, and as comrades in this war they honour and respect each other as never was possible

before, and we have all learned that in about equal pro-
portional numbers there are included in all the artificial
" class " divisions the industrious and the idle, the intelligent
and the stupid, the brave and the cowards, the honest and
the cheat, the truthful and the liar, the virtuous and the
vicious, the temperate and the drunkard, the strong and the
weak, the healthy and the sickly, the thrifty and the spend-
thrift, and that so long as these opposites of characteristics
exist there will always be the rich and the poor. Let us
uproot this habit of thinking of individuals according to
certain artificial so-called " classes." Nothing is more unjust
and nothing could be more dangerous.

Long before this war began we were experiencing the influence
in politics of a new Parliamentary Party, whose leaders scorned
the beaten tracks of old-school politicians, and who called
themselves the Labour Party.   The employee-workmen,
through their Trade Unions, have also become more active,
and have rightly and properly—so long as they respect the
just rights and liberties of others—organized to improve their
position. The betterment of the condition of the employee-
workers is declared, and I believe truly so, their sole objective
and goal, but so far as my knowledge goes the employee-workers
have not yet unanimously decided upon what might be the
best methods for them to adopt to realize betterment and
advancement. In short, whilst their aims, ideals and ambitions are clear and definite, their proposed methods for realization are most indefinite and hazy.

When the dissatisfied colonists in North America won,
under the leadership of General Washington, their severance
from Great Britain nearly a century and a half ago, they
declared as their ideals—and in these the whole English-
speaking world agrees to-day—that all men were endowed
by God with certain inalienable rights, amongst which were
life, liberty, and the pursuit of happiness. Washington and
his co-founders of the United States believed and trusted
that, if all men were given an equal opportunity, and if the
citizens of a country could frame their own laws and levy
their own taxes, the inequalities in wealth that existed in the
Mother Country could never exist in the United States. This
was the view held in 1776, and the founders of the United
States were convinced that the rich and wealthy were rich

and wealthy in consequence of some unfairness in the laws of the United Kingdom. But after nearly a century and a half, in spite of the Declaration of Independence as to equality, in spite of universal manhood suffrage, there are greater inequalities of wealth in the United States to-day than there are or ever were in the United Kingdom, and it is clear that neither Acts of Congress nor the Constitution of the United States have been able to make all men equal in wealth any more than in health, weight or stature, brains or muscle, piety or morals, character or worth. But this inequality of wealth, although infinitely greater in 1916 than in 1776 (at which time, as often is the case to-day, it was thought to be the cause of all the poverty of the poor), has been proved to have relieved the extremes of poverty and wretchedness, and to have greatly raised the average of comfort and betterment, and to have resulted also in actually a better distribution and more plentiful supply of wealth amongst the employee-workmen. The United States has produced millionaires in greater number and of greater individual wealth than ever the United Kingdom produced, and yet the employee-workman in that country receives the highest rate of wages known in the world. In 1776 it was believed that in the United Kingdom the Government had somehow interfered with some great principle underlying all social well-being, and that in the United States, under the Constitution adopted in the Declaration of Independence, wealth would be more equally distributed and poverty would cease. But the result has clearly proved that, so long as some men are stronger, or more healthy, or more intelligent, or more industrious, or more virtuous, or more self-denying, or more thrifty than others, there will be inequalities of wealth, that the employer-capitalist was not responsible for these, nor was the employee-workman to blame, and that, if either changed places with the other by Act of Parliament, that change over would constitute no remedy for acknowledged inequalities nor be a stimulus to social betterment for all. Employer-capitalists in acquiring their wealth by hard work of brain and energy of body have benefited not only themselves and their families, but have, even if unwittingly, conduced to the betterment of the employee-workman and also to the progress of the whole of the industries of the United Kingdom.

And now I venture to assert, notwithstanding that all the above circumstances are inevitable and normal and natural, that still no employer-capitalist with a true feeling of brotherhood can be quite happy in the fullest sense in the enjoyment of wealth (the product of his own hard work, intelligence, self-denial and thrift, every penny earned without committing injury to any man, and the acquisition of which has resulted in enormous benefits to his employee-workmen) without feeling a sense of dissatisfaction with present industrial conditions and a strong desire to improve them so that the employee-workman may be raised to a much higher level in social well-being.

But this ideal cannot be achieved by an Act of Parliament for the conscription or confiscation of wealth.

The men and women of British stock who crossed the Atlantic and founded the United States did not state in their Declaration of Independence that all wealth must be confiscated to the State. What they did declare was that man was endowed by God with certain inalienable rights of life, liberty, and the pursuit of happiness. Do these rights mean that Government should conscript or confiscate the fruits of the industry of one man who had led a thrifty, wholesome, industrious life in order that Government might use the same for the benefit of men who had lived lives of exactly the opposite type? That was certainly not what the citizens of 1776 ever intended. What was meant was that every citizen had the fullest liberty to live his own life and to make his own livelihood in his own way so long as that was honest and true, and that he was entitled to the full enjoyment of the product of his labour, whether of muscle or brain, and for the pursuit of his own happiness—also within honest and true limits—in his own way.

And what was meant by liberty? One of the best definitions of liberty has been stated by—if I remember correctly—a French Convention in the following words: "The liberty of one citizen ceases only where it encroaches on the liberty of another citizen." And as to the pursuit of happiness, John Bright has given us one of the best definitions of happiness in the following words: "Happiness consists in a congenial occupation with a sense of progress." In addition, this Declaration of Independence laid down the axiom that Governments were instituted to preserve these rights to the people and that the people themselves were the source of all the power that Governments possessed. The force that has created the United States has not been Congress, nor was the British Empire built up by Parliament. There would have been no United States and no British Empire without the labour and toil and sweat of the people of the two nations. Governments create no wealth as such, and possess no money but what they receive from the taxation of the people. All Governments are paupers, and only exist in free democratic nations by the consent of the governed. All Governments being paupers, they have only two means for raising money—by taxation and by borrowing. In times of war or for great public undertakings such as waterworks, or municipal developments, such as docks, etc., borrowing has had to be resorted to in the past years as in the present years, and will have to be resorted to in the years to come when this war is over. The power and ability of a Government to borrow and the rate of interest to be paid depend entirely on the credit of the Government concerned, and on the assured belief of the lenders in the borrower's ability and good faith for the due payment of interest and the repayment of the debt. Our British Imperial and Colonial Governments and our municipalities have hitherto enjoyed the power to borrow all their requirements at the world's lowest rate of interest. This advantageous position is entirely due to public confidence in the honour, honesty, and good faith of our Governments. If we once shake confidence in either our ability or our willingness to repay our indebtedness, then our credit, our power to borrow, is either seriously damaged or may be hopelessly destroyed. And with this destruction of credit and confidence would come equally the ruin of our industries, and unemployment and hunger would be our chronic condition. If we, as British citizens, cannot realize these truths, then we are in greater peril than if the Prussians had landed on our shores and were marching through an undefended country on defenceless cities and towns. The British Empire might recover in time from defeat in war, but the British Empire never could recover from its own default to repay its war loan indebtedness. The credit and confidence enjoyed by the British Empire is the one and only foundation on which stand, foursquare to all attempts to overthrow them, the prosperity and stability of British industries and ability to provide full employment at full wages for the British workman. The repudiation of debt, or the so-called conscription of wealth, would be an assassin blow at the very heart of the British Empire. But even if it were a practical and honest policy, there would be two questions still that would arise and require to be answered —how could such conscription be accomplished, and what would it yield ? The suggestion is that we conscript sufficient of the wealth of the country on some graduated scale to enable us to repay at least £4,000,000,000 of war loan indebtedness. How would our Government collect this £4,000,000,000 and convert the same into cash ?—for it is obviously only as cash that wealth could be used for the repayment of war loans. At present this wealth exists in the form of furniture, pictures, china, works of art, houses, land, workshops, factories, machinery, ships, horses, cattle, sheep, and the thousands of other forms of wealth, including debentures, shares, mortgages in public railways, industrial companies, municipal and dock loans, Government War Loans, deposits in banks and building societies. And this wealth includes the savings of the frugal father for his widow and children equally with those of the millionaire. We know the depreciation that takes place when trustees are forced to sell some portions of an estate in order to pay death duties. But only some £30,000,000 a year are paid in death duties, and much of this we know has been received by the trustees in hard cash from banks and insurance companies. It is only a cautious estimate to assume that not more than two-thirds had to be raised by forced sales—say £20,000,000 a year. But to realize even this modest sum each year has tended to depress the market value of securities. So that it is clear that no market could be found for £4,000,000,000 of conscripted wealth at what I may call *par* value, and as practically every one with wealth would be sellers and there would be almost no British buyers, it is only reasonable to say that the £4,000,000,000 of conscripted wealth would not realize in cash as much as £400,000,000. It would be almost valueless and unsaleable, and therefore not available for the purpose intended of repaying war loans. The confiscation of wealth would carry the country icebound below zero. Left to fructify in the pockets of its owners, we should have its yield in income tax and death duties to the State, and in employment for employee-workmen not only of the then existing factories and workshops, but still more important, of extensions and additions thereto, and for the provision of capital for working and building the same to be obtained on the credit of the security available. But conscript 10 per cent. or 20 per cent. of the wealth of the country, and not only would the conscripted portion be unsaleable, but the balance would be depreciated as security for credit to finance our industries to the lowest level of the conscripted portion. This would be like cutting out the roots of the tree to anticipate the next year's crop of fruit.

But this cutting out of roots is certainly not what wise men would do. They would guard the roots, fertilize them, prune the dead roots, support the limbs and branches, protect from frost the blossoms, and finally reap an abundant harvest —growing larger in quantity and better in quality each year of patient care and cultivation. Therefore, our course for repayment of war loan lies in cultivating our industries and fertilizing them—root-pruning by death duties and collecting the harvest by means of income tax graduated so that all citizens with incomes of £80 a year and over contribute according to their means. In no other way can we realize so large a cash income to so speedily and quickly pay off our war loans, maintain British shipping and industries, find ever-increasing employment for British labour, and maintain British credit and the pre-eminent present position of our world-wide British Empire.

It may be asked how steeply can income tax and death duties be graduated; the answer can only be, that if our needs require them, the only limit can be that point at which they yield the largest return to the State with the least injury to our industries. If income tax at 5s. in the pound and death duties at 20 per cent. yield the largest return to the State with least injury to our industries, and if income tax at 10s. in the pound and death duties at 50 per cent. would yield actually less to the State and would also threaten our industries with ruin, then the lower figure without risk to our industries would be proved to be the only' practicable rate. In other words, at the higher rates you would be killing the tree that bears the golden fruit.

Every farmer and gardener knows that such a hint from Nature as to the limits of cropping as a decreased yield would, if disregarded, sour the land and the plants, with ruinous results. The reduced yield from the higher rate would also prove that trade and commerce, house-building, shipbuilding, and our manufactures were suffering from being denuded of capital by excessive taxation, and that unemployment would soon be stalking, with famine and sickness, through our land. And we should find that a just, fair, and reasonable scale of graduated taxation would not only yield the largest amount of cash to the State, but that the remainder, left to fructify in the pockets of its producers, would act as a stimulus to the production of ever larger and larger taxable incomes, and to the employment of an ever-increasing number of employee-workmen by employer-capitalists, to the expansion of British shipping, trade, and commerce, and to the maintenance of our present pre-eminent position amongst the nations of the world. So graduated income tax has its zero-point.

> All that Freedom's highest aims can reach
> Is but to lay proportion'd loads on each.
> Hence, should one Order disproportion'd grow,
> Its double weight must ruin all below.

No! there is only this one way available to enable us to repay our war loans, to re-establish our mercantile marine, our trade, commerce and manufactures after this welter of a World War, and that is to stimulate the production of wealth and to tax the annual income to the limits of utmost yield, but always so that the producers of wealth are encouraged, stimulated, and left with the necessary means for the production of more wealth. This production of increased wealth will demand and necessitate that every adult man and woman of all classes shall, up to the limit of their abilities and capacities, work hard and strenuously for its production. But human strength has its economic zero-point also. If in the production of this wealth either the employer-capitalist or the employee-workman is overfatigued by working a longer number of hours than the limitations demanded by health and strength, then the result can only be disastrous to the production of wealth. But if all adults, of both sexes and of all classes, peer and peasant, employer-capitalist and employee-workman, work each a reasonable number of hours per day, then, without overfatigue of any, we can produce a wealth of products sufficient for our own home markets and wants and for overseas exportation far in excess of anything we have ever previously accomplished. The exact number of hours that will produce overstrain and fatigue, with resulting lower production, will obviously vary with the nature of the occupation and with the conditions under which the work is performed. On the farm, for instance, and on board ships, surrounded by green fields or green ocean and fresh air, the hours worked may presumably be longer than would be possible in factories, mines, workshops, foundries, offices, or stores, where perfect ventilation is never quite attainable and where the occupation is more or less monotonous. But in every kind of work and employment there must be some limit to human strength and endurance, and experience has taught us that between eight hours a day as a maximum and six hours a day as a minimum, the safety-point may most probably be found to rest. These hours of daily toil are what may be called the income-making period—the remaining hours are available not only for sleep, eating, recreation, and leisure, but also for education and public service and all the refinements of life. St. Paul has told us that he " laboured with his hands that he might be chargeable to no man," and we know that he was by trade a tentmaker. The hours of labour for tentmakers were, I am told, at that time from 5 a.m. to 11 a.m., that is, six hours per day, and the remaining hours St. Paul devoted to his life's work— service to his fellow-man. Let us organize our time better At present all our time is devoted to gathering income for maintenance, as if we were so many cows and sheep, all of whose time we know is devoted to the work of maintenance. Our factories, foundries, mines, workshops, stores, offices, and farms, throughout the British Empire, are full of men or women with ideals and ideas for utilities and inventions, and who, in addition to their capacity for the work of income-earning for maintenance and support of themselves and families, are capable of, and keen for, work of enormous social value to their fellows and the Empire. What a wealth of inventive genius and ideas have we there running actually to waste through our bad organization of their hours of work

and their subjection to overstrain and fatigue in the performance of the daily round of routine duties for income-producing!
Under our present system, each day has to be fully occupied
beyond the fatigue-limit in work of income-earning for maintenance, with the result that our machinery is underworked
and our workers are overwrought, giving us less wealth, produced at greater cost than need be the case. Thought and
ideas for new inventions and processes require intelligence,
alertness, and leisure—all impossible under conditions of over-
fatigue during long hours of laborious toil. Then see how the
wage and salary fund is impoverished. We can only work our
machinery and mechanical utilities longer hours by working
human beings fewer hours. We have already exceeded the
limit of human endurance from schoolage to dotage. But we
can reorganize our factories so that by working a number of
change shifts of employee-workers six hours each shift we
can run our machinery twelve, eighteen, or twenty-four hours
each working day. The wages paid at present for longer
hours would require to be paid for the fewer hours, and in
order to do this the total cost of production, which is partly
interest, depreciation and repairs for machinery, all of which
would be little if at all increased by the additional hours
worked, would on an increase of from 50 to 200 per cent. in the
output give us lower costs out of which wages could be increased
and selling price to customers reduced. And, believe me, it
is impossible to lay too strong emphasis on this crux of the
whole proposal, which is the one and only basis which would
make reduced hours and higher wages possible, namely,
reduced final costs and lower selling prices for the consumer,
with more wages to the worker and fewer hours of toil. The
employer-capitalist could, of course, work with a lower percentage of profit and yet realize on his increased production
a larger income to meet the demands made upon him for
higher graduation in rates of income tax.

But in addition to a better organization of time in our
industries, we require to still further advance in the direction
of a more logical basis in the relationship between the employer-capitalist and the employee-worker. There must be
some consideration given to the division between these two
of the profit resulting from the joint labour of both. The
wages system alone is not sufficient, but the wages system

must of necessity remain the basis for the employee-worker. It is a system that has stood the test of time ; it is convenient ; it is logical and practicable. Under the wages system the employee-worker practically says to the employer-capitalist : " I cannot undertake to bear any of the risks of this business. I must receive a weekly or monthly income, regularly, upon which I can absolutely rely and depend for my household expenses : therefore, if I engage with you we must mutually first agree on a sum which you shall pay me as wages or salary in exchange for my services. If after paying this sum of money to myself and also after your payment of all other expenses of the business there is a profit remaining, I agree that profit shall be yours. If there is a loss, you must make good that loss yourself alone, even to the extent of bringing ruin and disaster upon yourself and your family. I cannot share with you your losses, and I agree to make no claim upon you to share in your profits." This, I repeat, is the logic of the present wages system, and it is perfectly sound and just in its basis and principles.

The admission to Co-Partnership is not a right that the employee-worker can of necessity claim. It is obvious that there must always be the right with each of us to choose our partners by mutual consent if the true Co-Partnership spirit is to be maintained. The employer-capitalist can choose his partners, and does choose them, from those who can give him the best help and can best strengthen his business, either by contribution of capital or assistance in the management of the business ; and in making this selection of partners every care and effort is directed to avoiding entering into a partnership that may prove undesirable in practice. The happiest and most successful relationships in business life have been realized under the partnership system, and it is equally true that occasionally, from various causes unforeseen at the time, private partnerships have proved disastrous, both from the point of view of prosperity of the business and the happiness of the partners. But the intention has always been the same, namely, to help and strengthen the business and to share the responsibility and risks of the business between the partners. I am confident that, viewed in this light and not as a profit-sharing device, which in my opinion would be wrong, a Co-Partnership relationship with the employee-worker would be an added source of strength to any business to which it could be applied, and increase the prosperity and happiness of both the employer-capitalist and the employee-worker. The principles of Co-Partnership between these two would be as logical and as sound and practical a business arrangement as between any body of partners, and one that might be just as wisely entered upon.

Under the operation of our modern industrial developments, capital is generally raised from a body of shareholders, in the form of ordinary shares. These ordinary shareholders divide amongst themselves the total remaining profits of the business after payment of all claims for salaries, wages, interest, and other prior charges. The ordinary shareholders of a company are practically the partners who control the destinies of the company by their vote, but it is very rare for any of them to be engaged actively in the business as employee-workers. It can never be a source of strength to the business that the whole of the surplus profits, after paying a reasonable and proper rate of interest, should be entirely devoted to dividends to ordinary shareholders. I am convinced that the best interests of the ordinary shareholders would be better served, both in regard to the rate per cent. of their dividends and the security of their capital, if the surplus profits could be divided, under some scheme of Co-Partnership, between the employee-workers and the ordinary shareholders of the business.

It is not in the best interests of the success of any business nor the progress and development of British industries as a whole that the entire surplus profits should take only one channel, and that channel a direction away from those most interested in the business, and upon whom must depend the continued success of the business. It would not be right to view this question of Co-Partnership from any benevolent point of view. There can be no philanthropy in business. But the cultivation of a spirit of Co-Partnership and of a keen interest in the firm in which the employee-workers are engaged is not philanthropy but sound policy. The whole of the goodwill of any business, which goodwill is often of greater value than the actual bricks and mortar, plant and machinery, depends on mutual confidence. The employer-capitalist and the ordinary shareholders to-day view the employee-worker solely as a liability. Employees are not liabilities, but the most valuable asset of any business.

An objection often raised to Profit-Sharing, and I think rightly raised, is that there can be no Loss-Sharing. Under the system of Co-Partnership, Loss-Sharing can be linked up with participation in profits. After all, what are the losses of capital for the employer-capitalist? His losses of capital are that certain shares that he holds, by purchase or original application and payment, have become valueless because they have ceased to have earning capacity. One has often heard of shares in some company that has entirely lost its earning capacity being only fit to make into spills to light cigarettes with—their capital value has become *nil*. Equally, the Co-Partnership certificates issued under a scheme of Co-Partnership to the employee-workers would be only so many specimens of printing and absolutely valueless, if the power of the business to earn profits had ceased, notwithstanding all the efforts of employer-capitalist and employee-co-partner.

It is quite obvious that under a system of Co-Partnership, whereby an employee-worker receives each year an allotment of Co-Partnership certificates, in proportion to the amount of his salary or wages and the length and value of his services, and which Co-Partnership certificates are, during the Co-Partner's connection with the firm, entitled to dividends in proportion to the dividends paid to the ordinary shareholders, the Co-Partner would see the number of Co-Partnership certificates growing each year. He would experience the fact and realize the cause why dividends in some years were higher than others, and why in some years, from unavoidable causes, dividends might fail to be earned or paid. He would realize the direct connection between profits and all the problems that the Management have to solve in a business, and in this way the employer-capitalist would have secured a partner whose brain would be at work as well as his hands in effecting economies and avoiding waste in the business, and in making suggestions for the improvement of processes and improvement in the organization of the time of himself and comrades, so that profits might be increased and higher dividends be paid.

I claim that the employer-capitalist is not reasonable if he expects, in exchange for wages, any more than the per-

21

formance of the services which he has contracted for. But in addition to services that could be rendered on a wages system, there is that constant thought and care outside business hours equally as during business hours for the good of the business which the employer-capitalist himself does constantly manifest, or his capital would be in danger and his profits might never materialize.

Under a system of Co-Partnership the employer-capitalist would have all his employee-workers who had been with him a certain number of years as Co-Partners, now realizing that their interest in the business equally with that of the employer-capitalist ran along the lines of increased output and of cheaper costs of production, and there would come what I may call "team-work," which in the Army is, as you know, called *esprit de corps*, and which results in a spirit of comradeship in overcoming all obstacles, and which spirit is specially manifested in times of difficulty and danger.

And now let me say a word on the value of a better organization of time devoted to income-earning in its effect on education of brain, body, and mind, and the power it would give the State for training citizens for military service. In all change shifts the shift workers who one week worked in the morning would the next week work in the afternoon, so that there would be for every one the morning or afternoon free each week alternately From fourteen to eighteen years of age there would be for boys and girls two hours morning or afternoon each day required by the State to be devoted to higher grade education and physical training. From eighteen to twenty-four the State would require that these two hours be devoted each day to technical and higher education, such as is provided to-day only in our Universities, and for physical training, and from twenty-four to thirty years of age the State would require that these two hours each day be devoted to military training and preparation for National Service. After thirty years of age the citizen would have completed his period of compulsory attendance under State Regulations, and would be fully equipped by education and training for all the duties of citizenship, and might reasonably be trusted to make, as did St. Paul, but in his own way, his own voluntary contribution to social advancement and betterment.

But whilst my endeavours have been to record the views

I hold, and hold very strongly and sincerely—that Governments of themselves cannot create wealth, and that the power of Governments to confiscate or tax wealth is strictly limited within the range of such rates as will produce the largest cash income for the service of the State without danger of check or hindrance to the production of wealth and opportunities for employment—and whilst I have endeavoured to show that we shall require the labour of all adults of both sexes and of all classes, from peer to peasant, to repay our war indebtedness and to provide products for home consumption and for exportation overseas ; and have, further, endeavoured to show that work also has its limitations of profitable production, and that to overstrain employee-worker or employer-capitalist is not to produce the best results from either, I hold equally strongly that Governments can render such services of the State as will furnish opportunities and facilities, encouragement and stimulus for the creation of wealth by the citizens who have entrusted the State with powers of government. The State should and could make concentrated and well-considered efforts to provide every facility for honourable enterprise and honest industry. Our mercantile marine must be protected at sea and provided with ample harbour and dock facilities in the ports of the Empire. Shipowners, manufacturers, and merchants must be encouraged and helped by an efficient Consular and Foreign Office service so that our ships may sail over every sea and our flag be flying in every port. The State can improve our banking system by encouraging and stimulating our bankers to render increased credit facilities for the manufactures, trade, commerce, and mercantile marine of the Empire. In our Crown Colonies our Government can construct roads and bridges, build railways, open up new and rich territories of virgin forests, fertile soils, and rich minerals to developers, planters, and traders on terms that would encourage and justify private enterprise in the investment therein of capital. The State can improve the sanitation and healthiness of our villages, towns, and cities at home and in the Colonies, and so not only lengthen human life but reduce the toll on productiveness caused by ill-health. Government can protect child-life and see to its welfare, and can improve our educational system so that we get the utmost in the finished product for the many millions we spend upon education, so that the child of the employee-workman can have the opportunity of becoming as well educated as the child of the employer-capitalist. Government can remove all incidence of taxation and rating, local or Imperial, from improvements on land such as houses and buildings of all kinds and from machinery, and provide that all such taxation and rating shall, in future, be provided from local and Imperial income tax source and on site values. All obstacles, in short, for the development of the resources of the Empire at home and overseas must be removed and every facility, encouragement, and security be given to stimulate the production of wealth, otherwise what right or title have we members of the British race at home and overseas in the possession and enjoyment of a world-wide Empire on which it is our boast that the sun never sets ? If our Government is not sufficiently far-sighted or so wise as to foster facility and encourage great industries capable of producing enormous surplus wealth by the enterprise of her citizens within this world-wide Empire, which would not only find employment for all but provide a basis for taxation of incomes that would enable us to repay our war debts, then the British Empire is suffering from the palsy of old age, and we shall soon cease to exist as a World-Power. Empires rise and fall as they are well and wisely or badly and stupidly governed. Under wise government they become rich and powerful, their ships sail over every sea and carry the national flag into every port ; their Colonies cover whole continents ; their peoples are happy and contented, well housed and well fed, and not overwrought to maintain themselves in comfort in homes where, with wife and children, life lengthens and joy deepens ; their rulers and statesmen are honoured and respected by surrounding nations, who can view without bitter feelings of wrong to themselves a world-wide Empire wisely governed with every facility and opportunity, and where welcome is given to all right-minded citizens of all right-minded nations. Nothing can be better for the progress of civilization and the well-being of the whole world than such a government of such an Empire. And it must with equal truth be stated that there can be no more pitiable sight in the whole world than such an Empire held and possessed by a nation that has neither the vision nor the intelligence to wisely develop or justly govern. " Where there is no vision, the people perish."

V
DAY-WORK OR PIECE-WORK—WHICH?

PORT SUNLIGHT, *January* 13, 1904.
[Submitting theory to the test of practice, and keeping the two
in close mutual touch, Lord Leverhulme, in this paper, which
was read before the Port Sunlight Mutual Improvement
Society, communicates his thoughts on the resources, possibilities, and consequences of Socialism and Individualism.]

IT has always appeared to me that the question of Socialism
or Individualism resolves itself very largely into a question
of Day-work or Piece-work. We require to produce commodities for mutual consumption, and Socialism would appear
to be a question of whether these can best be produced by a
system of Day-work, and Individualism to be a question as
to whether it would be more profitable to the community as
a whole to produce them by what may be called Piece-work.
We all agree that evils exist in the great extremes of wealth
and poverty in the world to-day, but when Socialists propose
remodelling society on a very high plane of intelligence, they
do so without first endeavouring to find out what are the lines
on which society can best make progress. If Socialists would
content themselves with pointing out the goal which we are
all aiming for, namely, the greatest possible amount of social
well-being and comforts for all, and then if they would join
in concentrated efforts to the discovery of what direction
ought to be taken to ensure these benefits in accordance with
the principles underlying all society, I venture to think that
we should make greater progress in the future than we have
done in the past. Sometimes we can see, say in Switzerland,
a beautiful mountain whose summit is clothed in perpetual
sunshine, but if in attempting to reach that summit we disregard all the precipices and ravines that have to be crossed—
make no effort, in fact, to discover the only road that can

safely be taken—in all probability we shall never arrive at the summit.

So with a higher civilization we cannot disregard the constitution of society, nor can we disregard the very slow rate of progress we can make in the future, as we have made in the past, during the countless ages mankind has taken to develop to our present not very high state of civilization.

Now, before we come to the question of its distribution, let us consider what are the elements that enter into the creation of wealth. The principal elements are three : Labour, Capital, and the Employer. It is not a question of Labour and Capital alone ; the Employer is as essential as the other two, and the Employer may be a private individual, or a Board of Directors, or a Government or State. Labour is wisely represented when organized by Trade Unions working on their own individual lines. Now, in the production of commodities the payment of wages to Labour is under the present conditions the first fixed charge which has to be met. The next fixed charge is the payment of interest on capital. The payment to the employer comes last and is not fixed : it is variable. In fact, all that the employer can get for his labour is the leavings after Capital and Labour have received what has been agreed upon.

Sometimes there will be a loss ; that is to say, not only no leavings at all, but an actual loss, in which case, after the employer has been exhausted, Capital may share in that loss. But under the present conditions not only is it a fact, but it is a law of the land, that the payment of wages must not suffer loss under any circumstances whatever. Therefore, under the present state of society, payment for labour is a first charge on production, equivalent to a first mortgage or a debenture bond.

Now, what do the Socialists propose ? They propose to nationalize all the implements of production and to make the State the owners of all capital, and therefore the one and only employer. But, by nationalizing the implements of production they will not have abolished capital : they will have altered the nominal ownership of capital, but they cannot abolish capital, and for this reason—that capital is essential to production. Now, let us suppose it was considered that as a first step towards nationalizing the implements of production, mills, tools, machinery, and railways should all be confiscated. I don't suppose that this is seriously proposed by Socialists or by any one, but we will imagine for the moment that confiscation would be carried out and private ownership cease. That would not abolish capital. Railways would wear out, mills would become old-fashioned as to machinery, and would want renewing ; and how would this wearing out be remedied and machinery be renewed ? It could only be by the employment of labour to build fresh mills, to make fresh railways, and for this work labour would have to be paid. To provide payment for labour, loans would have to be raised on the credit of the nation as a whole and interest on them would have to be paid. Therefore, although temporarily, for a few years only, by the confiscation of all the means of production, the private ownership of the capital of the country might cease, this would not be permanent. From the very moment the nation took over the implements of production there would be decay going on, renewal would become necessary, and capital would again assume its position and would again be a charge on the undertaking.

Neither would Socialists have abolished the employer, whose salary is at present a variable quantity. The employer would still be required just as much in the nationalized industries as when enterprises were carried on by private individuals, but under the new conditions the employer—that is, the State—would be represented by managers, who would have to be paid fixed salaries. Then we should have effected this change only : that whereas formerly the employer took for remuneration only the leavings (if any) of Capital and Labour, the employer would now take, as manager representing the State, a fixed salary to be added to the cost of production.

We have still got Labour to consider. Now, we have seen that under the present system Labour receives wages whether production is successful or not, and we have also seen that under the altered system proposed by Socialists, managers, representing the employer, would require to receive fixed salaries, whether production was successful or not, and would rank equal with Labour as a prior charge on production. When accounts came to be balanced in these nationalized industries, they could only be balanced by advancing the prices of the articles produced, at the expense of Labour, because Labour is always the greatest consumer. The consumption of products being mainly by Labour, it would result that the wages of Labour would cease to be real and become nominal; that although wages had apparently not been reduced, their purchasing power had been reduced, and that therefore Labour would actually be receiving less in real wages, although the same in nominal wages : consequently, under the system proposed by the Socialists, Labour would have changed places with the employer.

Now, with regard to the employer. Management, to be really effective, must have a direct interest in the results of its labour. There is a peculiar quality, call it temperament or what you will, about management, that is produced under the present system by which management is the employer and is compelled to take risks, inculcating that alertness and activity of mind, that perfect mingling of caution with audacity, that grasp of possibilities, opportunities, and contingencies, which makes all the difference between success and failure. Therefore, Management, being paid a fixed salary, would not be brought into that state of tension, that bending of the bow, as it may be called, which is so essential to good management. Not being controlled by Labour, because Management would still have to control Labour; not being controlled by Capital, because Capital would still be a fixed charge on the business, but being controlled perhaps by some elective body, taking the form probably of a council appointed or elected for the purpose, the whole temperament of Management would be changed, and I venture to say it is not in that way that we can improve the position of Labour. The bow would be unbent and useless.

The profits earned by employers are not great, if averaged over the whole of the industries of the country. If we include those undertakings which, instead of making profits, are making losses, and take the average over all, I venture to say that employers as a body would make more money as managers under a system of fixed salaries than under the present system, and that the production of goods would not be cheaper but dearer under the system advocated by Socialists than under our present system, imperfect as that system is and wasteful in many directions.

Well, now, we want to consider another point in the case :

I refer to the statement that Labour is the source of all wealth. I think it was Adam Smith who first uttered this fallacy. It is a great fallacy, and one that has done the greatest possible harm. But supposing it were the truth, then I think we should agree that if Labour created all wealth, Labour must possess all wealth, and any attempt to take any portion of wealth from Labour was an act of robbery. Well, let us see what the income tax returns will teach us as to what is the wealth that is created, and what it would amount to if equally divided amongst our 42,000,000 of population. Now, the first portion of the wealth we have in this country is the land, and the income received from the land. To the extent that land is a monopoly it ought to be the property of the people ; to the extent that land yields an income to private enterprise, there would be no gain in it becoming the property of the people. But all monopolies in every free country ought to be retained in the hands of the people. Now, the income tax returns for 1902 show that the income in the United Kingdom received from land and occupation of land was about £70,000,000 sterling. Let us try and divide this income amongst all the inhabitants of the United Kingdom on the grounds that all good government must have for its basis the greatest good of the greatest number, and consequently that we have the right to nationalize the land without paying a penny piece of compensation to the owners of it ; in other words, to confiscate it—and we shall have one penny per head per day to give to every man, woman, and child in the United Kingdom. That would not be any great wealth. That will not lift us very far. None of us will be very wealthy on one penny per head per day more than we have got now Now, let us come to the houses that are on the land, and let us suppose we confiscate these also, whoever they belong to : the widow, the orphan, the building society, or the millionaire. Let us consider how we should stand if we confiscated all the houses on the grounds that if Labour created all wealth— and houses are a very substantial form of wealth—then the income from the houses so created ought to belong to Labour. Let us confiscate the income from all houses and try if that will help us. The income, as shown by the income tax returns for 1902, received from houses in the United Kingdom is £184,000,000 a year. Let us divide this amongst the inhabitants. It comes to 3d. per head per day when divided amongst our 42,000,000 inhabitants. That won't make us very rich either. We have got a penny from the land and threepence from the houses. Well, this is not very encouraging, and as we go through the remaining income tax returns, I am afraid the next item is less so, since when we come to consider the income that is received from the National Debt, we cannot confiscate that, because later on we are likely to want to borrow money to rebuild our works, and if a nation does not pay its debts it would not be able to borrow money at all. Therefore we cannot, for the sake of our own future, confiscate the interest paid on our National Debt, and we must pass by that source of income. We come next to the salaries of Corporation officials and civil servants. It is a very large item. We see from the income tax returns civil servants and Corporation officials receive amongst them £79,000,000 a year. We cannot confiscate that, because we shall want servants, and we cannot get a man unless we pay him a salary. It is quite clear that, if the workman in the factory is to have his wages, we cannot confiscate the salary of the man in the office, and therefore we cannot confiscate this income, but must pass it over. We now come to foreign investments, which bring in about £65,000,000 a year. We have no power to confiscate this income, because if we attempted to do so, such income would never reach this country. Suppose that the holder of investments in American railways found that the minute the dividends from the same reached this country they were confiscated, the holder would write abroad stopping this flow of dividends to this country and would invest the same abroad, and our country would be the poorer and not the richer, owing to the fact that these dividends would never reach us. Therefore, we could not confiscate them.

Now we come to something at last we can confiscate. We can confiscate all the profits of all employers, and of course our grounds for doing so would be that if Labour creates all wealth, Labour ought to possess all wealth. I quite agree with that view, if it is a fact that Labour creates all wealth. Let us see what would be the wealth we had to divide. It appears from the income tax returns to be

£361,000,000 a year, but this also includes the salaries of all salaried servants receiving £160 a year and over, and also the earnings of all professional men. We can certainly confiscate that, and we ought to confiscate it, if Labour has created it all. Still, we should want managers, lawyers, doctors, etc., and supposing the number of managers, lawyers, doctors, etc., would not be less, nor the salaries paid less than we now pay Government and Corporation officials, then we should have, after deducting for salaries, etc., as above, £282,000,000 that we can divide. If we divide £282,000,000 sterling, we get 4½d. each per day more for every man, woman, and child in the United Kingdom. There is no great wealth there.

Add this to the 4d. a day from land and houses, and we get 8½d. each per day for every man, woman, and child to receive. Therefore, we find that if Labour does create all wealth, as it is said to do, when you come to divide the product there is nothing to divide. It has vanished. It has been a shadow, this 8½d. per day. Now compare that with the benefits that Labour has received during the last thirty years through the operation of natural forces and of its Trade Unions. The Board of Trade Returns show that Labour has received 20 per cent. increase in wages, accompanied by 25 per cent. decrease in the cost of commodities, which means that for every 20s. paid in wages thirty years ago there is now 24s. paid, and the commodities that cost 20s. thirty years ago now cost 15s., a solid gain of 9s. per week for Labour.

So we find that by peaceful processes, working in the ordinary way, Labour has secured benefits solid and substantial, more surely and probably more lasting than it would have secured by confiscating the capital of the country and all the implements and means of production.

Therefore, we may adduce from this that Labour has received the whole of what Labour has created, and that any attempt to enrich any one section of the community at the expense of any other section is not likely to be successful. We can only improve the well-being of the whole nation by improving the well-being of every section of the community.

Now let us see whether, if Socialism could only have brought us to this point, profit-sharing could not have brought us any nearer to our ideal. I think you will agree with me that the profits we should have had to divide would have been

£347,000,000, and against that we should have had to deduct
the salaries of salaried servants and the earnings of lawyers,
doctors, and other professional men, and in addition interest
on capital. The result would probably be that we should
not have so much as 2d. per day for each man, woman, and
child in the United Kingdom. Therefore, I think you will
agree with me that those Trade Unionists who have always
looked on profit-sharing schemes with distrust, and who prefer
to depend upon their own organizations for increases of social
comforts and increases of wages, have acted wisely. They
are more likely to get increases of social well-being and comforts in that way than by any profit-sharing scheme. We
now ask ourselves how it is that, if it be true that Labour
creates all wealth, Labour is not better off than a paltry
8½d. per head per day if all wealth that we could confiscate
were divided equally. The answer to that is that Labour
does not create all wealth ; the wealth is created jointly by
Labour, Capital, and Employer, and of those three Labour
is in the most favoured position, but none of the three
can create wealth without the other. My objection to
Socialism is that it would attempt to benefit some at the expense of others. You cannot increase the wealth of any one
class by lessening the wealth of any other class, as stated
already. You cannot increase the wealth of the community
or of any class permanently by any method of confiscation
or redistribution whatsoever.

Then what means have we for increasing wealth ? First
of all, let us consider the three elements that go to the production of wealth : Capital, Labour, and Employer. In the
first place, what is capital ? I have endeavoured to show
that we cannot get rid of capital under any system whatsoever
—that capital would exist under Socialism exactly as it does
to-day. Mere abstract capital is owned by widows, by orphans,
by minors who are living on the money left them by their
parents ; by retired people who are living on the savings of
their life, and by frugal people who have saved ; by co-oper-
ators ; in short, by everybody who has saved money by
spending less than their income. Those are the only abstract
capitalists we have to-day. How did capital come into existence ? Suppose we just imagine our earliest ancestors.
They would be living on roots, on fruits, and on seeds that

they gathered. They would have no cultivation ; they would also be living on the game they were able to trap or capture, or the fish they could catch. Let us suppose a community of one hundred of these ancestors of ours living in this way. Every member would have to gather in for himself or herself ; they would have to be constantly at work, just as the birds are, to feed themselves and their young. And now we will imagine that ten men and women of this hundred offer to make spades for the purpose of digging up the roots, another ten offer to make bows and arrows, and another ten offer to build boats to go fishing, and another ten offer to build huts for protection from the weather, on condition that in exchange for the providing of these implements of production by these forty people they should receive clothing, food, and shelter as consideration from the sixty who would be using the implements of production they were going to create.

Now, the sixty remaining would find that with the aid of these implements of production they could obtain for the whole community of one hundred more food and clothing and better shelter, with less labour to themselves, than they could under the old conditions have provided for themselves alone. That is to say, that with the aid of these implements of production they were able to make enough for themselves and the other forty who created these implements, and that notwithstanding that they now produced for the whole community, they had more leisure and less exhaustion for themselves than when they worked without implements for themselves alone. And being better off under this system, they would adopt it permanently, and in future their community would be conducted on these lines. This would then be the first introduction of capital—the implements of production—and some members of the tribe would permanently devote their lives to the creation of these implements of production, and receive their return in food, shelter, and clothing. Therefore, you see that capital and the implements of production must have had a very long history. And what do we find to-day ? We find that the production of wealth and its distribution is most general and most equal where capital is most plentiful. I want you to think of that—that the production of wealth and its even distribution is most general where capital is most plentiful.

In the United Kingdom the productive capital per head is two and a half times that of the Continent of Europe, and the income per head averages double. In the United Kingdom the capital per head is five times that of Italy, Spain, and Portugal, and the income per head is increased in proportion again. In England, capital is twelve times that of China and India, and the income per head is thirteen times that of China and India. In England, labour itself is only 4 per cent. of the productive power, and capital is 96 per cent. of the productive power as represented by machinery—that is, labour represents 4 per cent. of the productive power, and machinery—in other words, capital—represents 96 per cent. In Spain, labour is 24 per cent; in Italy, labour is 34 per cent.; and in Portugal, labour is 42 per cent.; and consequently we find that the productive power of four Englishmen is equal to that of twenty-four Spaniards, thirty-four Italians, and forty-two Portuguese, and it is probably equal to sixty Chinamen and Hindoos, and that wages are proportionately higher in England. Therefore, this extra earning power, just as in the case of our first forefathers, when it was provided by bow and arrow, has been provided by capital. When this fact is grasped, I venture to say that workmen will cease to rail against Capital, and will view Capital as the friend of Labour.

The next element in the productive wealth is the employer; and by the word " employer " I refer to the owner in private enterprises and to the Board of Directors in public companies, or whatever constitutes the supreme responsibility. As we have pointed out, at present the employer takes all the risks of the undertaking, guarantees labour its wages, capital its interest, and is willing to accept for himself the leavings. By adopting such a system we bring reward or loss into direct contact with the employer. If you turned a man under such conditions as these on to a bleak rock, you would have adopted the surest way of making it into a garden. The successful employer can only be a man working on piece-work.

Now we come to the consideration of the position of labour in the production of wealth. There are two classes of labour: there is labour engaged on productive work, and there is labour not engaged on productive work. I think it was Adam Smith who said that a man got rich in proportion to the number of servants he employed in productive work, and he got poor in proportion to the number of servants in his domestic employ. However, we do not need to go into the question of domestic servants, but I would like to point out two facts in connection with domestic servants. First, they are a wonderful force, working in the direction of the more even distribution of wealth. Second, although entirely unorganized, their wages have advanced at a greater rate than any other class of labour.

Well, now, in considering labour and the position of labour, we come to this great fact—that a large production and a large consumption go together with high wages. You could not have low production and low consumption and high wages, but you can have large production and large consumption and high wages. Wages may be real or nominal. I will give you an illustration of wages that were only nominal. At the time of the outbreak of the rebellion in the United States under Washington, when our American Colonies made war against us, Washington had to issue paper money. He issued the first in March 1778, and then one dollar cash could be exchanged for $1.75 of paper money. Twelve months after, one dollar cash would exchange for $19.00 paper money. Twelve months after that again one dollar cash would exchange for $40.00 of paper money, and three years later, in May 1781, one dollar cash would exchange for $500.00 paper money, and after that it got up to the point when one dollar cash would exchange for $1,000.00 of paper money. Now we find at that period there was a minister at Brookfield, Mass., named the Rev. W. Appleton. In 1776, before the war, his deacons had a meeting and voted the Rev. W. Appleton a salary of 400 dollars a year, paid in cash. In December 1778 the deacons had to meet and voted the Rev. W. Appleton 1,100 dollars more in paper, in addition to his 400 dollars which, no doubt, they were then paying him also in paper money. Twelve months after they had to give him 3,600 more dollars in paper money, and in 1780, 12,000 dollars of paper money was required to keep the gentleman going. Therefore, in the last year he would receive 12,000 dollars in paper as the equal of 400 dollars in cash, but this was poor pay to the Rev. Mr. Appleton, because he would be enjoying fewer advantages on 40,000 dollars a year paid in paper in

1780 than on 400 dollars paid in cash in 1776. We must distinguish between nominal wages and real wages, and the only way you can distinguish between them is the amount of social well-being and comforts that the wages will purchase. Those wages are most real that will purchase the largest amount of social well-being and comforts. Consequently, to improve the position of labour, you must increase the product of labour, make it more abundant and cheaper, and then you can also improve wages and also make them more real. Wages can only be paid out of the product of labour, and it is for this very reason that employers make their first and most serious mistake, because, knowing that wages are paid out of the product of labour, they consider that the lower the wages they pay the bigger the margin of profit that will be left to themselves. On the other hand, labour, knowing that wages are paid out of the product of labour, considers that restriction of output will tend to keep wages at a higher level. These are two most remarkable fallacies, because both employer and employee overlook the important fact of the power of increased consumption. Labour overlooks the question of the difference between real and nominal wages, and the manufacturer overlooks the enormous power of a large consumptive demand. Every increase of wages gives increased power of consumption to labour, and consequently a larger production for the manufacturer, with a cheaper cost of production and the possibility of increasing profits. A larger volume of production, by lowering prices, gives increased consumption of the products out of which labour is paid. This pressure is constantly operating in the direction of the raising of wages and the lowering of prices at the same time that it operates in the direction of making wages more real and less nominal. Therefore, all combines on the part of employers to raise prices and all strikes on the part of labour to raise wages defeat their own ends by lessening the consumption and by lessening the production. Don't let us forget, and don't let employers forget, that the profits of employers are merely the leavings of labour and capital—the greater the product and the greater the consumption of products the greater the possibility of profits. The increased power of consumption of the people and their ever-increasing wants are the basis of the employer's margin for profits.

We now come to the consideration of another point : Supposing we had no increase in requirements, all wants being already fully satisfied, whether wages would increase. Happily we are none of us content to live to-day as our forefathers did. If we were, there would be no increase in consumption, and consequently no increase in production and no increase in wages. But, fortunately for all three partners in production, Labour, Capital, and Employer, the standard of living is rising even more rapidly than wages, and this fact brings us to the consideration of the next factor governing the rate of wages, and that factor is that the standard of living determines the rate of wages. This factor partly explains why wages are higher in one country than in another, and also partly explains why wages of skilled labour are higher than the wages of unskilled labour ; but the standard of living, for it to be effective as a wage-raiser, must always be in advance of wages. As soon as wages get in advance of the standard of living, progress stops. The navvy with ideas of a higher standard of living aspires to become a ganger, or by increasing his power of production to obtain an advance in wages ; but the navvy with no desire for a higher standard of living remains content with his wages, and has no wish to raise his wages by increased efficiency. It is the same with the mechanic, and every other department of labour. Therefore it is as important to develop the desire of Labour to consume wealth as it is to produce wealth.

Social progress is promoted just as much by consuming wealth as by saving wealth, and it is as true that the cost of production is governed by the standard of living as it is true that the standard of living depends upon the social character of the people. Now let us see how this is. The successful investment of capital in machinery is only possible in proportion to its power to cheapen production whilst raising wages, and so giving increased power of consumption to Labour. The higher the wages the higher will be the power of consumption, provided the social standard of living is also rising ; and consequently the higher the wages the better will be the return for capital, provided the use of capital can increase and cheapen production and can also increase the rate of wages, but not otherwise. Capital recognizes this fact, and flows into channels where it can effect the greatest

22

saving in the cost of production. If what we call "hand-made" goods can be produced the cheapest, quality and suit-ability considered, then it is clear "hand made" will be in the most demand ; but if what we call "machine made" goods, in other words, "capital and labour made" goods, can produce the cheapest, quality and suitability considered, then "machine made" will be in greatest demand. That which is able to undersell will always supplant that which is undersold. Consequently the increased use of capital and machinery is only possible on the basis of cheaper production and higher wages, because the higher wages are necessary to give the increase of consuming power. If wages do not rise with increased and cheaper production, there will be very little increased demand and little advantage to be gained by the use of machinery of greater producing powers. We see how these two elements act and react upon each other, and that rises in real wages depend upon increased production with decreased cost, and that the successful use of capital and the profits for the employer depend on rises in real wages to bring about this increased consumption which is possible only with decreased cost and increased wages.

Now let us see if we can illustrate this statement. We will imagine a nation of Hottentots, Eskimos, or Zulus, with no capitalists and no employers, for the reason that their standard of life, their social condition, was so low and their consumption of commodities was so small that all their require-ments could be supplied by hand labour. If machinery and capital were employed, this could serve no useful purpose, but would, from lack of increased demand, actually raise the price of production. Under these circumstances it is clear that production of commodities by hand labour would be cheaper for the limited requirements of Hottentot, Zulu, etc., than production of commodities by capital and machinery.

All increase of wages to be permanent must be accompanied by cheaper production and by increased standard of living. Let us take the cotton industry, because it is the chief industry in Lancashire, and most of us know something about it. At the beginning of the last century the capital employed in the cotton industry is estimated to have been £130 per operative, and the production 936 lb. per operative, or 7 lb. per sovereign of capital employed. By the middle of last century we find that capital had increased to £240 per operative, and the production had increased to 3,519 lb. per operative, or 15 lb. per sovereign of capital employed. To-day it is estimated that the capital per operative is £500, and the production has correspondingly increased. To find how this has affected wages in Lancashire, let us compare the wages of cotton operatives a hundred years ago, fifty years ago, and to-day, ever increasing, ever getting more real, and better able to purchase more social well-being and comforts.

I will now endeavour to illustrate how increased production and increased wages cheapen production.

We will take the manufacture of watches for our illustration, owing to the important part that machinery plays in the production of watches. Imagine four employers manufacturing watches, whom we will call No. 1, No. 2, No. 3, and No. 4, and suppose that No. 1, with inferior plant and old premises, can barely make watches to cost 10s. each, No. 2, with a little better plant, can make watches for 9s., No. 3, with better plant still, can make watches for 8s., and No. 4, with up-to-date modern plant and machinery, can make watches for 7s. Now it is clear that No. 1 must sell at 10s. or else become bankrupt, but if No. 1 is able to sell at 10s., it could only be for so long as Nos. 2, 3, and 4 also sell at 10s. And this they would continue to do provided they had nothing to gain by adopting a different policy. Now suppose that No. 4 saw that by selling at 9s. he could make more net profit for himself, having knocked No. 1 out and so increased his own production, than by continuing to sell at 10s. If he adopted this course he would then find that his watches cost him less by reason of increased production, and that instead of costing 7s. as formerly, they now cost him only 6s. He would probably next boldly lower his price to 7s. 6d. and would find his total profits greater than when selling at 9s., because of his increased production which brought down his cost to only 5s. per watch. No. 4 would also find that as his cost of production per watch came down he was able to increase the weekly wages of his men far beyond what Nos. 1, 2, and 3 could do, and so he would secure a better class of workmen, and his workmen would find that as they got better and more regular employment, with higher wages, they were in consequence larger consumers of watches and all other articles than they had ever been under the old conditions. The trade of No. 4 would be helped in every way and his success would be certain.

How does this reduction in the cost of watches come about ? I will endeavour to give you what would be called a *pro forma* balance-sheet. We will assume the prices of raw materials were fixed. We can assume that, because they would be affected only by the world's supply governing each of the four watch factories. We will suppose each of the four factories produces 52,000 watches a year, 1,000 a week each, and that the cost of the up-to-date plant of No. 4 was £50,000. Now, the raw material for the watch would probably cost about 1s. We will say No. 4 employs 200 workpeople at an average of 20s. per week for men, women, and boys. This would be 4s. per watch for labour. The interest and depreciation would come, you will see, to 2s. per watch, making a total of 7s. as the cost of the watch. By selling watches at 10s. each he would make a gross profit of £7,800, out of which he would have to pay selling expenses and provide a margin of net profit for himself. After No. 1 had gone, his production, we will say, would be about 104,000 watches, and he would have cost of increase of plant, £20,000, making total cost of plant now £70,000. His raw material would again cost him 1s., and he would probably require not 200 additional workpeople, but 100, making a total of, say, 300 workpeople, and would pay them, say, an average of 24s., instead of 20s. as formerly, making labour now 3s. 7d. per watch. The interest and depreciation would be 1s. 5d., making the total cost of the watch 6s. Selling the watches at 9s. each, there would be a gross profit of £15,600 to provide for selling expenses and for his own net profit. After Nos. 1, 2, and 3 were gone, his production would be 208,000 watches, and the cost of plant would probably be increased a further £30,000, making a total of £100,000 for plant, raw materials again costing 1s. He would probably now have 400 workpeople, whom he would pay now at the average rate of 30s., which would make labour now cost 3s. per watch, and interest and depreciation 1s., amounting to a total cost of 5s. per watch, and by selling at 7s. 6d. he would make £26,000 of gross profit out of which to pay selling expenses and leave a margin of net profit for himself.

Now what becomes of the 400 workpeople thrown out of employment ? We saw that the total amount paid to the workpeople under the old conditions, men, women, and boys, was £800 per week ; the total paid under the new conditions for 400 workpeople was £600 per week. The 400 workpeople formerly engaged in making watches are now liberated, and as the 400 workpeople who are left in the business have £200 a week more to spend than formerly, they have increased the demand for clothing, houses, and for all the things that make for social well-being and comforts ; consequently the 400 workpeople who left watchmaking find occupation in supplying this increased demand for commodities from the 400 workpeople who were left in the watch business and for others, because these rises in wages of watchmakers affected not only the watchmakers, but also tended to raise the wages of the 400 workpeople who went out of watchmaking and of all other workpeople. That is the case so long as our social well-being is continuously improving, but no longer.

Now all these things are very gradual. No sudden dislocation occurs, for the selling price of a commodity is always nearer to the dearest cost of production than it is to the cheapest cost of production. The balance between the dearest cost of production and the cheapest cost of production represents the margin of profit available for the capable employer, and for increasing wages. Therefore, instead of all losing money and having to reduce wages except the one fortunate employer who can produce the cheapest, all make money and are able to raise wages except the employer who manufactures the dearest. These industrial movements are like the Yeomanry regiment : they move at the speed of the slowest horse, and not the fastest.

The next point for us to consider is that in addition to the standard of living the social opportunities of Labour affect profits and wages. We have seen that we can only increase profits and wages by increased production, that we can only increase production by increasing consumption, that we can only increase consumption by raising wages and the standard of living. Now, we will try to prove that we cannot improve the standard of living without as a first step increasing the social opportunities of life, and that this latter can only be done by reducing the hours of labour. Two conditions have to be observed in reducing the hours of labour. The first essential is that it shall be general, for you could not have one section working one set of hours in an industry and another section working another set of hours. The second essential is that it must be gradual. Well, now, we must look into history to see what the effect of reducing the hours of labour has been. In 1800, you will hardly believe it, the hours of labour of adults in this country were fourteen to sixteen hours a day, and children commenced to work at the age of six years and worked for twelve hours a day. The hours for adult labour and children were gradually reduced, and the age limit for children was gradually raised until you have the present scale, which is as well known to yourselves as to me. It varies from nine and a half hours to eight hours a day for adults, and we have an age-limit of twelve or thirteen years for children. As each Act came into operation the benefit was so marked that the efforts of friends were strengthened and the position of opponents was weakened. In 1847 Lord Ashley, better known as Lord Shaftesbury, proved that wages had not fallen, but had risen ; that profits had not fallen, but risen ; production had not diminished, but increased ; that the general prosperity of the whole country had not suffered but had been benefited by each reduction of working hours. And now to-day, fifty years later, we can state that all these assertions have been still further proved to be correct, and with even more astonishing results. The reason for this is that increased time for social advancement has improved the standard of living, that increased leisure has raised the tastes and habits and intelligence of Labour. Shortening the hours of labour, therefore, has brought about a natural rise in real wages for labour, and, consequently, more opportunities for profitable employment of capital and larger profits for employers. At the same time, it must not be overlooked that shorter hours do require intensified labour in the hours devoted to labour, but that need not and must not result in greater exhaustion, but rather in less exhaustion for labour.

Our factory system is not perfect, but it does give more equal opportunities to skilled and unskilled labour, to the strong and to the weakly, than we have had under any other system. Every automatic machine we possess is simply a storage battery for the brains of the inventor, enabling a less gifted intellect to intensify production without intensifying exhaustion. Let me now give you an illustration to show this. The whole quantity of yarn produced by hand labour in Lancashire two hundred years ago is estimated not to have exceeded the quantity that 50,000 spindles of our present machinery can produce. One man and two boys can superintend 2,000 spindles, and therefore twenty-five men and fifty boys with modern machinery can produce by intensified production, but with less exhaustion of the individual, as much product as all the cotton operatives, men, women, and children, of Lancashire, working for fourteen to sixteen hours a day, with excessive exhaustion, could produce two hundred years ago.

Our engine power in England to-day is estimated to represent a greater power of production than 120,000,000 of adult workmen, working day and night without rest or sleep, could produce by hand labour with the implements of production of one hundred years ago. And yet the product is all too small for our wants. Whatever poverty we have to-day is due to the fact that the commodities produced are not sufficient to satisfy the requirements of the people. We have a more even distribution of social well-being and comforts, and less poverty to-day than we had one hundred years ago, simply because production is greater, and when production is sufficient to satisfy requirements, nothing except bad laws can prevent an equitable distribution. We have seen the enormous advantages brought to Labour, Capital, and the Employer working along natural courses. Socialism could not have secured this, because the wealth of any one class, as we have endeavoured to prove, cannot be increased by lessening that of any other class. Nor could we secure this by means of any method of redistribution whatsoever. We can only increase social well-being and comforts, and secure a more even distribution of them, by increasing the total wealth produced. We can only increase the total wealth produced by intensified production and increasing the wages of labour, and consequently Labour's power of consumption. This we can in turn secure through elevating the standard of living by enlarging social opportunities made possible by a general and gradual reduction of the hours of labour—brought about by means of intensified production, but which must not be accompanied by increased exhaustion.

By these methods only can we succeed, for the natural order of social progress must always be from the material to the intellectual, moral, and social, and the progress of every nation must depend mainly on increasing the opportunities for improving the material condition and social well-being of its people.

VI

SOCIALISM, OR EQUALITY AND EQUITY

[From " Bibby's Annual," 1918]

ONE of the most clearly defined of our human aspirations is a desire for Equality. It is upon this yearning of humanity for Equality that the Socialist, the Anarchist, and the Bolshevist found their hopes for the realization of their ideals as to the re-organization of Society.

But they are following a mirage of the desert—a will-o'-the-wisp—that can only lead them into a waterless, barren land, where hunger and famine are the constant accompaniment of life, or into a quaking bog where mankind would sink into slime and ooze and death.

For let it be noted that this yearning for Equality is never coupled with any basis of Equity. It is a desire for an equality that would divide the wealth of others amongst those who consider that such division would bring gain—not loss—to themselves.

The Trades Unionist, Artisan, or Socialist desires to share with his employer, but will not agree that his labourer should share with himself, nor even receive the same rate of wages as himself. His interpretation of Equality is that he should say to his employer, " I am equal with you," but not that he should also say in Equity to his labourer, " You are equal with me." When the Socialist wears khaki he has to accept the gradations of rank and pay that follow from Private to Corporal, from Sergeant to Lieutenant, from Captain to Colonel, and so on up to Field-Marshal, but in industries the Socialist claims equality with all above him, whilst denying equality to all others beneath him. We all wear khaki throughout our lives, invisible to all eyes but our own, but our own conscience sees our uniform, and we appoint ourselves to our own rank, and no man chooses for us.

The basis of all social conditions and advancement is the law of service to others, and in this only can we realize Equality and Equity with both the man above and the man below us. The earliest manifestation of selection amongst most primitive men was that they chose as their King and Ruler the man most distinguished by prowess in defending them from their enemies, and right down to the present day Kings are looked up to to serve their peoples. When Kings cease to make service to their peoples their title to Kingship, and demand instead service from their peoples, that moment Kings have themselves signed their own abdication. Neither King nor Priest, nor politician, nor people, nor capitalist, nor employer, nor employee-worker who has ceased to serve can survive, and no Socialist " cure-all " can produce equality in value or fruits of service until our Creator sends us into this world all equal in health, strength, energy and ability. There will always be gradation of rank of service from King to peasant, from Field-Marshal to Private, from Admiral to Jack Tar. Equally by service and by service alone in Business, Science, or Art come gradations in rank and advancement.

Gigantic combinations, whether called Trade Unions or Trusts, or Labour or Capital, which are solely concerned with their own selfish, narrow aims and ideals cannot succeed or continue any more than a one-winged bird can fly. Their continuance depends on their fulfilling the eternal law of service. That great truth is as immutable as the law of gravitation, and service means, to work for and to serve others. It does not mean " ca' canny " by a " Trade Unionist," or slackness and competition dodging by the Employer-Combine; nor does service for others mean overstrain or work beyond limits of continuance in frenzied competition with fellow-man—that is War, not Service. The Employer-Capitalist or Employer-Worker, or Socialist, or Anarchist, who thinks only of Equality and ignores the Equity of service, will stand no chance of survival under modern social conditions of life. Life is a game that must be played with scrupulous fairness. The outstanding law of life is service to others and just and equal rights and liberties for all. Life will not surrender a bishop for a knight, nor a queen for a rook. However alert we may be we shall never catch Equity napping in that way.

Either by ourselves directly, or by our fathers or forefathers, the corresponding service must have been rendered. We can inherit good health or ill-health, strength or weakness, strong mentality or feeble-mindedness, energy or slackness, application or inertia, with their corresponding rewards or punishments " to the third or fourth generation of those that serve." No typewriter or calculating machine more correctly records the key we ourselves or our ancestors have struck than does Life record our service, be it high or low, noble or mean. Equity is depicted as silent but scrupulously just and pitiless. Nature or Equity—call it what we will—knows no pity. The game of life is difficult and our antagonist Equity is wary and adept, but victory always rests with the man whose life conforms most successfully to the rules of service. Equity or Nature is always more than willing to be checkmated by the man of boldness who brings courage and efficiency and noble service to the game. And equally true it is that Equity will exact the fullest price for every false move and for every error and blunder of ourselves or of our forefathers. Nature or Equity—call it what we will—is absolutely infallible. Judas thought to sell his Lord for thirty pieces of silver and make a profit on the deal. But he only sold himself and brought about his own suicide. Cain sought his own happiness by killing Abel, but he only achieved his own misery and undoing. And these truths are written large through all the pages of History. All down the echoing vaults of time there comes only one recorded note as the basis of success, and that note is—service to others.

It is quite out of the power of any one of us to escape from our ego any more than we can escape from our own shadow in an open field on a sunny day. Our ego is the central force of our very life and being, and consequently we are all by nature Individualists and not Socialists. We are all egoists just as surely as snow is white and coal is black. All snow is not alike in whiteness, but all snow is white. All coal is not alike in blackness, but all coal is black. And so we may each of us differ individually, but we are all egoists—

we cannot avoid being so if we would and we would not if
we could.   But rich or poor, 'high-born or low-bred, saint
or sinner, peer or peasant, philosopher or fool, wolfish or
lamb-like, bold or timid, courageous or cowardly; we are all
egoists.'

Even whole nations are egoists. The Germanic nation are
egoists in their ideals of " Mittel Europe " and world domina-
tion.   Great Britain, France, Italy, United States and their
Allies are egoists in opposing this Germanic ideal. All our
best Heroes, Statesmen and Citizens have been egoists, and
believing in themselves have worked for human happiness,
have saved mankind from disaster, or have deluged the world
with blood, suffering, hardships and misery according to
their ideals and ideals of their ego. Lincoln, Washington,
Cromwell, Pitt, Wellington, Nelson, Napoleon, Cæsar, and
Alexander were all egoists of different ideas and ideals. An
ignoble idea of self, a weak, feeble egoism is the root of all
evil more surely than any other cause.

As is the compensating balance to the watch, or the safety
valve to the boiler, so is the power of self-criticism and self-
valuation to our ego. The power of self-criticism must be
as true and exact as a beam scale with just balances founded
on accurate self-knowledge. It is when our ego is self-judged
by the power of self-criticism that it leads us to power and
dominance over all the forces which oppose our aims and
ideals. We can only fulfil our full and useful service when
we have impartially subjected our ego to the searchlight of
self-criticism.

The unique attribute of the successful man, who does
accomplish results as compared with the mere dreamer, is
this power of self-criticism. The great power of an ideal
is not so much in the ideal but in the balanced egoism of
the idealist. If he be a true egoist then he possesses the
inward strength to realize his ideal. Without this inward
force of the egoist the ideal will never progress beyond a
dream.

The world owes its position and advancement to-day not
to self-distrust and self-effacement, but to the self-centred
individualists, well-balanced egoists who, with confidence in
themselves and faith in their ideals, have dared and done
all for their realization and achievement. It has been said

that the British are a nation of shopkeepers ; that the Americans are thinking only of the dollars ; and Bismarck had a saying that Germany was a nation of servants. Her soldiers are drilled units of humanity. Her workmen are dragooned into service, but they are consequently, as rank and file, not equal in ego to the rank and file of other races. They lack the ego of individualism and its power of initiative.

We are egoists because we are human. We serve with our ego the happiness of others because we are Divine as well as human. It is the Divine in us that triumphs always and ever ; it is the base in our ego that lowers and destroys us. But through it all our ego is to each of us what the sun is to Nature, and we can no more triumph without our ego than Nature can produce food and flowers without the central radiance and power of the sun.

But whatever we call ourselves—Individualist, Socialist or Anarchist—we cannot escape by adoption of any name or badge the obligation laid upon us of service for others. That must be our highest ideal and the goal to which we travel in our national and personal aims and ambitions. And let us consider the joy of ideals founded on service to others. First, there is the joy of the ideal itself, the inspiration. Then our inspiration to achieve that ideal. Then the joy of tireless and ceaseless application to overcome all obstacles and difficulties, and, lastly, the final joy of realization.

But we so often fix our attention too much on the goal of our ideals rather than on the best methods to adopt to make sure of reaching that goal. The point is not how high we can climb or how far we can travel each day, or year, or life-time, to reach our goal, but to see that our methods are true and right for ourselves and posterity. If we are to concentrate solely on our ideals and not equally concentrate on methods that will stand the test of all conditions of time, then we are no more likely to reach the summit than would be an Alpine Climber who, with eyes fixed on mountain peaks, ignored the ravines, precipices, rivers and glaciers he had to traverse and overcome.

The Socialist would look to attain a higher state of civilization by the giving of all power to Governments. The Anarchist would hope to attain the same ends by the denial of any power to Governments. There have always been two types of Government—one nearest to Socialistic ideals, and the other nearest to Individualistic ideals, but there is no record of social life in communities without Governments. From the days of ancient Egypt and ancient Rome there have been Governments that pauperized the people ; that gave doles for a cheap loaf ; doles for house-building that the workman might pay less for his bread and less rent for his house than he had received for his labour as the cost of their production. This type of Government is considered by Socialists to be the protector and guardian of the people, and is said to live and exist for the people. The other type of Government gives no doles for cheap bread or cheap houses. It believes that the individual should be a freeman and self-supporting. It concentrates on Justice and Equity and equal rights for all ; favouritism or pauperizing for none. This Government is proud of its reputation that its policy is to encourage the people to live for themselves.

Every act of the Socialistic Government makes each man's penny—the penny of those who receive Government doles equally with the penny of all others—worth less than one penny. Every act of the Individualistic Government makes each man's penny worth more than one penny in the comfort, health and happiness it places within his reach.

Reward must be linked to effort, and without effort there can be no reward. It is only when we play the game of life, not on the basis of asking and looking for doles and grants from Governments, not on the basis of " ca' canny " or cunning, but on the basis of whole-hearted service for others, that we can reach the sublime heights for ourselves, and make it the easier for all others to reach there and to attain to a full and complete life of happiness.

Who can set a limit on the influence of a human being for good or ill ? But we are poor and feeble whatever may be our wealth or health, if we lack the leisure to satisfy healthy wants of mind and soul as well as of muscle and body. Material, individual and national progress is inseparably interlocked with the progress and development of men, women and children as individuals. We have seen in Russia the collapse of hopes for betterment founded on the fallacies of Socialistic theories. We are a democratic nation living under the finest and most sane and stable form of

Government the world has ever known—a Constitutional Monarchy—and it would be nothing less than a scandal if we, a democratic nation and empire, could organize successfully for War at short notice, as we have done, and could not equally successfully and rapidly organize for Peace.

There is a saying amongst sailors that if the wind were always south-west by west then children might take ships to sea. But we British with our brave Allies have for over four long years on individualistic, democratic principles successfully weathered the tornado hurricane of this present World War, and surely we can successfully navigate in the calmer winds of Peace. Our only ally that has dropped out has been the Ally misled by Socialistic fallacies, but that Ally will, let us all hope, yet turn from these fallacies and, rejoining her friends, achieve liberty and freedom.

Our greatest hindrance for betterment reconstruction after the War will be that we always find it difficult to shake ourselves clear of prejudice and preference for former habits and lines of thought. The inertia of former habits of thought and habits of action is difficult to overcome, and inertia makes cowards of us all. But science was making rapid progress, and moving with accelerated speed during the War, and will move with still more rapid strides immediately Peace follows on War.

It is true that as marked by figures on a Calendar there is a greater interval of time from the days of Adam to the days of Sir Isaac Newton than from the days of Sir Isaac Newton to to-day. But as marked by the progress of science, civilization and of the unlocking of the secrets of Nature by man, and his acquisition of correct knowledge of the universe and of the infinite power of such natural forces as electricity, there has been a greater span and interval from the days of Sir Isaac Newton to the present time than in all the preceding centuries since the foundations of this world were laid.

It is Science, and the wealth of Capital and mechanical utilities made possible by Science, that have raised mankind from a race of cave-dwellers clothed in skins of beasts into house-dwellers clothed in scarlet and fine linen. And yet it is these very modern conditions of life that have given us power for increased production, accompanied by lessened exertion, that are viewed as powers that can be made to produce greater well-being if they are accompanied by a policy of " ca' canny." The workman fears the mechanical utility, believing it reduces employment, and is obsessed with the fallacy that Capital and the Capitalist, which have made Science and machinery possible, are the sworn enemies of the workers, whilst a closer examination of these operations would prove that both are the best friends the workers and mankind have ever enjoyed for the service of man. But to the ignorant or partially informed the truths of knowledge and facts of history do not exist any more than if they were not. The present-day attitude of Trades Unionists to labour-saving machinery is just as logical as if our cave-dwelling ancestors had decided that the first inventors of bows and arrows, canoes and fishing nets or clubs and spears for the men who hunted, fished or fought, were likely to bring about periods of distress through over-production by giving increased facilities for securing more game and fish, and better defence from attack, involving social danger that might bring ruin in its train if not " cabined, cribbed, and confined " by " ca' canny " methods.

We are told that the cave-dweller had a shallow, receding skull fashioned like an inverted saucer and which skull held little more than a spoonful of brains. He did not worry about Socialism or any other " ism " ; and let us thank God that he had brains enough to see that the inventor who invented for him the mechanical utility, crude as it was, of a bow and arrow that enabled him to kill the fleeing deer without the necessity of running himself off his legs on foot chasing after the deer, or who invented the mechanical utility of the canoe and nets which enabled him to catch more fish in an hour than he could take in a month without them, or who invented the club and spear that enabled him the better to defend his wife and children from attacks of enemies, and so live in greater security and comfort, could not possibly be other than his friend ; and that every mechanical utility that enabled him to produce more food and clothing with less exertion, and in greater safety for his wife, children and himself, was something to be sought after and to be employed without hesitation or doubt as to future ill effects.

The greatest of our utilities to-day for the production of

more food and clothing, with greater safety and comfort for our wives, our children and ourselves, is Capital ; for Capital is the result of the developed heart and mind of man which has enabled him to produce more than he consumes. Hence we get stored-up Capital. Capital to-day is mankind's best friend, which with magic wand, harnesses the waste forces of Nature into the service of mankind, making the desert places and wildernesses of the earth to blossom and bring forth food and clothing and to provide comforts for our sheltering homes. And yet Capital and the so-called Capitalist system is the most abused, the most misunderstood and probably the best hated of our institutions. Without Capital and the Capitalist there could be no machinery, no mechanical utilities, or opening up and development of our Colonies or of the distant waste lands from the frozen North or South poles through the torrid tropics and temperate zones. Unless some one had rendered service to others by self-denial, in order to save up Capital with which to purchase machinery and mechanical utilities, our feeble physical strength could not produce one-hundredth part of the food, clothing, shelter and bare necessities of life required to maintain our highly civilized modern life at one tithe of its present level of comfort, health and happiness.

Capital, machinery and mechanical utilities, plough, sow, cultivate and harvest our fields ; milk our cows and prepare our food ready for consumption ; spin, weave and make our clothing ; dress our leather and make our boots and shoes ; make our furniture and carpets, and erect our houses, build our ships, locomotives and engines ; and by electricity can light and heat our homes, cook our food, clean our knives and our boots. A vacuum cleaner will sweep our floors, carpets and curtains. Machines typewrite our letters, add, subtract and multiply our calculations for us, set up the type for and print off our newspapers, and, in fact, perform for us, without entailing strain or overwork on ourselves, thousands of services too numerous to describe, which, without the aid of Capital, machinery and mechanical utilities we could never by our own feeble strength accomplish.

Capital, machinery and mechanical utilities bear our heaviest burdens for us and prevent our own backs from being broken under the heavy load we would otherwise have

23

to bear, or be forced to return to the misery and discomfort
of the life of our ancestors, the cave-dwellers. If Capital,
machinery and mechanical production were withdrawn from
the world to-morrow, or their service to mankind curtailed,
or hindered, or arrested, this would cause millions of our
fellow creatures to perish, and force the remainder to exist
in abject misery and wretchedness. In awe and wonder we
exclaim this is a machine age, and that it is all too wonderful
for us to understand or realize, or adequately appreciate.

But the modern street-corner orators and Socialists, and
large masses of employee-workers, and ill-informed Trades
Unionists attack what they are constantly denouncing as
the " Capitalist system," and they speak of " Wage Slavery,"
" Capital," " Machinery " as the cause of each and every
ill that a distorted imagination can depict. Even religion
and Christianity are described as part of the Capitalist system
of " Wage Slavery." If our Christian religion and its Founder
teach us that our own well-being and happiness are absolutely dependent for realization on the extent of our own
services and the services of our fathers and forefathers to
our fellow-man, and that service to our fellow-man is a duty
we can never disregard without bringing suffering also on
ourselves, then revolutionary orators declare that religion is a
device of the so-called " Capitalist system " for the enslave-
ment of mankind, and is " fundamentally " wrong, and one
that must be abolished by the " proletariat " as the enemy
of the people. Talk to the man who would carry the " Red
Flag " through the land, talk to the Socialist or Anarchist of increasing production, or of volume of output and its relation
to the costs of production, and you receive a vacant stare from
out their bloodshot eyes and a scornful reference to " Capital-
ism " and " Wage Slavery." They hold all increases in production as solely the exploitation of the workers, and they
view machinery and mechanical production as part of a
" Capitalist System " and " Wage Slavery " to be met and
defeated only by Trades Unionist secret rules for limiting
output by " ca' canny " methods. Abolish the " Capitalist
System," abolish " Payment of Interest," abolish the " Wage
System," confiscate all wealth, let all the industries of the
country be run by Committees of Workmen without Capitalist heads to guide, direct and control, and they declare we

shall then have discovered the secret of " Perpetual Motion " in our industries, the " Philosopher's Stone " of Government, the " Elixir of Life " for social well-being, and the " Transmutation " of baser metals into gold for every employee-worker, and finally that but for the so-called " Capitalist System " and so-called " Wage Slavery " mankind would bask in the perpetual sunshine of satisfied wants and realized ideals without any corresponding labour.

This mental outlook of the Socialist and Anarchist has been cartooned by a satirist in a French journal, who depicted some Bolshevik workman reading a poster put out by the Bolshevik Russian Government, which reads, " Our soldiers and citizens are without bread and all other necessaries. Let every citizen do his duty and work "—the Bolshevik workman's comment being, " Work ! ! Our Government has betrayed us. The Capitalists have triumphed."

But " if a man will not work, neither shall he eat " must always be the law of the universe, and instead of Capital, machinery and mechanical utilities being the foes of the worker, making his laborious task the harder, they are just as much his friends and more surely improvers of his condition, and are even more necessary to his civilized existence than were the first club, spear, bow and arrow, canoe and net invented for the use of our cave-dwelling ancestors.

Who and what are the Capitalists ? Every man or woman with good health, good character, common sense, who exercises self-denial and practises the essential law of service to others, can become a Capitalist.

Capital and wealth or health are the results that Equity records in the game called Life, when we strike the keyboard letters and figures with habits of industry, economy, attention to duty, service to mankind, and hard concentrated work. Every man or woman lacking in these qualities will become bankrupt in Capital, wealth or health, even if he or she inherited the same from father or remoter ancestors, who had possessed and had practised them. Nor can Capital, wealth and health be fraudulently acquired and retained. Poverty and ill-health are the record of Equity in the game called Life when the keyboard letters and figures of fraud or of idleness, extravagance, slackness, selfishness in regard to others have been struck by ourselves or our fathers. But when we see Capital, wealth or health, poverty or ill-health, we view them as causes not as effects. It would be as reasonable to view the rosy flush of health or the pustules of smallpox as the casue of health or disease. But with these manifestations we do not fall into any such error. We know they are not causes, and we recognize them as effects, and as the outward and visible sign of good health or ill-health.

It would be just as logical and productive of service to mankind to declaim against health and strength as it is to declaim against Capital and Wealth. The more we desire to produce conditions that result in rosy cheeks of health and strength, the more we find ourselves dependent on the conditions that equally are necessary for the production of Capital and Wealth. Do we wish mankind to become each succeeding year the possessor of more Capital and of more Wealth, Health and Strength, then we must make easier the practice of the qualities that lead to the acquisition of either and both. We must do nothing to discourage the acquisition of Capital and Wealth, any more than we should discourage the acquisition of health and strength ; otherwise we shall bring suffering and distress on the whole human race—on ourselves equally with all others.

If we could bring greater prosperity and happiness on mankind by preventing the fertile valley from yielding a more plentiful and a richer harvest as compared with less fertile soils, or by preventing the cow that was a good milker, the hen that was a good layer, from producing more than the poor milker or poor layers, we might then achieve prosperity and happiness by preventing or discouraging the man or woman of exceptional powers for the acquisition and the production of Capital, Wealth or Health, from producing more than was produced by those of feeble powers for the acquisition of either. Any attempt at limiting the powers of the individual to acquire wealth is like endeavouring to lower some one's standard of health because it is higher than the average. The healthy of a community are a source of strength to all others, and so are the wealthy. What we require to do is not to weaken the strong or impoverish the wealthy, but to show to the weak and the poor the way to become healthy and wealthy.

Our hope for the future is a deeper and wider knowledge

and a broader outlook, a frank discussion without prejudice or temper. We are, in our industrial and economic conditions, merely like a healthy, strong child that has grown faster than it could be provided with new clothes. No blame attaches to Capital for this, and no blame attaches to Labour ; both have become entangled in the strong currents bearing along the drift weeds of previous growths. The strong and wealthy are as helpful and generous as the sickly and poor would be if they were to change places. Men work and are saving and frugal, not only for themselves, but for their wives and children. If we abolished distinctions between men there would still be the strong and the weak, the healthy and the ailing, and consequently the rich and the poor. The healthy and strong of to-day may be the sickly and weak of to-morrow, and the wealthy of to-day may become the poor of to-morrow, and the children of the poor of yesterday will then take their places. The brightest hope for the future is our ever-increasing healthy wants and ever-increasing desire to live and enable our children to live in greater happiness and comfort. The old wages will not supply the new wants, and science and the better organization of our industries enable us by increasing production to reduce the hours of toil, increase the wages, and cheapen the product.

On these lines our future happiness lies, and not on dreams of an impossible Socialism. Already we see the coming of a new day, and are warmed by the glorious rays of its rising sun.

INDEX

Printed in Great Britain by
UNWIN BROTHERS, LIMITED, THE GRESHAM PRESS, WOKING AND LONDON

CHARGE FOR OVER DETENTION TWO CENTS A DAY
ALTERATIONS OF THE RECORDS BELOW ARE STRICTLY PROHIBITED

DUE	DUE	DUE	DUE	DUE
Ap18 '22	B 18 '41			
My 12 '				
Jy 27 ''				
Jl 17				

40 M. P. L. 670   1-5-20   11746-20

THE PUBLIC LIBRARY
WASHINGTON, D. C.

HF45   L575s

366008

All losses or injuries beyond reasonable wear, however caused, must be promptly adjusted by the person to whom the book is charged.

Fine for over detention, two cents a day (Sunday excluded).

Books will be issued and received from 9 a. m. to 9. p. m. (Sundays, July 4, December 25, excepted).

KEEP YOUR CARD IN THIS POCKET.

MOUNT PLEASANT BRANCH

Lightning Source UK Ltd.
Milton Keynes UK
UKHW01f0609210818
327557UK00010B/535/P